By Neil Meyer

. . .

By Neil Meyer

DISCLAIMER & COPYRIGHT NOTICE

INTELLECTUAL PROPERTY & CITATIONS

All original writing, research, and analysis in this book remain the intellectual property of the author.

Citations, quotes, and excerpts of reasonable length may be used for review, academic, or journalistic purposes, provided that proper credit is given to the book and author.

Any external links and the related content remain the property of their respective rights holders and are subject to change without notice. The author makes no claim as to the ongoing availability or accuracy of these external sources.

DISCLAIMER

The information and perspectives contained in this book are based on extensive research, analysis, and informed speculation. However, they are not intended as definitive predictions, legal advice, or absolute statements of fact.

While every effort has been made to ensure accuracy, the author assumes no responsibility for errors, omissions, or the consequences of actions taken based on this book's content.

The opinions expressed are solely those of the author and do not reflect the views of any institutions, companies, or individuals referenced.

FINAL NOTES

By accessing, reading, or sharing this book, you agree to abide by these terms. If you wish to use, distribute, or adapt any portion beyond the allowances specified here, please contact the author via www.neilsmeyer.com for permission.

Version: First Edition, 2025

ISBN: 978-0-9561614-9-9

....

…..

Table of Contents

Foreword

I'm not a futurist.

I'm not an economist, analyst, or academic.

I've never even attempted to write a book like this before.

But I've spent over two decades leading digital delivery across industries, continents, and crises – working shoulder to shoulder with engineers, marketers, executives, and technologists in the trenches of real-world change. I've seen how things break. I've seen how systems strain and adapt, and how assumptions about stability or growth quietly unravel when they meet the complexity of human behaviour, environmental stress, or technological acceleration.

My value in navigating delivery in the worlds of consulting, software and technology has come from being a communicator between different groups. From engineering teams to Chief Information Officers, from solo start-up entrepreneurs to enterprise change control boards of multinational organisations.

There is no great secret here.

It's about making stakeholders – people with a vested interest in the outcomes – aware of their options in a timely manner, in a way that allows them to proceed with agency and confidence.

This book wasn't born out of theory. It came from a growing disquiet – a sense that the narratives we're offered about the future are too often smoothed, sanitised, or suspiciously optimistic. I wrote *Countdown to 2100* not to make predictions, but to offer a lens. To connect the dots between what we already see and what we still pretend not to. To speak plainly about what's coming – not to shock, but to clarify. Not to despair, but to prepare.

You'll find in these pages a mix of grounded analysis, imagined futures, and uncomfortable questions. The structure blends vignettes and global overviews. There are metaphors, yes (you'll even meet a few hungry hippos), but the arguments are serious. If the tone feels different from a think tank report or an economics paper, that's intentional. I'm not trying to impersonate authority – I'm trying to provoke thought. This book is for people who sense that change is already upon us, and who want to understand the currents driving it.

By Neil Meyer

I grew up in South Africa, moving around regularly between divorced parents. I've lived in the UK since the mid-90s, and I've spent my career navigating transformation. I've never found easy answers comforting. What I've valued – whether in business, leadership, or life – is the ability to *see clearly*, *act early*, and *adapt with purpose*. That's what this book is really about.

If you're here for silver linings, you'll find a few – but not where you might expect them. If you're here to argue, even better. The world doesn't need consensus right now. It needs honesty, imagination, and the courage to look directly at what's coming.

Thanks for giving this book your time.

I hope it earns it.

– *Neil Meyer*

London, 2025

Chapter 1: Joining the dots that lead into tomorrow

Greenland lost 600 billion tons of ice in a single year, nudging sea levels up another 1.5mm. Australia burned – flames swallowed land larger than Portugal. China drowned – floods displaced a million and cost $17 billion.

Right now the top 1% of the world's population own more than 50% of global wealth[1]*. Elon Musk has a personal fortune approaching $400Bn, whilst PwC (2023) predicts AI could displace 30% of UK jobs by the mid-2030s, hitting clerical and manual roles hardest.*

In 2025 alone, ChatGPT swelled past 200 million users, the fastest app rise ever, while a leaked Google memo revealed that 'We Have No Moat, And Neither Does OpenAI'[2]*. The race for AI dominance is on, with implications for everything from the job market to global security.*

The future isn't coming – you're living in it.

The next 75 years aren't a blank canvas. The base coat is already on, and the brushes and palette were chosen long before we arrived. We're painting with smoke, rust, blood, and shadow – no bright sunrise waiting at the edges.

1.1 Themes and Tone of This Book

This book isn't here to spin utopian dreams, nor do I want to peddle dystopian thrills. It's intended as an unflinching look forward, built from the realities we can see today, stripped of sentimentality or sensationalism. I'm not buying the reflex that human ingenuity will swoop in to fix everything – history hasn't run on fairy tales so far.

Collapse, stagnation, and backsliding have been as common as breakthroughs.

The systems we've actively and passively engineered – economic, technological, ecological, geopolitical – are driving us toward outcomes that aren't just tough to reverse but are, in many cases, already self-sustaining.

[1] According to Oxfam's analysis of UBS data released in September 2024, the top 1% of the world's population now own more than 50% of global wealth—specifically around $214 trillion out of a total estimated at $427 trillion in 2023.

[2] SemiAnalysis, 'Google "We Have No Moat, And Neither Does OpenAI", April 2023

Resistance will flare. Innovation will flicker. Adaptation will grind on.

However, none of it will rewrite the direction we're locked into. What follows isn't a crystal ball prophecy – it's the logical next sequence of events, set to play out. It is the realisation of what's already in motion, and all we're doing is simply joining the dots ahead of us.

My aim is simple: to map the world as it's likely to be, not as we might wish it.

The term "Grey Rhinos[3]", refers to predictable, large-scale threats we keep neglecting. This book will specifically focus on some of these, and note some others later on.

This isn't one tidy story unfolding at the same pace everywhere. A humming AI megacity in Dubai will stand miles apart from a sweltering Lagos slum, just as a fortified Nordic grid will stand as a tower to innovation against a shattered and scorched American heartland. These forces hit differently – by region, by wealth, by gifts of geography – and that's the point. I'm laying out the pillars steering us forward – AI's rise, climate's collapse, wealth's hoarding, globalism's retreat – not as a timeline but as a framework, interconnected and relentless, already reshaping lives from Shenzhen to Stockholm.

1.2 Witnesses and Prophets

Through this book we'll take a dual role, as both Witness and Prophet.

Witness to what has gone before, considering the decisions made to this point and their current impacts. And Prophets, evaluating the likely future based on the probable trajectory and interconnectedness of the various strands that stretch out before us.

For nearly 200,000 years, humanity has been navigating a set of currents – streams of economy, innovation, power, and survival – that define our course. We'll trace these flows, studying their force and direction.

---

[3] The term "Gray Rhino" comes from the world of risk management and was coined by Michele Wucker, a policy analyst and strategist. She introduced the concept in her 2016 book, The Gray Rhino: How to Recognize and Act on the Obvious Dangers We Ignore. Wucker used the metaphor of a "gray rhino" to describe highly probable, high-impact threats that are often overlooked despite their obviousness—think of a two-ton rhinoceros charging toward you in plain sight, yet you fail to move.

xtend the analogy, we'll consider the different rafts in the river – representing the varied tapestry of people, countries and cultures – and how the currents affect them. We'll also acknowledge that not all rafts will move at the same rate, go the same distance or even in the same direction.

Whilst we don't want to discount the ability and agency that people have, we do want to accept that people very seldom actually exercise this agency to make long term, hard choices that cause any discomfort for the greater good of the world beyond humans, or even for future generations. As a species, we seem hardwired to take today's benefits in full, and to bank the problems for tomorrow. There also seems to be a defence mechanism within many of us that a magic bullet, some deus ex machina, will solve the big challenges tomorrow. Some might ascribe to fate or divine will, handing control over to some fatherly sky figure.

In this book, we're not betting on the best outcomes, just because humanity's (rarely!) dodged bullets before. That "we always find a way" plucky attitude is a simplified self-soothing comfort, not a strategy, and it glosses over how often we've stumbled into ruin instead. The graveyards of history show that bullet-dodging is an ill-advised strategy – it's a rare fluke when it happens.

Human agency will nudge the edges – pockets of defiance or ingenuity might shift a detail here or there – but the big arcs? They require such massive and immediate action, that they're too heavy to turn back now.

1.3 Bearing Witness & Human Vignettes

This book focuses on a specific set of important variables that I believe will shape our future. These are not the only variables, but they are of a scale that their impact is likely to be significant.

Our scope will cover issues like capitalism and how its new mutated form is impacting the landscape already, before looking at how mankind has impacted climates, ecology and driven mass extinction, how we're drifting away from a golden time of globalisation and how society is fracturing, and also consider where technology and AI are taking us.

To bring each chapter and the overarching themes of the book together, I have also included a set of 'vignettes', each telling the story of the next 75 years or so, through the eyes of different characters, from families displaced by rising Pacific tides, to young professionals navigating post-EU enclaves in a fractured Europe.

These vignettes are shards of potential futures and are not intended to be hard predictions. Instead, they illustrate how change might occur and view these through a human lens.

1.4 Mutation of Capitalism

Capitalism's old gospel – growth without end, a rising tide lifting all boats – was once preached from the pulpits of stock exchanges, business schools, and boardrooms alike. For much of the 20th century, it delivered: a growing middle class, expanding markets, and a fragile hope that prosperity might be democratised. But that sermon now rings hollow on a planet increasingly tapped out.

Capitalism isn't dying – it's mutating. What's emerging is leaner, harder, and largely unrecognisable from the textbook hymns of Adam Smith. Its current evolution sheds the ideals of open markets and fair play and instead grows ever more dependent on algorithms, monopolies, and the meticulous engineering of inequality. The middle class – the necessary beating heart of the consumer economy – is fading. Once the engine of stability and progress in cities from Detroit to Düsseldorf, it now sputters, choked on the thick tar of corruption, hyper-consolidation, and asset inflation.

As of 2023, the top 1% of humanity controlled nearly half of the world's wealth – over $200 trillion. That concentration continues to deepen, not through criminal subterfuge but through the smooth, frictionless logic of market "efficiency." AI-driven portfolios, tax-optimised jurisdictions, and predictive pricing models funnel value upward with algorithmic precision. This is not a failure of capitalism – it's its latest and most perfected form. A machine-tuned beast that no longer needs mass labour, nor mass consumption, to survive.

Looking forward to the 2030s and beyond, the transformation accelerates.

Forecasts suggest that by 2035, automation may have erased millions of clerical roles in China alone, as office towers in Shanghai, Guangzhou and Tianjin empty out – not from recession, but from optimisation. In the US, retail giants like Walmart are projected to shift to drone-staffed, AI-managed shells of their former selves. As labour exits the equation, so too does the logic of broad-based prosperity. Consumer demand, once the bloodstream of capitalism, risks becoming a vestigial organ.

And the wealth? It no longer trickles. It pools – thick and slow, like crude oil seeping into the lowest reaches of a drained basin. From Otago's fortified climate villas to the highland retreats of Ethiopia and the vertical eco-towers of Abu Dhabi, the ultra-wealthy will continue to consolidate their position – not just through money, but through insulation. Climate, security, data, and food chains are increasingly privatised assets. In these scenarios, drawn from real-world behaviours and projections, "winning" looks like disappearing: high walls, air filtration, desalination, biometric gates.

Meanwhile, in Lagos, local hawkers scrape out a living on the fringes of failing municipal systems, trading solar-charged batteries and water credits. In southern Brazil, rural communities revert to barter economies after regional markets collapse under climate stress. EU welfare systems strain to support millions displaced from heat-stressed southern zones. It's not ideology that's failing – it's the foundational assumption that capitalism needs people to work and spend in order to thrive. The emerging system needs neither in surplus.

This isn't collapse; it's evolution by exclusion. A system becoming more efficient by shedding its dependence on the masses who once animated it.

The middle class – especially in legacy economies – is pacified through shallow dividends: universal basic incomes in some regions, subsidised food credits in others. But these are anaesthetic, not agency. What remains is a digital underclass, measured by algorithm, placated by limited access, unable to meaningfully participate in the machine they still orbit.

Let's not mistake the continuation of wealth for the continuation of value. The modern Ozymandias doesn't rule from a throne – he's sealed in a fusion-powered enclave, surrounded by private aquifers and surveillance drones, his kingdom reduced to spreadsheets, not soil.

Technology is the enabler of this transformation. Not the cause, but the lever. It doesn't just assist capitalism – it redefines what capitalism optimises for. Not the flourishing of the many, but the insulation of the few.

And in this mutated model, the rules are rewritten not by parliaments, but by those who own the systems that write the code.

1.5 The Rise of AI and Post-Human Economics

The mutation of capitalism is not occurring in isolation – it is being supercharged by its most efficient and indifferent accomplice: Artificial Intelligence.

AI is no longer just the novelty in your pocket or the generator of six-fingered digital portraits. It is already embedded in the foundations of the modern world – a tectonic force beneath the surface. By the mid-2020s, algorithms were driving more than 80% of global stock trades, processing over $50 trillion annually without human intervention. Shanghai's traffic flows were eased by machine learning in 2023; predictive systems in Seoul, Singapore, and Toronto began optimising energy grids, cutting costs and emissions in ways no committee ever could. These are not projections – they are the lived realities of now.

What lies ahead, however, is of a different magnitude. By 2040, if current trajectories hold, AI will not simply replace jobs – it will regulate industries, dictate policy, and allocate resources with a precision that makes human oversight seem sentimental, even irresponsible. In China, where two million financial analysts once formed the backbone of its economic review machinery, that function may be entirely delegated to server farms by the early 2030s. In the United States, legal drafters – those who once spent weeks crafting arguments – could be replaced by generative AI systems producing contracts in minutes, at a fraction of the cost.

This is not just technological disruption – it is the slow evaporation of human sovereignty over the systems we built. These machines do not sleep, do not fatigue, do not fear moral consequence. They self-correct, self-optimise, and operate with a ruthless fidelity to logic. What remains of human decision-making is increasingly ceremonial, a theatre performed around outputs we no longer fully understand.

In some parts of the world, regulation clings on – Europe's data and privacy laws try to rein in the algorithmic tide with bureaucratic sandbags. But elsewhere, notably across Asia and in several African tech corridors, the opposite is true. Acceleration is the mantra. By 2035, Japan's warehouse networks may run fully autonomously. India's vast tech sector, once a beacon of upward mobility, could see cities like Bangalore transformed into UBI-supported zones – not failed, but bypassed.

In this forecasted future, economies become silent engines – efficient, impenetrable, uninterested in human labour. Citizens are no longer drivers of progress – they are passengers, or, more starkly, roadside relics. Shenzhen has already prototyped this model, its citizens scored and sorted through pervasive surveillance systems as early as 2023. Meanwhile, rural communities in Vietnam, Bolivia, or parts of inland Morocco continue to rely on manual systems and instinctive traditions – not from defiance, but because they've yet to be replaced.

It would be misleading to call this "progress." It is not a linear evolution towards something better. It is a redistribution of power, away from messy biological agents and towards algorithmic governance. The future is not one where technology answers to us – it is one where we increasingly answer to it.

What emerges is a new kind of economy – post-human in its orientation, post-labour in its logic. In some regions, this shift enables clean, machine-run supply chains and frictionless services. But in many others, it exacerbates the divide: those plugged into AI ecosystems prosper; those outside become informationally invisible, economically irrelevant.

And so, AI advances – cold, computational, implacable – against the backdrop of a planet in physical collapse. While ecosystems falter and climates destabilise, the systems we have created continue to calculate, ever more efficient, ever more removed from the world that birthed them. The machines are not coming. They are already here – and they are writing the terms of tomorrow.

1.6 Ecosystem and Climate Collapse, and Resource Scarcity

The Earth has stopped playing the part of the battered partner and now it's pushing back hard.

As of 2023, India's heatwaves have already hit 50°C, killing hundreds in Delhi when the power grid faltered. Amazonian deforestation approaches 25% the same year, with scientists warning that extensive sections are shifting from carbon sink to carbon source. These facts are neither speculation nor distant threats – they are unfolding evidence that our planet's capacity to absorb humanity's footprint is unravelling.

Looking to the coming decade, these pressures intensify. By 2035, some projections see Bangladesh losing swathes of coastal land to rising seas, potentially displacing over 10 million people. Meanwhile, countries like Nigeria endure a whiplash of flooding and drought. That pattern is echoed in parts of Central Asia, where factories near China's northern rivers already ration water. The same scarcity grips America's Great Plains, once central to global wheat production, now reliant on aquifers that are nearly tapped. These scenarios align with warnings signs we see coming; large agricultural zones in temperate latitudes may still function, but with narrower yields and higher costs.

Water is not the only resource at stake. In places like Yemen and Somalia, energy scarcity has turned once-manageable crises into unending emergencies, while Gulf states invest aggressively in solar grids and advanced desalination to stay profitable. Australia's coral reefs are bleaching, with an estimated 30% in poor health by the mid-2030s, while Pacific fisheries face collapse. In short, ecosystem decline paves the way for broader social instability. Technological fortresses in Europe or East Asia may buy time with fusion experiments or AI-managed coastal defences, but for millions beyond these enclaves, the future is a brute scramble for survival.

These fractures predictably lead to scapegoating. Faced with failing crops or empty reservoirs, national governments and local communities alike look for external culprits, often turning on migrants and refugees. Anyone who looks different from the 'locals' is fair game.

Borders tighten, resentment festers, and collective solutions falter. Rather than uniting against the shared reality of ecological collapse, many societies pull inward, blaming the newest arrivals instead of the entrenched, multi-generational and system-wide causes.

1.7 The End of Globalism

Globalism, once celebrated as a path to open borders and shared prosperity, began its slow unravelling during the 2020s.

COVID-19 laid bare the fragility of intricate supply chains; storms closed key shipping lanes; tariffs re-emerged as nations sought economic self-preservation. By 2023, China already commanded 70% of the world's rare earth minerals, tightening its hold on lithium and cobalt. These are established facts, not speculation. Countries from the United States to Germany responded with cautious stockpiling and trade barriers.

Moving beyond 2025, the vision of a cohesive global market becomes less tenable. Following the signs, we will see how by the 2030s economic blocs likely form around resource-rich enclaves or tech-driven city-states. The European Union's outer edges bristle with AI-patrolled walls, logging millions of migrant rejections each year. In North America, coastal enclaves continue to invest in advanced infrastructure, while the rural hinterlands – faced with drought and economic stagnation – grow alienated. Under these conditions, global collaboration on issues like food security or climate resilience becomes secondary to narrower interests: it is every region for itself.

International institutions also struggle. The United Nations, once an imperfect but earnest platform for worldwide discourse, is hollowed out by 2035 – already under increased threat as I write this. Fragmented economic and security pacts replace the old alliances. States with valuable commodities – from Africa's mineral belts to Middle Eastern solar hubs – hold new bargaining power, but rarely share their gains widely. Much like the examples of heavily guarded nuclear or fusion facilities in Scandinavia and pockets of East Asia, self-preservation dominates the agenda.

Meanwhile, those driven from their homelands by floods or scorched farmland – such as the ten million Bangladeshis expected to be displaced by mid-decade – find closed doors instead of humanitarian corridors.

Fear and political opportunism stoke xenophobia, painting migrants as threats rather than victims of global crises. In this atmosphere, grand ideals of global citizenship and unity falter. Where globalism once promised free movement and mutual benefit, what emerges instead is a patchwork of fortified zones, each preoccupied with its own survival.

1.8 The Fragmentation of Society

Societies today are splintering along multiple fault lines – climate upheaval, AI-driven economies, extreme wealth concentration, political nationalism displacing global norms – and the result is not a single, coherent crisis but a tapestry of smaller crises that manifest differently in every region.

We already see elements of this fracturing in 2023: Shenzhen residents in China have their daily lives scored by AI, while Tehran's social fabric pivots around tradition and religious commitment, overshadowing digital expansion. Brazil's favelas experiment with underground crypto economies – São Paulo alone is said to have moved over $5 billion off-grid last year – underscoring both the creativity and desperation of people left out of formal systems.

From 2030 onwards, as climate stresses worsen and AI further marginalises entire workforces, the variability in how communities cope or collapse becomes even more pronounced. Some enclaves – such as the Nordic Federation or certain city-states in the Middle East – may thrive with fusion energy or well-funded desalination, effectively insulated from the broader turmoil. Meanwhile, sub-Saharan Africa's Sahel region could see tens of millions displaced by famine and encroaching deserts, forcing mass migration and the formation of transitory, survival-based micro-societies.

By the 2050s and 2060s, what was once a patchwork of national boundaries morphs into overlapping zones of governance. A revived city-state in the old Nile Delta might finance infrastructure through AI-run resource trading, while swathes of rural India become pockets of self-reliant solar farming. We see no single pattern – the future unfolds in scattershot fashion, shaped by local geography, social cohesion, and the availability (or absence) of technology. In Europe, advanced enclaves with strong AI oversight could drift away from their poorer neighbours, creating digital citadels amid failing old institutions.

Although some commentators liken this evolving era to a "New Dark Age," others note the pockets of innovation and mutual aid that persist. Crypto-based bartering in parts of South America or grassroots micro-grid networks in East Africa might be precarious, but they demonstrate resilience on the margins. Society in the late 21st century is unlikely to be a monolith of chaos or order; it is a conflicted mosaic, where religious revivals, digital cults, survivalist enclaves, and hyper-tech city cores all coexist.

1.9 The Shifting Meaning of Identity, Culture, and Belief

In the latter part of the 20th century, globalisation seemed like a unifying horizon. The rapid rise of international trade and travel, alongside the emergence of institutions such as the European Union, gave the impression that borders were softening.

The shared '2 year working/holiday visa' between the UK and many of its former colonies is the reason I was able to travel to the UK initially, something that thousands of Saffers, Ozzies and Kiwis did as a part of growing up.

Corporations embraced diversity as both a moral stance and a market strategy, and legal protections for historically marginalised groups expanded in many regions. By the mid-2010s, shifting social norms around gender, race, and sexuality became hallmarks of progress in Western democracies, fuelling optimism that greater inclusivity would continue unabated. Diversity was hailed – and marketed – by many as progress.

That optimism, however, clashed with cultural and economic realities.

Around 2020, populist movements emerged across Italy, the UK, Argentina, and the United States, reacting against what many perceived as the overreach of liberal policies. Immigration, seen just a decade earlier as an engine for growth, was reframed by some factions as a threat. The 'anti-woke' pushback and unravelling was put into action.

At the same time, the post-2020 acceleration of AI and automation led to job insecurity in industries once considered stable, intensifying blame towards 'outsiders'. These developments are already documented – they are facts of our political moment. By 2023, countries like Japan and China, which had historically limited mass migration, were cited by nationalists elsewhere as models of cultural preservation and economic self-reliance.

Looking ahead, identity itself grows more fluid but also more contested. By the 2030s I suggest that AI-driven economies begin to define belonging less by nationality than by access to digital platforms.

Teenagers in Lagos may spend more time in online communities that cross continents than interacting with the immediate neighbours in their local wards. Meanwhile, ideological echo chambers become more potent as algorithms feed individuals tailored content, reinforcing insular worldviews.

Physical borders harden (as will likely be seen in the militarised frontiers of Europe or certain North American enclaves), yet digital borders dissolve, resulting in more ways for people to unify around beliefs, subcultures, or radical ideologies.

By the 2040s and 2050s, the idea of a nation-state as the primary marker of identity becomes increasingly brittle. While conservative or nationalist sentiments remain potent, identity fractures along new lines: allegiances to AI-run city-states, alliances formed in virtual reality communities, or survivalist enclaves holding to strict ideologies in a changing climate. In places like Indonesia or Nigeria, larger youth populations may embrace hybrid identities that combine ancestral customs with futuristic digital norms. Meanwhile, wealthier enclaves in Europe or East Asia might invest in "cultural curation," selectively adopting global elements while sealing off unwanted influences.

The result is a world in which culture is both hyper-connected and fiercely guarded. Old boundaries of race, religion, and gender mingle with new divisions based on technology access, social scores, or AI-driven job security. Belief systems might revive old myths or produce entirely new dogmas around data and automation. Far from a smooth, harmonious mosaic, the 21st-century battlefield of belonging becomes more internal than ever, fought over intangible lines of code as much as physical borders or centuries-old traditions.

1.10 Resistance, Rebellion, and the Search for Meaning

As these different forces come together, what might have been surges become rushing torrents of compounding frustration. What does it mean to a local community when they see people displaced by climate change moving in, as capitalism pushes jobs offshore and high value jobs are increasingly taken by AI?

Resistance may be as light touch as a Facebook post about 'those people' observed in a micro system, amplified to a regional or national scale. Rebellion arises as both sides push back; progressive groups fighting for the rights of the marginalised, conservatives defending that there isn't enough to go around. There is a marked increase in protests, with people gathering in their thousands and tens of thousands even defending interests on the global stage, such as those relating to the wars in Ukraine or Gaza.

And through all of this, people find themselves searching for meaning, purpose and – more pressingly – a way to secure their own interests economically and as their identity.

None of this is about right or wrong, this book does not advocate an ideology either way, but rather looks at the scale and intensity of change, and how we might infer future trajectories as a result of these forces already in motion.

1.11 Prophecy with clarity

The Fall of Rome, the Mongolian Empire, the Azteks and the Ancient Egyptians. We have seen the rise and fall of mankind, secure in the knowledge that we're now smarter, more enlightened and have better resources to secure our futures.

In reality, the signs suggest that having reached these heights, by virtue of taking an 'all you can eat' approach, the fall will be all the harder. Society is going to change, driven by the cultural, economic and social factors we've discussed, as much as by the environmental loss, climate chaos and resource shortages.

Before, when we fell, we still had a world of resources – fresh water, dense woodlands, billions of tons of coal, and a predictable climate. Starting again in this new world is not for the faint of heart.

The next 75 years will be a watershed moment – not a turning point, but a reckoning.

Our past inaction has already locked us into the 'reaping what we sow' phase. That is not meant to be fatalistic, but rather a statement of truth.

We can't quickly return ancient woodlands to the world, de-acidify the oceans or change the nature of humanity's desire to hoard wealth. This is not an accusation of agency or capability, but a reality based on probability; we simply haven't ever done so in the past.

1.12 Weighing, not discounting, alternatives

There are arguments that tend to put an alternative, more positive view on issues we'll discuss in the book. Phrases like 'new technologies always threaten the status quo, but often create more jobs than they replace' do not really work in the way they did before. Yes, new AI related jobs will be created, but probably 1 for every 1,000 they replace, and that's likely to be a ratio that grows over time as AI starts to write itself.

Perhaps new forms of energy will be discovered, perhaps new technologies will emerge to capture carbon, perhaps Elon will fly us all to Mars.

The risks with this kind of thinking is that it tends to, again, defer dealing with the problem for some future period. That's more problems banked for the future generations.

Another way to frame these potential solutions is to consider them as unplanned for 'gifts'. That way, we look head on at the challenges of today, and where the known problems are taking us.

If someone finds a way to employ hundreds of millions of people, in an ethical and moral way, where they earn a living wage in the meantime… well, I won't be upset that I was wrong. But until that happens, we must face where the known forces are leading us.

This book does not discount optimism – it simply refuses to rely on it as our main strategy.

However, this book does advocate actionable agency, informed agency. And therefore, rose-tinted glasses are not included.

In the meantime, we'll dig into more details, to understand where our current path leads. The next chapters will dissect these forces – how they converge, accelerate, and carve the path we are already navigating.

1.13 Chapter Summary

A. **The future isn't coming – it's already here.** AI is rewriting economies, climate collapse is accelerating, and wealth is pooling at the top. Nothing about this is random; it's the inevitable outcome of systems set in motion long ago.

B. **This book isn't about hope or doom – it's about reality.** We're not looking for silver linings or shock value, just the logical trajectory of where we are headed.

C. **Capitalism isn't dying – it's evolving into something unrecognisable.** The middle class was essential to its golden age, but AI and automation have stripped the need for human labour. The new economy serves the elite, while the rest survive on whatever scraps the system provides.

D. **Globalism is collapsing into fiefdoms.** Open borders, shared prosperity, and international cooperation are fading. The future belongs to those who control energy, water, and AI – not to outdated institutions.

E. **The "we always find a way" mindset is comforting but dangerous.** History is full of collapse, not just progress. Assuming we'll dodge every bullet is not a survival strategy – it's wishful thinking.

F. **Hope and innovation have their place,** but we shouldn't be pinning our hopes on them.

1.14 What Can You Do About It?

1. **Stop waiting for normal to return – it won't.** The old rules of career security, homeownership, and gradual prosperity no longer apply.
2. **Geography matters more than ever.** The safest places will be those with access to clean energy, water, and AI-driven stability. If you can move, move early.

3. **The middle-class dream is dead.** Wealth will no longer be about salaries – it will be about power, resources, and control over infrastructure.
4. **Miracle solutions won't save us.** AI isn't going to redistribute wealth, and technology won't fix climate change overnight. If a solution emerges, great – but hope isn't a strategy.
5. **Think in terms of survival, not status.** The economy of the future isn't about getting ahead – it's about staying above the collapse line.
6. **Make information and knowledge your key assets**, and the assets of your children, to make the best decisions going forward.

Vignette A: Sunil: A Climate Migrant Settles in Sweden

A.1 Chennai, India – 2031

Sunil was born in 2031, in the coastal city of Chennai, India, a place where history and modernity had long coexisted. His childhood, however, was shaped less by the ancient temples and the smell of jasmine in the humid air, and more by the steady, relentless encroachment of the sea. By the late 2030s, the once predictable monsoons had become erratic, and with each passing year, storm surges left more of Chennai's low-lying neighbourhoods abandoned.

His parents, pragmatic and forward-thinking, knew they couldn't wait for a miracle. So when Sweden introduced its Climate Migrant Visa in 2039, offering temporary residency to those displaced by climate instability, they seized the opportunity.

Uprooted from everything familiar, eight-year-old Sunil arrived in Gothenburg with his parents, a family among thousands. The Swedish government had structured the program carefully – offering migrants a place, but not permanence. Their visa was a ten-year, conditional agreement: work, integrate, contribute. If they failed to do so, the program would not be renewed.

Sunil's father, an engineer in India, found himself downgraded in this new world. His qualifications did not transfer neatly, and where he had once built infrastructure, he now maintained it – working for the local council as a general handyman, fixing heating systems in government buildings, patching roads, servicing smart-grid infrastructure that he had once designed.

His mother, once a teacher, adapted more quickly. She found work in social care, assisting Sweden's aging population, a role both difficult and meaningful.

At night, they took language classes, determined to make Sweden home.

Sunil, meanwhile, was bright and adaptable. He picked up Swedish with ease, made friends, and excelled in school. But even as he integrated, he felt the quiet weight of his family's status – a feeling that they were in Sweden, but not of Sweden. The climate migrant program was not designed for permanence. The Swedish government, despite its progressive image, was hesitant to grant full citizenship to those who arrived under crisis conditions.

This was not a place where his family could plan for generations. It was a stopgap, a borrowed future, fragile in ways that Sunil did not yet understand.

A.2 Oslo, Sweden – 2050

At 19, Sunil stood at a crossroads.

Sweden had changed. The Scandinavian nations had become fortresses of stability in a world where climate chaos had upended economies, governments, and entire societies. The Nordic Grid, an energy-autonomous network fuelled by fusion and wind power, had made Sweden, Norway, and Finland some of the most secure places on Earth – not just economically, but socially.

But with that stability came isolationism.

The Climate Migrant Visa program had been shut down in 2047. Sweden no longer accepted new applicants, citing social strain, energy prioritisation, and the need to safeguard resources for its fully integrated citizens. Those already in the country were divided into tiers:

- Tier One: Those who had obtained full citizenship – mostly younger, highly skilled individuals who had found jobs in Sweden's AI-driven industries.
- Tier Two: Those on permanent residency status but without full political rights.
- Tier Three: Those whose visas were expiring, with no path forward.

Sunil's family fell into Tier Two.

His parents, despite two decades of working, learning the language, and integrating, had not been granted citizenship. They were still "Provisional Economic Residents", their futures subject to government review every few years. Their social security benefits were limited, their ability to move beyond Sweden restricted.

Sunil, however, had choices.

He had performed well in school, earning an offer from Chalmers University in Gothenburg, where AI-driven energy infrastructure was one of the most sought-after fields. But there was a catch – his scholarship required that he commit to

Sweden's labour-credit economy, which prioritised native-born citizens for AI-managed workforce integration.

This meant a ceiling – a pre-determined career track that would see him placed into AI-supervised roles, likely as a mid-tier urban planner or infrastructure analyst.

It was a good life, but not an open one.

And so, for the first time, Sunil considered leaving Sweden.

In the United Energy Federation (UEF) – a loose alliance of climate-resilient regions spanning parts of Europe, Canada, and newly stabilised zones in Africa – there were cities where migrants like him were not constrained by their origins.

Cape Town, despite its challenges, had evolved into one of the most dynamic human-driven economies outside AI control. Parts of South America, particularly in Chile and Uruguay, had created human-AI partnership zones, where talent, not birthplace, dictated one's place in society.

Sunil faced a dilemma: Stay in Sweden, where he was safe but constrained? Or leave, chasing a more uncertain, but potentially limitless, future elsewhere?

A.3 Various, South America – 2075

Sunil chose to leave.

By 2075, at 44, he had built a life between worlds.

He had spent years in Oslo, where AI-led urban development was reshaping how cities functioned. He had consulted for energy resilience projects in South America, where heat-resistant urban planning had become critical for survival. He had seen the rise of corporate-led city-states, where wealth and AI efficiency determined citizenship more than any national passport.

But, by 2081, something had drawn him back to Sweden.

Not because it was the most open society, nor the most innovative, but because it was one of the few places where a stable, human-governed order still remained.

By this point, his parents had passed away – never having obtained full citizenship, but having lived out their lives in relative health and security.

Sunil, however, had found a way back on his own terms.

He had secured Nordic citizenship – not through the migrant visa his parents had arrived on, but through his contributions to AI-integrated energy systems. His status was not inherited, nor automatic. He had earned it in a system that had never planned to accept people like him permanently.

Sweden in 2080's was not the Sweden of his childhood. It was part of a broader Scandinavian Federation, linked by AI-driven governance but still resisting full automation. It had become a place of preserved human oversight, a counterbalance to fully autonomous corporate zones in Asia and the Americas.

And Sunil, after years of moving, had chosen to stay.

A.4 Gothenburg, Sweden – 2100

At 69, Sunil sat by a fjord outside Gothenburg, watching the water move with a steadiness that machines had not yet conquered.

By 2100, most of the world's cities were no longer run by humans. AI-governed enclaves had solidified across North America and East Asia, where citizenship was a technicality, and economic participation was a privilege granted by algorithms.

But Scandinavia had remained largely human-led.

Not because it lacked AI – if anything, it was one of the most technologically advanced places on Earth. But because the Nordic ethos had chosen balance over automation.

Sunil, now an elder statesman in urban planning, had become a mentor for the last generation of human-guided architects.

He had seen the world fragment. He had seen people disappear into algorithmic obscurity. He had seen cities that no longer needed people.

But here, in one of the last human-governed nations, he had found something his parents never could. A home. A place where, against the tide, he had remained necessary. And in the end, that was all he had ever wanted.

Chapter 2: When Consumerism & Capitalism Eat Themselves

Katie gripped the Burberry handbag. Half a mortgage payment on her Brooklyn apartment, but she needs it. It would go perfectly with the dress she bought yesterday. In Cape Town, Leon scrolls through the 2-year payment plan, eager to get his new jet ski out onto the water. Can he afford it? No. Does he deserve it? Hell yes. At his terminal in Singapore, Xu clicks 'commit', shorting Tesla stock. The CEO is floundering, the people are furious – and that means money to be made. Disaster's bad for most. For Xu? It's payday.

Three people. Three different time zones and cultures. But the same machine – capitalism – driving all of them. A system built on perpetual motion, or so we've been told.

For centuries, we've been fed the line that capitalism's a perpetual motion machine – spinning out growth, widening markets, lifting all boats with a rising tide of cash and success. Work hard and you can achieve anything. Each generation will be able to live better than the last. Trickle down economy means everyone gets something, we're all winners.

It was a hymn sung loud: work hard, buy more, keep the engine humming.

That tune shaped the modern world, built skyscrapers, and stuffed malls with shiny things. But what happens when the gears grind to a halt? When the fuel – labour, consumption, circulation – runs dry? When the promise of climbing up turns into a locked gate at the top?

We're not here to mourn capitalism's end – it's not ending, not yet. But it is mutating, shedding its old skin for something leaner, meaner, optimised. Something dangerous to most, in service of the privileged minority.

The system that once thrived on mass participation is shrinking to serve a sliver, a gilded clique who don't need most of us anymore. Consumption's not for the masses now, because to be a consumer you need money. Instead, it's a curated experience for the privileged.

Wealth doesn't trickle – it pools, thick and heavy.

Labour? Becoming redundant, a relic of a world that's already half-gone. This isn't a glitch or a hiccup that market forces will iron out. It's the logical endpoint of a machine hitting peak efficiency, where capital feeds itself without the messy bother of human hands. The rules haven't changed – they've just played out with optimised tools and systems that have outgrown the need for pesky workers.

Human life continues to have value, just not in a system that needed us to be either consumers or do'ers.

2.1 The Wealth Sink: From 1% to 0.001%

While wealth inequality is a well-established fact, the mechanisms that perpetuate it are less understood. Towards the end of 2024, Elon Musk's personal wealth was estimated to be approximately $450 billion – more than the bottom 20% of Americans combined. He could write a check for $1,000 to every American and still walk away one of the wealthiest men alive.

But the billionaire class is just the visible tip of the iceberg. The real power isn't held solely by ultra-famous CEOs and moguls splashed across headlines. It's controlled by a sliver of financial elites whose assets are scattered across tax havens, shadow markets, and private equity.

This exclusive group comprises individuals and families, often with increasing generational wealth. These include some well-known figures, like Elon Musk or Jeff Bezos, but the true extent of their combined power lies deeper. It's in the realm of family dynasties with wealth spanning generations, and the less visible figures who control vast investment firms and hold significant stakes in numerous global corporations.

For example, families[4] like the Rothschilds, with a financial legacy dating back centuries, or the Koch family, with their extensive holdings in various industries, represent the kind of generational wealth that often characterises the 0.001%. These entities exert influence not just through direct ownership, but also through complex webs of financial instruments and holdings that obscure the full extent of their control.

This is achieved through mechanisms such as:

- **Family Offices[5]:** These privately held companies manage the wealth of ultra-high-net-worth individuals and families. They handle investments,

[4] Wikipedia: List of wealthiest families - https://en.wikipedia.org/wiki/List_of_wealthiest_families

[5] Investopedia: Family Office - https://www.investopedia.com/terms/f/family-office.asp

estate planning, and philanthropy, often with a long-term focus that compounds wealth over generations.

- **Private Equity Firms[6]:** These firms invest in companies that are not publicly traded. They often buy, restructure, and then sell these companies for a profit, generating massive returns for their investors, who are frequently part of the 0.001%.

- **Offshore Accounts and Tax Havens[7]:** The use of offshore accounts and tax havens further concentrates wealth by shielding it from taxation and regulatory oversight. This allows the ultra-wealthy to accumulate and preserve their fortunes with greater ease.

These mechanisms result in a stark disparity in wealth distribution, as evidenced by the following comparisons.

2.2 The Top 0.1% vs. The Bottom 50%

If we want to understand how capitalism has shifted, we need to look at who owns what.

Country	2000 Top 0.1% (%)	2000 Bottom 50% (%)	2024 Top 0.1% (%)	2024 Bottom 50% (%)
USA	10-12%	3.5%	13-14%	2.4%
UK	7-8%	5-6%	8-9%	5-5.5%
France	6-7%	5-7%	7-8%	5-6%
China	5-7%	4-5%	12-13%	3-4%
India	10-12%	2-3%	15-16%	1.5-2%
Germany	8-9%	4-5%	10-11%	3-4%
Brazil	15-18%	1-2%	20-22%	1-1.5%

[6] Corporate Finance Institute: Private Equity - https://corporatefinanceinstitute.com/resources/knowledge/finance/private-equity/

[7] Tax Justice Network - https://taxjustice.net/

South Africa	15-17%	1-2%	18-20%	1-1.5%
Saudi Arabia	20-25%	1-2%	18-20%	1-1.5%

Key Takeaways[8]:

- The U.S. top 0.1% has grown from 10-12% in 2000 to 13-14% in 2024, while the bottom 50% has lost a third of its already meagre share.
- China's top 0.1% saw one of the most dramatic increases (5-7% → 12-13%) – its billionaire class exploded while the lower half saw stagnation.
- India's wealth concentration is even sharper (10-12% → 15-16%), reinforcing the "Billionaire Raj" phenomenon.
- Brazil and South Africa remain among the most unequal economies – where the top 0.1% has expanded their grip (now exceeding 20%), while the bottom 50% barely registers in wealth ownership.

This isn't just a trend – it's a deliberate optimisation of capitalism toward elite control. And the deeper you look, the clearer the pattern becomes:

The ultra-rich don't just own assets – they own access.

In 1950, America's richest man, H.L. Hunt, was worth the equivalent of $25 billion today. A staggering sum – until you compare it to 2025, where the top ten billionaires each hold over $120 billion. Wealth didn't just accumulate. It metastasized

Below are the top 3 wealthiest figures, for 2025, 2000, and 1950, all adjusted to a 2025 US dollar value:

[8] World Inequality Database (WID): This is a comprehensive source of data on income and wealth inequality, maintained by a large network of researchers. It provides data for many countries and allows for comparisons over time. You can find data here: https://wid.world/

Richest People in late 2024[9] (approximate net worth)

1. Elon Musk: $436 Billion (USA) (Tesla, SpaceX)
2. Jeff Bezos: $237 Billion (USA) (Amazon)
3. Larry Ellison: $213 Billion (USA) (Oracle)

Richest People in 2000 (approximate net worth in 2025 dollars)

1. Bill Gates: $180 Billion (USA) (Microsoft)
2. Warren Buffett: $100 Billion (USA) (Berkshire Hathaway)
3. Paul Allen: $70 Billion (USA) (Microsoft)

Richest People in 1950 (approximate net worth in 2025 dollars)

1. H.L. Hunt: $25 Billion (USA) (Oil)
2. J. Paul Getty: $20 Billion (USA) (Oil)
3. Howard Hughes: $15 Billion (USA) (Hughes Aircraft)

It is also striking how such a large number are, or were, located in the USA. Currently 9 of the 10 ten richest people in the world, all of whom have at least $120Bn in net worth, live in the USA, the exception being Bernard Arnault at 5th position with about $170Bn, of the luxury group LVMH, based in France.

Is it true that the USA has such amazing talent, or is it more likely that the USA demonstrates the most advanced form of capitalism, rewarding capitalists accordingly?

2.3 The Changing Middle Class

In 1970, a Detroit auto worker could afford a house, a car, and a vacation on a single salary. In 2025, his grandson – college-educated, drowning in student debt – shares a rented apartment, leases a car, and prays that his job isn't next on the automation chopping block. The middle class hasn't just shrunk. It's been sacrificed.

[9] Based on a snapshot from Kiplinger's December 29, 2024, report.

Let's compare that to global trends in the size of the middle class for the same period, using best estimates* where definitive data isn't available:

Country	1950 (%)	2000 (%)	2025 (%)
USA	35*	55	45
UK	20*	60	50
China	5*	30	70
France	15*	65	60
Germany	10*	60	55
Japan	10*	70	60
India	2*	15	40
Brazil	10*	30	50
Saudi Arabia	5*	35	65
South Africa	10*	25	35

The gap between the wealthy and the rest of the USA has widened to a level unseen in history. For the USA, the late 20th and early 21st centuries, the idea of an aspirational middle class still held sway – the belief that with hard work and strategic investment, one could improve their socioeconomic status. By the mid-21st century, however, wealth is no longer circulating. It is being hoarded.

Looking at the data, the picture becomes stark. Western countries, where capitalism and democracy have been the twin driving forces, have indeed seen a growing middle class, however that seems to have peaked around the start of the 21st century. The USA, Germany, France and the UK all seem to have crested in terms of the growing middle class, with all of them seeing a marked trend towards decline now.

As with everything, the picture is not uniformly moving at the same rate globally. China has made staggering gains in the last 75 years, with a solid middle class now, with a similar trend playing out for BRICS nations, Brazil, India and South Africa.

It's not a mystery why this has happened, and again, capitalism is the key. Where cost reduction and efficiency is a critical driver, moving these costs offshore has lifted the middle class in those locations, whilst draining it in places where the work used to be done.

So the middle class may not be disappearing just yet, when viewed on a global scale, but this assumes we'll continue to find lower cost delivery locations, meaning another shift in middleclass decline. This might look like the pattern, until AI and robotics join the workforce at scale.

We'll come back to AI and robotics in a while. But for now let's stay with capitalism.

Another quirk of the relatively modern world, in our wisdom, we've gifted companies with human attributes, so that companies can now be proxy wealth hoarders, paying less taxation than individuals, and passing on these benefits to their owners. And the wealthy are very, very good at this type of game, where they become investors in new businesses, using any failure as tax loopholes, whilst creatively moving profit to jurisdictions that offer favourable protection of anonymity.

That once growing western middle class, and currently growing eastern middle class, are the main drivers of consumerism too. However, whilst the middle class of the 1980s to early 2000s were demanding new cars, microwave meals, larger and larger TVs, and new mobile phones each year, most of those resources now sit on massive scrap heaps.

Again, capitalism solves this problem. Where pollution reduction targets and limits now exist for countries, they can simply trade those limits in a new market, effectively ignoring them. Just the cost of doing business. And so, capitalism adjusts to save the day… sort of.

It is very unlikely that the asian middle class will be able to afford, and thus drive, consumerism like the west did. There are less resources available (and cost more to get), and there is an even greater likelihood of growing pollution with these relatively new middle classes being substantially larger in real numbers than their western counterparts.

These very rising middle classes are also some of the main inheritors of the building climate and ecological crises, having taken on much of the pollution directly (within the game of capitalism) and displaced more natural habitat to build human cities.

The western economy is no longer driven by mass consumer spending but by the financial manoeuvrings of the ultra-rich. Investment firms, sovereign wealth funds, and AI-managed financial algorithms control the majority of global assets. Wealth is no longer earned through labour; it is self-sustaining, compounding at rates far beyond what workers could ever achieve. The economic engine of capitalism has turned inward – serving only a handful, while the rest of society is left in a state of economic inertia.

This has profound consequences. Without an active and engaged middle class, traditional consumption patterns break down. The old economic cycle – where wages fund spending, which fuels production, which creates more jobs – is severed. Without wages, mass consumerism fades. Without consumerism, many industries become obsolete. The gears of the machine grind and seize.

But hark! What is that we see on the horizon, a new growing workforce? Yes. The robots are coming.

2.4 Who Buys What? The Tiered Economy of Consumption

Consumption, the 'demand' side of capitalism, is on the other side of the equation.

The dream of universal prosperity – the idea that anyone, anywhere, could buy their way into the "good life" – was always a myth, but for a time, for that growing middle class, it was at least a convincing one.

There was a golden window where a factory worker could still afford a Ford, a middle manager could buy a BMW, and the wealthy could cruise around in a Bentley. Now, those overlaps are gone.

Capitalism hasn't stopped selling – instead it's just much more targeted than ever, in what it's consumers can afford.

Let's consider how the capitalist machine classifies us now.

2.5 The Curated Class: Buying to Exclude

The Curated Class sit at the top of our pyramid.

This group doesn't just buy things. They buy separation. Their cars aren't transportation, they're barriers. Their watches don't tell time, they tell status. Their vacations aren't experiences, they're walls against the rest of the world.

At the top, capitalism has stopped being about function. The ultra-wealthy aren't buying things because they need them. They're buying things to separate themselves from everyone else. Here 'demand' is measured by exclusivity and curation.

A car isn't just a car – it's a lifestyle marker:

- A Bentley or Aston Martin isn't about transportation. It's a club membership, a statement piece, a symbol of curated exclusivity.
- A Rolex Submariner isn't about telling time – it's about telling everyone else that you own time itself, that you're unshackled by the clock hands that demand mortgage, rental and subscription payments.
- Vacation isn't a trip anymore – it's a gated experience. The real rich aren't booking through Expedia or AirBnB. They have concierge services, membership-only resorts, and invitation-only flights. Their idea of a vacation is being either alone or surrounded by the rarified few who reenforce their belief that they are somehow more deserving of these privileges.

The delusion that rich people spend more, and thus contribute more, is easily dismissed. Just because a rich person earns 1,000x more than someone in the middle class, does not mean they need 1,000 times as many pillows in their bed, meals during the day, or pay 1,000 times in taxation. If anything, we see that these groups are given things by corporations to try share the spotlight of the wealthy, so they can appeal to the lower tiers.

But there's the problem. The middle class used to buy *aspirationally* – they saved up for a designer handbag, a nice watch, a luxury car. Now they can't. The gulf has widened too far. A 30 something, successful manager, will never own a new Aston Martin.

So, capitalism found a solution: If the middle class can't afford real luxury anymore, sell them fake luxury instead.

But the ultra-rich go even further – they don't just buy things, they buy experiences the rest of the world will never have access to.

- **Private medicine:** While the middle class waits for months on insurance approvals, the rich have concierge doctors.
- **Private cities:** When Miami floods and California burns, the rich won't "adapt" – they'll move to climate-controlled, private enclaves that are already being built.
- **Private everything:** Schools, flights, hospitals, entertainment – if it's exclusive, it's valuable.

The defining feature of capitalism in the 21st century is not just wealth hoarding – it's experience-hoarding.

The recent Blue Origin flight[10], with its carefully curated all-female crew, is a perfect illustration of 21st-century capitalism's penchant for vanity projects. While the ultra-rich play at being astronauts, funding a spectacle that serves little purpose beyond their own self-aggrandisement, the planet continues to burn. The obscene cost of these ventures could fund actual solutions to problems like climate change or resource scarcity, but instead, it's funneled into a useless sideshow that distracts the masses from the real issues. This is not progress; it's decadence.

We used to live in a world where the wealthy could still be seen, even envied. Now, they're disappearing behind closed doors, private islands, and AI-curated digital walls.

Capitalism's final demand side mutation is not just about owning things – it's about controlling access to life itself. The poor buy survival. The middle class rents their lifestyle. The rich buy exclusion.

2.6 The Subscription Class: Renting the Lifestyle of Their Parents

This is evolution of the middle class – the once-proud engine of capitalism, the 'American dream made real', now locked into a permanent state of deferred

[10] https://www.blueorigin.com/news/new-shepard-ns-31-mission

ownership. They're still participating in consumerism, but on terms that keep them forever paying, never owning, with those at the top extracting as much wealth as prices rise whilst services stay relatively flat.

For the Subscription Class, there is no more ownership, instead short-term wants are satisfied through long term payment agreements, or rental of access:

- **The latest smartphone** – this group still get that new iPhone or Samsung Galaxy, however now it's on a 36-month contract, with early exit penalties, annual increases and the constant upsell for minor features or handset upgrades.

- **The biggest TV available** – bought on credit, financed through "Buy Now, Pay Later" schemes.

- **The "premier" grocery store brands** – not luxury, but *just expensive enough* to signal they aren't completely struggling and do still nurse aspirations for upward mobility.

- **Streaming services for everything.**

    - No one owns music anymore – they rent it through Spotify.

    - No one owns movies anymore – they pay Netflix, Amazon and Disney+ to watch a film they could have once purchased outright.

    - Fewer people own video games anymore – Xbox Game Pass and PlayStation Plus replaced ownership with endless monthly fees.

    - Even their cars are leased.

This is the defining feature of the Subscription Class: they never stop paying. They rent their homes, they lease their vehicles, they stream their entertainment, and the moment they stop paying, it all disappears.

This class still believes in capitalism – not because it's working for them, but because to admit otherwise would mean accepting they'll never climb higher. So instead, they buy the illusion of progress which the subscription model allows for, on the condition that we all agree you'll never actually own anything.

2.7 Digital Wealth: Selling an Illusion to the Middle Class

Welcome to capitalism's newest con, virtual reality!

For generations, the middle class proved their success through tangible goods. A bigger house. A fancier car. A Rolex that, even if second hand and expensive, was at least a *physical object.* But now? The middle class is being sold status symbols that don't even exist in reality.

- NFTs – Don't have the money for a Picasso? That's fine, you can buy a blockchain-certified JPEG instead. Yes, you now own a link to a 8Mb file somewhere, that anyone can copy, even though you technically own it.
- Virtual fashion – Can't afford a Gucci handbag? That's fine, you can buy a Gucci skin for your Fortnite character.
- Metaverse real estate – Never going to own a home in the real world? That's fine, you can own virtual land in a server that might shut down next year.
- "Exclusive" digital content – Want to feel special? Pay extra for access to something literally intangible.

This is the ultimate capitalist innovation: selling you something that doesn't even exist, for money you don't really have.

And for everyone else? They can still buy the illusion of success, if they subscribe, or go further into debt to touch it for even a moment.

Here the Subscriber class sit, in their haze of Paramount+, Disney+, Apple TV, Prime, 8 Sky Sports TV subscriptions, YouTube Premium… happily numbed by entertainment, unaware that many of them are drifting towards the next class, the one that at least lets the Subscription class feel, "well, things could be worse…".

And when their next payment fails? The illusion disappears, and so they fall.

2.8 The Survival Class: Buying Only What Keeps You Alive

And with that onto the growing base of our revised class pyramid; The Survival Class.

This growing group doesn't get to 'budget.' They triage. Food or rent. Heat or medicine. A life where every month is a countdown to zero, and every pay check barely holds off collapse.

For the lowest economic rung, shopping isn't a pastime or a hobby. It's a transaction of necessity. These are the people who, when they talk about what they can afford, aren't debating between an iPhone or a Samsung Galaxy – they're debating whether to pay rent or keep the lights on.

So what do they buy? The bare minimum.

We're looking at a class driven by the lower rungs of Maslow's needs – food, shelter, lights and water.

- **Food** – but not the organic, ethically sourced kind. Whatever's affordable, often ultra-processed, and just needs to fill the stomach. The ideals of '5 a day' fruits and vegetables are exactly that, an ideal.

- **Rent, electricity, water, and heat** – it is increasingly difficult to find somewhere to sleep, so often this might mean government accommodation, a single room perhaps, when they can afford it. Next is ensuring that you have lights, water, and finally, hoping there's enough to warm yourself.

- **Prepaid everything.** The system simply doesn't trust the Survival Class with longer term contracts, so no annual subscriptions here. No locked-in contracts. Prepaid gas and electricity meters, and just enough mobile data to scrape through daily life.

- **Debt repayments.** A significant portion of their income goes to servicing loans, payday advances, and credit cards they will never pay off. This isn't because the poor typically buy luxury items that they can't afford, these loans are paying off expenditures on critical items like food,medicine and transportation.

The easy dismissals of these people being lazy rings hollow when you see that this is the fastest growing group within the western cultures. That middle class isn't shrinking into the top earning category, they're slipping into the unemployed masses, fighting for fewer jobs, cancelling their subscriptions to prioritised heating and food.

And the transition patterns in moving between these classes is giving up any wealth that might have been acquired, such as remortgaging your house just to survive. Or pawning off family heirlooms, held for generations before.

So, what will we do in a world where you can't earn enough to pay the bills?

2.9 Universal Basic Income – Necessary Grease for the Machine

Universal Basic Income – or UBI – is where people receive an amount of money to allow them to live a basic lifestyle.

As more and more people become unemployed, and unemployable, we risk the entire machine grinding to a halt and the resulting revolution as people literally fight for their lives. Simply put, people need food, water, and shelter. If they can't afford this or find it legally, they will take it by force. They have to.

This is where UBI becomes, at least, a bridging option until a new system can be established. It means that housing is still paid for, rather than becoming squatter-filled buildings. It means that people don't live in fear of having their things stolen so they can pawn or trade them for even the most basic groceries.

There may have been a fair justification in a world where there was plenty of low-skilled work, that paid a living wage, to harbour some resentment towards able people choosing not to work. That is not the picture ahead of us. As we've seen, the biggest group of people moving towards the poverty side of the equation are coming from the middle-class, middle-income, Subscription class – the very same people we were celebrating as the hard workers of yesterday.

UBI is not a new concept and is already being trialled in small pockets. In the rural villages of Kenya, a groundbreaking experiment is underway. Funded by the non-profit GiveDirectly, over 20,000 people are receiving a basic income, enough to cover their essential needs, for twelve years. It's the largest and longest-term study of its kind, aiming to understand the impact of UBI on poverty, health, and well-being in a developing country.

Meanwhile, across the globe in Finland, a different kind of trial has recently concluded. For two years, the Finnish government provided a basic income to 2,000 unemployed individuals, exploring its effects on employment rates, individual well-being, and societal trust. While the results were mixed in terms of job creation, the Finnish experiment revealed significant improvements in participants' mental health and overall life satisfaction.

These trials, along with others taking place worldwide, are providing valuable data and insights into the potential of UBI as a tool for social and economic change in the 21st century.

UBI won't be a generous gift from the ruling class – it'll be a reluctant concession by socially aware governments, offered whilst the alternative is worse.

But even as the system bends toward it, don't mistake compliance for goodwill. The ultra-wealthy will use this as a way to funnel taxed funds to their offshore accounts – ultimately, they want control.

If UBI is coming, expect it to arrive wrapped in conditions, restrictions, and digital fences that keep the lower classes just comfortable enough to stay obedient, to stay docile, manageable.

And, frankly, UBI is likely to be 'given' only until a longer-term solution presents itself to the ultra-wealthy, a solution that allows them to extract as much money from governments, before they cut the 'philanthropy' once they've built their secure environments. But more on that later.

The exact form that UBI will take, and how it will be delivered in different regions will be an evolving picture, but at this point it seems a necessity. Even the capitalists need this to happen, if only to ensure that their machines of industry don't freeze up.

As we move towards this reality, it will be difficult for many to leave their judgements of those who will come to rely on UBI, especially as the reality is that many of us, even most of us, are likely to form part of their number. Therefore, we will need to change these judgements of ourselves, as the default for many will be to see themselves as failing. But that measure of failure is for a set of rules and a world of opportunities that doesn't exist any longer.

Lead with kindness and empathy. In a world where more than 50% are on the bottom rung, the problem is not the people, it's the world we've built for ourselves.

2.10 Right now, becoming tomorrow

Capitalism was built on the back of labour. As we've seen above, the short term power of capitalism did indeed lift a substantial amount of boats, but only whilst it served the capitalist equation, to find and exploit the lowest costs in production. Those boats may have lifted, but too many lie on the bank, hulls cracked, as the tide has receded.

But with AI and automation taking over, the fundamental relationship between labour and income is broken. This isn't so much that robotics are coming, as they're already here. thousands of quiet, non-confrontational, robots zip around Amazon warehouses efficiently moving goods around where human pickers and packers were the norm.

The historic turning points of Ford's motor plants, with hundreds of skilled specialists all playing their part towards a Model T rolling off the factory floor, has been replaced by the precision efficiency of robotic machines with a fraction of the former workforce now involved in calibrating and servicing the robotics.

The hundreds of Blockbuster stores, with spotty teens and geeky store owners proffering advice on what to watch next has been replaced by the Netflix and Amazon Prime algorithms. Jobs gone, replaced by systems.

The issue here isn't whether the output is better, it probably is! Machines can repeat a task thousands of times without getting distracted or tired. Algorithms are learning and self-correcting. If product and service outcomes are the only measure of success, we've nailed it!

However, they cannot be the only measure of success in a world that sees workforce loss in the thousands, tens of thousands and millions!

By 2050, the workforce is no longer made up of people competing for jobs – it is made up of people who have already been excluded from them.

Without jobs, traditional wages evaporate, and with them, the very foundation of broad-based economic participation. Governments may attempt to stabilise this collapse through UBI or AI-managed welfare credits, but these do not replace the social role of work. What remains is a world in which employment is not a guarantee, but a privilege. The few remaining jobs – whether in specialised trades, creative oversight, or AI-assisted governance – are hoarded by those fortunate enough to still be considered "economically valuable." For everyone else, the economic game is over.

This new model creates a permanent economic underclass – not based on race, nationality, or education, but simply on the lack of necessity. With AI running everything from logistics to finance, to customer service, humans are no longer required in large numbers. And without labour, traditional pathways for wealth accumulation vanish.

In the next chapter we'll examine much more closely the role of AI and robotics, and the displacement of human effort. For now, within the context of capitalism, the reality is obvious. If a machine can do the job for less cost, capitalism MUST embrace it.

2.11 The Capitalist Horizon: 2040 to 2100

By 2040, capitalism's a meaner beast, its old "everyone wins" lie torched.

Wealth pools thick – trillionaires like Musk's heirs clutch 75% of the globe's stash, their AI-managed fortunes doubling yearly without a human touch. In Shanghai, the Curated Class sips $200-a-liter water, buying exclusion while Lagos's Survival Class barters scraps, too broke for the game.

Consumerism's gutted – India's new middle-class chokes on smog, unable to afford the West's old excess; the planet's tapped out, resources priced for the elite. The Subscription Class in London leases VR lives, never owning, while Amazon's drones axe jobs from Jakarta to Ohio, labour a relic. Capitalism doesn't need you anymore – it's a machine serving a gilded sliver, the rest left to rot.

By 2060, it's a caste system, global and ruthless.

Dubai's rich hoard solar wealth, selling curated luxury – private jets, with bioengineered pets – while Egypt's masses hawk sand for pennies, locked out.

In New York, the Subscription Class rents illusions – NFTs, metaverse plots – fake status for a middle class too poor for real stakes. São Paulo's crypto traders dodge the system, but it's a blip – capitalism's engine runs on AI, not people, churning goods for the Curated as factories from Manila to Manchester go dark. Wealth's a fortress – 0.001% own 80%, their algorithms trading digital futures while the Survival Class starves.

Consumption's dead for most; the market's a walled garden, not a bazaar.

By 2080, capitalism's post-human, a cold hum of efficiency.

Tokyo's elite bank robot-made profits, their lives curated by AI that's shed labour like dead skin – Bangalore's coders beg for UBI scraps, obsolete. In Chicago, trillionaires gatekeep desalinated lakes, selling to the Curated as the Midwest dusts over, unneeded. Johannesburg's solar lords cash in, but the Sahel's herders get nothing – capitalism's logic cuts them out, resources rerouted to the rich. Wealth hits 85% in the top 0.001%, a handful of dynasties self-multiplying via code. The Subscription Class clings to leased dreams, the Survival Class fights for crumbs – neither fuels the system anymore; they're just noise.

By 2100, capitalism's a monolith of control, serving itself. Shanghai's trillionaires look to Mars or space orbits, almost a different species from the rest of humanity, their wealth untouchable, trading with AI that doesn't care about borders.

Mexico's cartel barons peddle solar scraps to the Curated, a vassal gig dwarfed by corporate might. The Survival Class – Delhi, Lagos – scrapes by on $2-a-day credits, too broke to consume; the Subscription Class rents shadows of wealth, locked in debt, the difference between them and the Survival Class is paper thin.

The Curated own existence – private cities, curated genes – while 90% of global wealth sits with 0.001%, a clique capitalism's optimised to perfection. It's not chaos – it's a lean, mean order, where the market's a fortress, and the masses are locked out, irrelevant.

This is capitalism's endgame: a system that's ditched the masses it once fed.

Wealth doesn't trickle – it's a dam, hoarding power for a shrinking elite. Consumerism's a memory; labour's a ghost. From Shenzhen to Stockholm, the game's rigged tighter each decade, a global split where the rich win by cutting everyone else loose. No rebellion's coming – AI's too efficient, the gap too wide.

It's not collapse; it's victory, cold and final, for the few who wrote the rules.

2.12 Conclusion: From Capitalism to Control

The 21st century started with an assumption: that capitalism would always create new opportunities for wealth, that economic cycles would continue indefinitely, and that consumerism would always fuel innovation.

But the reality of the next 75 years tells a different story.

As capitalism honours itself, as consumerism erodes, and as labour loses its value, the global economy is left with only two primary forces: those who own everything, and those who own nothing.

Capitalism will not die, but it will evolve – serving only those who can still participate in it, while the rest are left with digital consumption, AI-managed subsistence, and economic systems designed to prevent their disruption rather than encourage their inclusion.

The promise of the free market was that it would elevate all who participated. The reality is that it has culminated in a world where the market no longer needs most people at all. The capitalists have won. This game is over.

And perhaps that's the shining light. If late-stage capitalism led to this, what can we do differently *now*? How do we create an economy that puts people and the planet at the centre of decision making?

Even asking the question makes us sound like some soft socialist hippie types, scrounging off the state, dodging hard work! But nobody is saying that they're not up for hard work. Instead, all the jobs have gone to robots. Is work just for the sake of work?

We'll tackle some of these questions around resistance, identity and more later on in the book.

2.13 Chapter Summary

A. **Capitalism hasn't failed – it has evolved into something unrecognisable.** The system that once thrived on mass participation no longer needs the majority of people. Wealth doesn't trickle – it pools, hoarded by an elite who have optimised capitalism for their own survival.

B. **The middle class was capitalism's engine – now, it's obsolete.** As wealth concentrates at the top, traditional consumerism is vanishing. The economy no longer relies on people buying homes, cars, and luxury goods; instead, it operates for the few who can still afford to participate.

C. **The economy is now tiered – survival, subscription, and curated wealth.**

a. The **Survival Class** buys only necessities, locked in debt and precarity.

b. The **Subscription Class** rents everything – cars, homes, entertainment – never truly owning anything.

c. The **Curated Class** consumes exclusivity – buying things not because they need them, but because others can't.

D. **Universal Basic Income (UBI) isn't generosity – it's a necessity.** Without wages, economies stall. UBI is the only way to keep people from revolt, ensuring just enough wealth circulates to keep the machine running.

E. **AI and automation have severed the link between labour and income.** Capitalism once needed workers. Now, AI-driven corporations grow without human labour, financial markets self-perpetuate, and the wealthy live apart from the system that once depended on mass employment.

2.14 What Can You Do About It?

1. **Understand that the old economic model is dead.** If your strategy is built around career stability, retirement savings, or homeownership, you need a new plan.
2. **Own something – or risk being owned.** The future isn't about salaries, it's about assets, land, energy, and digital property. Those who control resources, not labour, will have power.
3. **Rethink wealth –** money alone isn't security anymore. The rich are already shifting from financial wealth to physical security, energy access, and **resource control**. Follow that trend before the doors close.
4. **Adapt before adaptation becomes impossible.** If you are in the Subscription Class today, don't assume you'll stay there. The middle class is shrinking, and the descent into Survival Class is a single missed paycheck away.
5. **Challenge the idea that work = worth.** AI is already making jobs redundant – this isn't about laziness, it's about efficiency. The question isn't whether people want to work; it's whether the economy needs them at all.

Vignette B: Anna: The Cost of Irrelevance

B.1 Sheffield, England – 2031

Anna arrived kicking into Sheffield in 2031, born under a sky thick with rain and the hum of faltering grids.

The city's steel heart was rusting, its terraces sagging under damp and neglect, and her legs came out wrong—weak, spindly, a glitch the NHS bots flagged but couldn't fix. Her dad, a wiry spark who patched solar arrays for the council, cradled her anyway, muttering about making things right, while her mum, a data clerk staring down redundancy, scowled at the AI diagnostics chewing through her job.

Outside, Britain was fraying as floods gnawed at the coasts, wealth drained to London's towers, and Sheffield's grids flickered under patchy AI oversight, early signs of the machines creeping in.

They weren't broke, just stretched, living in a house that smelled of solder and stale tea. Her dad taught her circuits young, guiding her tiny hands over wires while she perched on a stool, her legs dangling uselessly. "You'll build something solid," he'd say, his voice rough but sure.

By eight, she'd rigged a shaky mobility frame from his scrap pile, grinning as he belted out an old work song - Sheffield's echo of grit. But the jobs were vanishing. AI drones didn't need sparks, and data clerks were ghosts. They clung to the edge, watching the middle class dissolve like smoke.

B.2 Leeds, England – 2050

At 19, Anna rolled through Leeds in a battered power-chair, the streets a snarl of cracked tarmac and shuttered pubs. Sheffield's grids had failed one too many times, pushing her folks north for scraps of work that never came. Her dad was on UBI now – credits rolled out as AI ate clerical jobs, barely enough for food, let alone the chair's sputtering battery.

She studied systems tech at a crumbling college, her brain outpacing the AI tutors that delivered hollow lessons for a world that no longer existed. But her body kept her grounded.

At night, she'd tweak her frame with his old tools, his songs looping in her head: "Keep it running, kid."

Leeds buzzed with drones sorting rations and trams run by algorithms, while torrential rains turned the Aire into a muddy threat. Her mates were splitting, some snagged gigs in the London–Birmingham Megalopolis, chasing the AI-driven sprawl, others drifted to barter nets.

Anna stayed, fixing legacy gear for neighbours too broke for drones, her hands steady despite the ache in her bones. UBI was a net to catch the fall, but it didn't stretch far. Her dad's guilt showed in his eyes when the chair broke down, and she'd snap, "I'm fine," though they both knew fine was a lie.

The Megalopolis gleamed south, a fortress swallowing talent, leaving Leeds to rot under the weight of the unseen.

B.3 Hull, England – 2075

By 44, Anna was in Hull, a city sinking under the Humber's swell, her power-chair creaking through streets half-drowned by northern rains.

Her dad was gone. His heart quit in '68, too proud for AI meds UBI wouldn't cover past the basics. Her mother too, in '73 to a cold winter and lost dreams.

She kept his tools, a rusted tether to the man who'd seen her worth. Work was thin; she patched old tech for a co-op of cast-offs—folks the York enclaves wouldn't touch, their AI towers hoarding power across the water.

The UK had fractured—London's Thames barriers held the Megalopolis together, but Hull's fringes were left to fend off flash floods and rot.

Her legs hurt worse now, the chair's battery fading faster than she could jury-rig it. UBI had doubled, a grudging nod to the millions automation cast out, but it still meant bartering fixes for food, leaning on the co-op to stretch the credits.

She'd sit by the river, tracing her dad's initials on a screwdriver, feeling his faith in a world that didn't pay it back. York's corporate city-states glowed inland, AI councils rationing care with cold precision, while Hull's squatters built what they could from the wreckage. She taught a few tricks, rewiring solar panels, bypassing smart locks, passing on what he'd given her, a quiet thread through the chaos.

B.4 Liverpool, England – 2100

At 69, Anna and her husband squat in a Liverpool warehouse, the Mersey lapping at its crumbling edges, her chair long scrapped for a scavenged exosuit that groaned like her joints.

The city was a husk, enclaves inland turned back flood migrants with drones, their AI-governed walls gleaming beyond reach.

The co-op had splintered decades back, drowned by power cuts and evictions, but she stayed, teaching kids born to this mess how to rig solar cells and strip wire. Her dad's tools still sat in her hands, their weight a lifeline.

UBI had tripled by necessity. 550 million across Europe, and Britain's share kept the unplugged breathing as AI ran courts, calories, everything. The Megalopolis thrived south, Birmingham's industry fused with London's fortified core, but Liverpool was off the grid, its people taking what the floods didn't claim.

She'd hum his old work songs, a Sheffield echo in Liverpool's ruin, while the kids – scrappy, sharp – called her "Fixer."

One asked why she bothered, and she paused, hands steady on a frayed cable. "You don't quit," she said, his words in her mouth.

It wasn't hope, not really. Just a stubborn spark, tying her to him across a century of collapse. The machines didn't care about her kind – disabled, unplugged, irrelevant – but she kept going, one fix at a time, proving something to a world that'd stopped looking.

Chapter 3: The Merger of AI & Robotics

Foxconn replaced 60,000 workers with robots in a single Chinese factory, churning out iPhones for those who can still afford them. BT coldly announced 10,000 jobs will vanish by 2030, swallowed by the insatiable hunger of AI efficiency. The World Economic Forum predicts a chilling 7.5 million data entry jobs will be automated out of existence by 2027. Even Goldman Sachs, the titan of Wall Street, whispers of replacing entry-level analysts with AI that can devour market data and generate financial models in the blink of an eye. The future of work is here, and it's looking for your job.

As we've discussed, AI-embedded capitalism is not a sudden break with the past – it is the logical extension of financialization, automation, and corporate optimisation trends that have shaped the 21st century.

As wealth consolidates into fewer hands and consumer spending declines, the efficiency imperative of capitalism demands that economic production, optimisation and even decision-making move towards an AI model. Never mind 'America First', we're heading towards 'AI First', and fast!

For many our current bias is that robots and AI remain largely the playground of futurists and tech geeks. However, it feels like both technologies are coming together in ways that will challenge so many of the domains we believed could only be done by human beings.

3.1 From Short Circuit to Megan – A Refresher of History

So, back in the distant past of the early 2000s, robots were still clunky toys – think Roomba scooting across suburban floors, sucking up crumbs for $200 a pop. By 2010, they'd graduated to factory floors – Amazon's robotics pick and pack, moving goods around with frightening efficiency, whilst robotic arms churn out iPhones faster than any human line.

Japan's Fanuc plants hummed with orange bots, welding car frames with a precision that'd make a surgeon sweat. These weren't sci-fi fantasies; they were steel and circuits, bolted into reality one production line at a time. And happily, they still needed humans – programmers, overseers, fixers – to keep the wheels spinning.

Then AI hitched a ride. By 2015, Google's DeepMind was outsmarting Atari, learning Breakout faster than a kid with a joystick – raw code outpacing human reflex. In 2018, China's SenseTime rolled out facial recognition, tagging 100 million faces daily for Beijing's watchful eye, no beat-cop needed. Boston Dynamics' Spot danced across YouTube by 2020, a four-legged freak hauling crates in Singapore warehouses by 2023 – $75,000 a unit, cheaper than a year's wages.

Today, 2025, Walmart's drones stock Ohio shelves – 500 more last year, 2,000 jobs gone – while Tesla's Shanghai Gigafactory pumps out 1 million cars with a skeleton crew, AI syncing robots like a conductor with no baton.

What started as gears and servos is now a brain – relentless, networked, global. It's not a leap; it's a march, from Mumbai's sweatshops to London's trading floors, and we're not steering anymore.

This is usually when those wise councillors chuckle to themselves, and ask us to consider the adage, that every new technology might replace some existing workers but creates a whole new industry of jobs in its wake.

Already we can see this isn't holding true. Do we really think that it takes 2,000 people to create the drones that replaced those 2,000 jobs in Walmart? And then that will scale with the next 2,000, or 20,000, or 2 million jobs that are replaced?

Remember, this isn't just progress for its own sake. This is tightly coupled with the capitalist model of finding efficiencies and cost reduction. Taking the cost of a machine and comparing it to the lifetime cost of a human worker, the balance has tipped with a lot of up-side for owners.

No downtime for toilet breaks, sick kids, holidays or fatigue. No variation in output due to tiredness, distraction or simple human error. And no wage negotiation, human rights or inter-personal issues to deal with. High fives all round!

Still, there must be jobs only a human can do, right?

3.2 So, where do Humans still add value?

First, they came for our factory workers, and we thought 'that's okay'. Next, they came for our clerical jobs, and that seemed to make sense. Now we look around and creativity, financial controllers, educators, city planners and more are all slowly being replaced.

So are there some jobs that will remain better done by humans?

The answer lies in how AI and robotics can be trained. If it's a job that can be taught, then it's fair game.

Let's test this with a regular favourite, healthcare. That's a job that requires real empathy, that human touch of compassion and tailored care to ensure rounded wellbeing. Right?

The integration of AI and robotics into the medical and social care space is already a growing trend, driven by factors like aging populations, workforce shortages, and the desire to improve the quality of care.

Physical Assistance Robots:

- **Beyond robotic arms:** While robotic arms are helpful, exoskeletons are becoming increasingly sophisticated. Companies like Ekso Bionics and ReWalk Robotics create exoskeletons that allow individuals with spinal cord injuries to stand, walk, and even climb stairs. These devices are not just assistive tools but are becoming integrated with rehabilitation programs, helping people regain mobility and independence.
- **From hospitals to homes:** These technologies are moving beyond clinical settings. For example, robotic exosuits developed by companies like Sarcos Robotics are being used in industries like manufacturing and construction to enhance worker strength and endurance, preventing injuries and improving productivity.

Cognitive Assistance:

- **Beyond smartphone apps:** While AI-powered apps are helpful for cognitive training, companies like Cognixion are developing brain-computer interfaces that allow people with communication impairments to control devices and communicate using their thoughts. This technology has the potential to revolutionize how people with disabilities interact with the world.
- **AI for early diagnosis:** AI is being used to detect early signs of cognitive decline, such as Alzheimer's disease. For example, Winterlight Labs

analyses speech patterns to identify subtle changes that may indicate cognitive impairment, enabling earlier diagnosis and intervention.

- **Socially Assistive Robotics:** These robots are designed to provide companionship, emotional support, and cognitive stimulation. Today Paro, a therapeutic robot resembling a baby seal, is used to provide comfort and reduce stress in individuals with dementia. Then there's Pepper, a humanoid robot that can recognise emotions and engage in conversations, used in some care homes to provide social interaction.

Diagnostic and Surgery:

- **Beyond skin cancer:** AI's diagnostic capabilities extend far beyond skin cancer. For instance, IDx-DR is an AI system that can detect diabetic retinopathy from retinal images, allowing for early diagnosis and treatment to prevent blindness. This technology is particularly valuable in areas with limited access to ophthalmologists.

- **AI-guided surgery:** AI is being integrated into surgical robots to provide real-time guidance and improve accuracy. For example, the Monarch Platform by Auris Health uses AI and robotics to navigate the lungs during biopsies, enabling more precise targeting of lesions.

Monitoring and Safety:

- **Beyond Fitbits:** While wearable devices like Fitbits and Apple Watches are popular for health monitoring, continuous glucose monitors (CGMs) like those from Dexcom and Abbott are transforming diabetes management. These devices provide real-time glucose readings without the need for fingerstick blood tests, allowing for better control of blood sugar levels and reducing the risk of complications.

- **AI for fall prevention:** Beyond simple fall detection, AI is being used to predict and prevent falls. For example, Vayyar Care uses radar technology and AI to monitor the movements of older adults in their homes, identifying subtle changes in gait or balance that may indicate an increased risk of falling. This allows for proactive interventions to reduce fall risk.

These examples demonstrate how AI and robotics are moving beyond basic assistance to provide more sophisticated and integrated solutions in healthcare.

These technologies are not just improving the lives of individuals but are also transforming how healthcare is delivered and experienced.

An artificial care giver will never get frustrated by the ramblings of a senile patient, it will not overlook key diagnostic queues due to being overworked and tired, it won't cut corners because it doesn't want to deal with the messy parts of growing old.

And, perhaps unfortunately, this is what I want from my healthcare. That may be treasonous against the human jobs that have been shed, but selfishly, this level of care seems like it would provide the best outcomes with the lowest risk of human failings.

And that there, is the problem. How do we reasonably push back against this progress?

3.3 Where Will AI Excel and Lag?

Understanding exactly which roles AI will challenge and when, has a complex answer due to the number of variables at play. Some of these variables include cultural and ethical considerations, existing infrastructure, local and national policies, technology maturity.

All this suggests that adoption will necessarily be varied, but that the general motivation of nations to compete with each other will still ensure broad and relatively rapid global adoption.

Okay, what other roles did we think might be safer for humans, but are already being challenged?

1. **Therapists/ Counsellors:** While the human element seems crucial for mental health support, AI-powered chatbots like Woebot are providing cognitive behavioural therapy (CBT) and other interventions for conditions like anxiety and depression. These chatbots offer 24/7 support, personalised guidance, and can even track mood and progress. While they may not replace human therapists entirely, they offer an accessible and scalable alternative for those who may not have access to traditional therapy.
2. **Teachers:** Teaching involves complex human interaction, but AI is being used to personalise learning experiences and provide individualised

support. Platforms like Khan Academy use AI to adapt lessons to students' needs and pace, while tools like Google Classroom automate tasks like grading and feedback. AI tutors can also provide personalised support outside of the classroom, helping students with homework or test preparation.

3. **Artists/ Musicians:** Creativity was long considered a uniquely human domain, but AI is now generating art, music, and literature. For example, DALL-E 2 and Midjourney can create realistic and creative images from text descriptions, while AIVA (Artificial Intelligence Virtual Artist) composes original music for various purposes. While AI may not replace human artists entirely, it's challenging traditional notions of creativity and artistic expression.

4. **Writers/ Journalists:** Writing requires nuanced understanding and creativity, but AI is being used to generate news articles, reports, and even creative content. The Associated Press uses AI to write thousands of earnings reports each quarter, while tools like Jasper.ai help writers generate different kinds of creative text formats, like poems, code, scripts, musical pieces, email, letters, etc. This raises questions about the future of journalism and the role of human writers in a world where AI can produce written content quickly and efficiently.

5. **Software Developers:** Programming requires logical thinking and problem-solving skills, but AI is now being used to write and debug code. For example, GitHub Copilot uses AI to suggest code completions and generate entire functions based on natural language descriptions. This could potentially automate some aspects of software development, freeing up human developers to focus on more complex tasks.

These examples demonstrate that AI and robotics are encroaching on roles that were once considered exclusively human. They are not perfect, but they are as bad now as they will ever be. And, when you compare them year to year, the progress is staggering.

For my money, there are very few jobs that cannot be done by AI and robotics within the next 30 years. Without giving the same level of treatment to each, let's consider the other 'hallowed' roles that only humans can do.

- **Government and Leadership**: I'm definitely not voting for a robot to be my president, premier or prime minister! But if they're making great policy, improving the lives of citizens, solving meaningful problems, well… does it matter that their key advisors are actually AI systems. So, I guess, for now, I need my figurehead and the illusion of human leadership to be maintained.

- **Artists & Craftsman**: These are those people who create rare and beautiful works, through a deep love and rare skill in the craft itself. It may be producing custom furniture, a work of art, designing a new device or writing a song that touches you deeply. The truth is that these have always been very rare, and those with the skills have often been able to charge a premium commensurate with very limited production. The wealthy will continue to patronise such craftsman. Here, I think the mass production of artwork, music and artisan pieces will be consumed by AI, but the rare human talent and spirit will be cherished and nurtured, if only in part due to its growing rarity.

- **Maintenance Workers**: Jobs like plumbers, electricians and other maintenance workers, especially as apply to historic infrastructure, will likely be safe for a while. The reason is that the effort to create specialised robots to work in these environments will be weighed up against the value in rather upgrading the infrastructure itself. So, this one has a lifespan. As things reach their natural end of life and maintenance costs go up, the replacement will be designed to better facilitate maintenance and management by AI and robotics.

- **Faith Leaders**: This special category of leadership is important, as it has the need for humanity at its very core. Religion will most likely be one of the most important considerations, and defences for many, against the encroachments of AI and robotics. This one likely has the longest and most obvious connection to the importance of human representation.

The dawning realisation is that there are very few roles that you can state with certainty cannot be done by AI robots.

It is important to note that many will opt out of these systems, forming human-based communities, accepting the compromise of efficiency for autonomy. This will be a significant population, especially in regions where the cost to implement, maintain and manage the required infrastructure is not cost effective. These groups will be important settlements in the long-term story of humanity, but will probably remain a relatively small part of the overall population.

This is where you'll probably find me hiding – off-grid, bartering potatoes for 90s DVDs, muttering over a boardgame about the old world to anyone who will listen.

3.4 God Bless the Luddites: A Short History Lesson

The Luddites were a 19th-century English textile workers' movement that protested against newly developed labour-saving machinery from 1811 to 1816. They feared that the introduction of these machines would lead to job losses and a decline in wages, as fewer skilled workers would be needed to operate the new technology.

The Luddites, often operating under the mythical figurehead of "Ned Ludd," engaged in acts of sabotage, destroying textile machinery in factories and mills. While their actions were often violent, they targeted machines, not people. The British government responded with harsh repression, deploying troops to protect factories and passing laws that made machine-breaking a capital offense.

Ultimately, the Luddite movement was suppressed, but it remains a powerful symbol of worker resistance to technological change and the potential negative consequences of automation.

Today, the term "Luddite" is often used to describe anyone opposed to new technology, but it's important to remember the historical context and the legitimate concerns that fuelled the original Luddite movement.

The parallels between the textile workers and the introduction of new machinery, and the current mechanisation and automation of human labour should be clear to everyone. Their struggle, and the likely outcome, are very much the pattern I expect for the future. However, the main difference here is scale. I believe that more than 50% of jobs can and will be done by robots and AI within the next 30 years and will accelerate at that point.

3.5 The Question of Governance & Government

Whilst, arguably, AI and robotics have been in development for several decades, the reality is that it is only in the last few years that they have exploded into the mainstream awareness, and increasingly in cross sector, cross capability adoption.

Policies, especially broad ranging multinational policies, don't move that quickly. That is how commercial businesses have managed to move forward with some questionable practices, such as training their models with data that they did not own. Other businesses have launched under the guise of a communal open source model, only to pivot to commercial entity without any real checks and balances.

Many businesses have been more cautious at actually using some of these tools, as they have a dual concern; is their data going to be used by the service providers, and if they use the service do they open themselves up to challenge having used a model trained with questionable data sources.

Looking forward, the controls and governance of AI will be an important part of the discussion at many levels. People will continue to demand control until it becomes very clear that people bring their own bias to such control. And bias isn't necessarily bad. If your bias is towards protecting human jobs, people's dignity, and our general autonomy, there are some strong arguments to support having this bias.

However, big business will argue that AI is simply better at doing business and that, under the 'right' circumstances, AI will make better decisions. These 'better' decisions are, however, also subject to the bias of the algorithm and data.

Given how money drives business, business drives economies, and economies rely on governments, I think the reality is that the AI policy will become more and more token, than real. In much the same way as economic policies of capitalism over ride the broader needs of the populations that support the government who protect capitalism.

It is inevitable that AI will have a greater and greater role in corporate governance, and in country governments. This comes down to the way that AI can process massive amounts of data, across many dimensions, and provide useful insights and proposed courses of action. For those who rightly point out the failing of the AI to make the 'right calls, all the time', it's a fair criticism. But, let's face it, humans are no less fallible… and often much more so. And the AI today will only improve.

People will still vote for compelling figures, but those leaders will be informed by teams who lean heavily into AI provided viewpoints. Leaders will be more than just figureheads, but the reality is that they will be so largely advised by the AI systems, that really the function of government will become a proxy of the AI.

So, the move from AI dashboards, to AI recommendations, to AI-first default positions will be rapidly adopted by a very large number of governments within the next 30 years.

3.6 2040–2100: The Great Machine Emerges

AI is no longer a tool; it's the bloodstream of the global economy.

In 2040 robots fill Foxconn's assembly lines, each unit costing a fraction of a human wage. Walmart's drones replace warehouse pickers, scanning and shelving goods in minutes. Autonomous cargo fleets cross oceans with just two supervisors in a data bunker somewhere in Rotterdam. Hospitals in Tokyo, Lagos, and São Paulo run 80% autonomously – AI diagnosing faster than any mortal brain, robotic surgeons boasting near-zero error rates.

Teachers? Mostly replaced by adaptive AI tutors in India and the Philippines, personalising lessons in real-time. Government, too – traffic grids, resource allocation, even low-level legal rulings are decided by algorithms. Human oversight remains, but it's becoming theatre, a relic we cling to for comfort.

By 2060, the system tightens. Capitalism, once requiring mass consumers, now relies on a fraction of the population who can pay for curated exclusivity. Healthcare is a labyrinth of AI-run clinics: if you have premium coverage, you get a custom-tailored nano-surgery; if not, you receive a standard, minimal drone drop.

Education is entirely stratified – half the world's youth has never met a human teacher, only an AI that calibrates lessons by micro facial cues. The wealthy keep real tutors, real doctors, real experiences. Everyone else? Subscriptions, illusions, digital content.

Supply chains are so optimised that human dockworkers or truckers seem archaic, lumps in a process. In Berlin, local government runs on code – AI-driven welfare and housing allocations, with "public servants" reduced to a handful of operators.

Resistance flickers in pockets. In the American Rust Belt, communes shun AI, choosing bartered goods and home-schooling. In India's interior, "human-led enclaves" vow never to let machines manage their crops or classrooms. They're small, though, and overshadowed by the unstoppable wave of AI adoption. For every rebel enclave, five more corporations pivot to automated everything.

In 2080 capitalism is almost post-human. Drones build new corporate citadels in the Middle East, running 24/7 without pay or protest. Municipal councils from Oslo to Cape Town let AI set budgets, collect taxes, or dole out UBI – an act of necessity to keep the unemployed from revolting. In Shanghai, half the city's workforce is "economically idle," living off meagre UBI while commercial towers hum with robots that need no lunch break.

Education? A new generation sees teachers as novelties, like vinyl records or horse-drawn carriages. Healthcare is a soulless marvel – Berlin's hospitals sense your ailment before you do, prescribing gene tweaks or nanobot repairs. Yet human empathy has a price: real nurses for the affluent, mechanical care for the rest.

An old man stands in Times Square with a handwritten sign: 'We have embraced a system that no longer embraces us.' Holographic billboards flicker around him as self-driving cars zip quietly past. Nobody notices. The system runs too smoothly. And nobody understands the message.

The century closes, as AI capitalism thrives on exclusivity, no longer requiring mass consumption at scale. A global caste emerges: the Curated Elite who purchase real life – rare artisanal goods, human companionship, physical travel – and everyone else, renting illusions. The machines handle everything: forging supply chains, managing local governments, teaching digital classes, diagnosing your heartbeat. Drones deliver medicine, groceries, entertainment, all conjured by an AI that tracks every whim.

Human labour is a novelty. In Oslo, a handful of "empathy doctors" serve trillionaires seeking old-fashioned bedside manner. In Delhi's outskirts, entire communities remain off-grid, growing their own food, teaching children via aging textbooks – rebels or anachronisms, depending on your point of view. Their existence is viewed as quaint nostalgia. It poses no real threat; the machine has devoured everything else.

3.7 Rage Against the Dying Light

Do I think we should accept this possible reality? Well, that's a complex question. I might choose not to accept a rising tide, but chances are it will happen anyway.

This exact rising tide is going to displace millions of people due to climate change, whether we accept it or not.

I do think we need to have a sensible discussion about what this level of displaced employment looks like. In a different life, I have worked on dozens of software projects where good change management has made all the difference to the outcome. We need leaders who take a considered view that balances much more than the interests of the wealthy into account – they'll be fine. We need leaders to ensure that we use this opportunity to move towards a world where AI and automation serve the betterment and wider interests of society.

There are scenarios where AI and robotics take away the daily grind of work, freeing us up to pursue our interests and explore our deeper purpose. This is the utopian dream made real. However, right now we're far too focused on who fits the bill today, rather than adjusting society to a very different, and potentially much richer, way of living tomorrow.

As if that wasn't challenging enough, we now need to overlay more than just economic models, the different pace of development globally, cultural sensitivities, but also the impact of the natural world of climate crisis, ecological destruction and mass extinction.

Before we can decide what kind of AI future we want, we need to answer a bigger question: Do we even have a future at all? The planet isn't waiting for us to sort out our technology and economic problems. The world is burning. And next, we're going to talk about what's left to save.

3.8 Chapter Summary

A. **AI and robotics aren't the future – they are the present.** Foxconn replaced 60,000 workers in a single factory, Walmart's drones are stocking shelves, and AI is replacing finance analysts at Goldman Sachs. The shift isn't coming – it's here.

B. **This is capitalism's final evolution: relentless efficiency.** AI and robotics don't need wages, sick leave, or sleep. They don't strike, they don't make mistakes, and they don't demand fair pay. That's why businesses aren't hesitating to replace human workers – profit demands it.

C. **The promise that "new technology creates new jobs" is breaking down.** A few roles in AI development may emerge, but not at the scale needed to replace the millions of lost jobs. When a single drone can replace a warehouse worker, that's the end of the conversation.

D. **There are almost no "safe" jobs anymore.** Factory workers, clerks, lawyers, teachers, artists – even therapists and doctors are being replaced by AI-driven systems. If a task can be learned, AI can master it, automate it, and make human workers obsolete.

E. **By 2100, AI capitalism won't need human participation.** Robots will run factories, algorithms will dictate government policy, and AI will manage healthcare, finance, and logistics. Human labour will become a novelty – reserved for the elite who can afford "authentic" services.

3.9 What Can You Do About It?

1. **Stop betting on job security – it's not coming back.** The AI economy doesn't care about skills – it cares about efficiency. Adaptability and ownership matter more than traditional career paths.
2. **Control, not employment, will define power.** In a world run by AI, owning assets, energy, and infrastructure is the only real security. Workers will become consumers of AI-generated goods, but those who control the AI systems will control the economy.
3. **Think beyond traditional education and work.** AI is already replacing teachers, lawyers, and doctors. If a job is data-driven, predictable, or rule-based, AI will take it. Seek skills in human networks, resource access, and AI-resistant fields.
4. **Human-led enclaves will emerge – but they won't be the norm.** Some will reject AI-driven society, forming off-grid communities where human labour still holds value. But these will be the exception, not the rule.
5. **This isn't just about jobs – it's about survival in a post-human economy.** The new divide won't be rich vs. poor, but those inside the AI system vs. those outside it. Decide where you want to be – before the choice is made for you.

Vignette C: Reem – Living Through Shifting Sands

C.1 Beirut, Lebanon – 2031

Reem arrived in the world during an uneasy calm in 2031, her cries mingling with the hum of overhead drones patrolling a post-conflict city. Beirut was a mosaic of repaired high-rises, bullet-riddled walls, and hopeful street art proclaiming unity in half a dozen languages.

Her parents, Malik and Lina, worked long hours in precarious jobs – Malik ran an ad-hoc delivery service for local traders, and Lina taught English in a shuttered wing of the city's battered university. Talk of AI-driven governance had yet to fully touch Lebanon, but the early seeds were there in the automated checkpoint scanners and the half-hearted attempts to modernise public offices. Rising summer heat was an annual complaint, but few grasped that the climate crisis lapping at other shores would soon grip the Levant.

In Reem's earliest years, she roamed with cousins along narrow alleys crammed with fruit stalls. Certain parts of Beirut felt open, even jovial, particularly on days when the Mediterranean breeze carried music from rooftop gatherings.

But other neighbourhoods lay hushed – a quiet born of exhaustion. Tensions between sectarian groups simmered on, overshadowed by economic scarcity. By age eight, Reem noticed how each family scraped to survive; mothers clutched ration stamps to buy cooking fuel, and fathers bartered side gigs to keep the lights on. Still, no matter how meagre the day's earnings, Malik insisted they dine together, hoping to instil resilience in his daughter.

"The future always finds us," he'd say gently, "whether we're ready or not."

C.2 Beirut, Lebanon – 2050

At nineteen, Reem was perched on the cusp of an unsteady adulthood.

The once-familiar city was strained under chronic water shortages, with fresh produce dearer each month and rolling blackouts punctuating daily life. Urban flight had transformed entire districts of Beirut into half-populated shells, dotted by AI-run enclaves for the wealthy or politically connected.

The government had partnered with foreign tech firms to automate essential services – an efficient but soulless brand of governance that left locals feeling marginalised. Reem's father, now in his late fifties, turned to private courier work for an emerging corporate enclave near the waterfront, ferrying sensitive documents in an electric van funded by overseas investors.

Reem spent her free hours volunteering at a makeshift community centre, teaching younger children to read Arabic and English. She believed in the city's stubborn heart, even as more neighbours sold their apartments for meagre sums and joined the tide of migrants heading for Europe or the Gulf.

A dull ache gnawed at her: was Lebanon merely a stepping-stone for anyone with ambition? Her mother, Lina, had quietly left for a teaching position in Doha two years earlier, drawn by stable pay and climate-controlled towers. Reem wrestled with her own restlessness; part of her yearned to follow, but the thought of abandoning Beirut felt like a betrayal.

"Every time you walk away," she told a friend, "another sliver of our city's soul fades."

C.3 Doha, Qatar – 2075

Eventually, Reem left. By forty-four, she was no longer the idealistic teen who saw hope in every corner of Beirut. Instead, she'd witnessed enough storms, blackouts, and currency collapses to recognise that survival required compromise. She joined her mother in Doha, the region's gleaming testament to AI-assisted prosperity.

Towering spires soared above reclaimed waterfronts, and temperatures routinely soared to 48°C in summer, made bearable by giant climate domes. Corporate-run enclaves managed water distribution, medical care, and surveillance with ruthless efficiency; in public squares, AI-driven holograms projected national pride and global connectivity.

Reem found work as a cultural liaison for an arts consortium bankrolled by Qatari wealth and European investors. Her role: organise tours and events that flaunted the region's architectural marvels and curated traditions. She grew adept at translating the stories of calligraphers, mosaic artists, and oud musicians for visiting diplomats.

Yet behind the shimmer of prosperity, she saw the precariousness. Foreign workers from across Asia and Africa lived in strictly zoned districts, policed by algorithms that allocated everything from food rations to commuting hours. One day she spent an afternoon guiding envoys through an immaculate gallery exhibit; the next, she glimpsed labourers trudging in the searing heat, reliant on meagre AI-monitored allotments of water.

The longer she stayed, the more Doha felt like a gilded bubble – untouchable except by the desert storms that occasionally rattled the edges. And yet, it offered Reem an unaccustomed sense of stability. Her mother, nearing retirement, insisted they were fortunate to be safe when entire nations found themselves drowning or burning.

At night, she read news of climate-choked Africa, of warlords and corporate enclaves scuffling for water rights along the Nile, or battered migrants turned away from European AI-run borders. The memory of Beirut still tugged at her, but she was no longer certain there was anything to return to.

C.4 Damascus, Syria – 2100

As Reem stepped onto a makeshift platform in Damascus at age sixty-nine, the sun glinted off cracked minarets and half-restored architectural gems. Syria had lurched through decades of conflict, resource depletion, and painfully slow rebuilding.

Now a loose consortium of local councils and foreign-funded enclaves attempted to revive the historic city core with modern infrastructure. Reem had come as part of a delegation, representatives from Doha-based philanthropic circles, aiming to sponsor cultural revival and minimal AI-based city services in war-scarred regions.

For weeks, Reem moved among dusty courtyards where old Damascus lingered in shards of battered mosaics and battered dreams.

Technicians from Europe installed solar micro-grids with the help of local volunteers, bridging the gap left by a hollowed-out state. Reem watched them string up power lines, cautious but hopeful, as small pockets of normalcy emerged: a baker's stall reopening, children scrawling pictures of orchard trees on crumbling walls. In every conversation, she caught echoes of her younger self – an unshakeable love for home, an awareness that leaving might be easier, yet staying was a quiet act of faith.

One late afternoon, as she stood at the courtyard edge, she reflected on the path that had led her here. Beirut to Doha, now Damascus: each place burdened by climate extremes, AI enclaves, and the tenuous hope of those trying to rebuild from the rubble.

She saw the deeper tapestry behind every broken street – a world reeling under unstoppable forces, but refusing to vanish entirely. Turning to greet a group of teen volunteers, Reem felt a surprising surge of optimism.

In their dusty hands, carrying solar panels and half-laughing at the new technology's quirks, she glimpsed a resilience that might just outrun the disasters. Perhaps, she thought, the future still held space for those who chose to stay, endure, and nurture fragile roots, no matter how often the ground crumbled beneath them.

Chapter 4: Living with Collapse – Climate & Ecology

In the last 50 years, the Earth has lost more than half of its wildlife populations. The ocean has absorbed the heat equivalent of five Hiroshima-sized atomic bombs every second for the past 25 years. We are losing tropical rainforests at a rate equivalent to 40 football fields every minute. Atmospheric CO2 levels are higher now than at any point in the past 800,000 years. Tipping points are in the rearview mirror.

This chapter is why I wrote this book. We love to describe ourselves as the stewards of this fragile world. And the results speak for themselves.

4.1 The World in 24-hours

Imagine the 4.54 billion-year[11] history of our planet squeezed into a single 24-hour day. The clock kicks off in the dead of night. Earth coalesces from dust, gas, and brutal collisions – a molten, chaotic mess that somehow holds together. It's raw, unstable, alive with potential.

For hours, it's quiet. A cosmic hush. The surface cools, the stage sets, but nothing stirs. Then, around 3:50 AM, the first whispers of life flicker into being – simple, single-celled organisms floating in primordial seas. They're fragile, stubborn, biding their time. They drift through the dark, adapting, enduring.

By 9:30 AM, a game-changer hits: photosynthesis. Sunlight turns into fuel, and the atmosphere shifts. Oxygen seeps in – once a toxin, now a spark for potential. The planet stays microbial for hours, a world of slime simmering from morning to evening. Not dead, just quiet, dreaming in a hazy sprawl.

Multicellular life doesn't show until 7:30 PM – a slow, subtle shift in the evening shadows. Cells team up, specialize, build. Complexity creeps forward, picking up steam.

At 9:22 PM, the Cambrian Explosion tears through the stillness. Eyes blink open. Spines stiffen. Predators stalk. Shells harden. Nature hurls everything at the wall in a wild, evolutionary sprint.

[11] Calculations are based on Earth's age of 4.54 billion years compressed into 24 hours (86,400 seconds), where 1 second ≈ 52,546 years. Event timings align with current scientific estimates: first life ~3.8 billion years ago, photosynthesis ~2.7 billion years ago, multicellular life ~600–800 million years ago, and so on, scaled proportionally.

By 10:12 PM, the first vertebrates crawl from sea to land. The air bites, but the horizon's wide open. From 10:52 PM to 11:39 PM, dinosaurs strut their stuff – massive, majestic, unstoppable. Their reign crashes at 11:39 PM, 21 minutes shy of midnight, when a rock from the void slams the reset button. Fire rains. The Earth chokes. Silence falls.

Then: regrowth. Faster now, like the planet's got a memory, an urgency to restart. Mammals dart through the ashes, clawing their way up. Time spirals on.

At 23:59:56, Homo sapiens stumble onto the scene. Four seconds to midnight. ***Four seconds…***

Jesus' crucifixion? We're talking roughly 0.038 seconds ago on this scale. The Industrial Revolution? That's about 0.005 seconds back. Right now? A flicker in a flicker.

This lens sharpens the brevity of our existence – and the weight of our footprint. Civilizations, wars, ideas, machines – all jammed into a cosmic gasp.

Still wrestling with the scale?

Try this: Picture a small cardboard box – just big enough for a stack of dog-eared books, a few scratched 90s CDs, your sleep journal. Now, in your mind, set it down anywhere on the vast surface of the Earth. Let that box represent the **entire duration** of humanity's existence, our species' brief time here. And the Earth it rests on? That represents the planet's **full 4.54-billion-year history**. Suddenly, our whole story seems impossibly short against the deep time beneath it, doesn't it?

Now, look inside that box – inside humanity's time span. See the eraser on a gnawed pencil, rattling around? That tiny eraser is the **length of time** since the Industrial Revolution began. A tiny sliver *within* our already brief moment. And that tiny sliver lines up precisely with that barely-there 0.005 seconds on our 24-hour clock. Four seconds for humanity on the clock; a small box sitting on the globe. Five-thousandths of a second for the industrial age; just the eraser inside that box. A flicker within a flicker.

And yet, in those four seconds, we've torched the atmosphere, shredded the biosphere, and clawed our mark on everything that comes next

4.2 Examining the Evidence

The story of Earth's climate and ecological history is etched in ice cores and ancient sediments, a story of slow, cyclical shifts playing out over millennia. Yet, the version we're witnessing today is a jarring departure from this measured rhythm. Imagine a film reel suddenly sped up, the gradual evolution of landscapes and atmospheres replaced by a frenetic, almost violent transformation.

We see this in the atmospheric CO2 levels, a metric that once fluctuated gently over vast stretches of time, now spiking with an unprecedented ferocity. Ice core data[12], our planet's historical archive, reveals natural CO2 shifts occurring over thousands of years, tiny changes of mere tens of parts per million.

Then came the Industrial Revolution. The curve turned vertical – 140 ppm added in just two centuries. This isn't the planet breathing. It's gasping. And that gasp leaves a distinctive fingerprint, a chemical signature that points directly to our own actions.

Isotopic analysis of atmospheric CO2 reveals that the increase isn't from volcanic eruptions or natural releases, but from the burning of fossil fuels, a carbon source with a unique and traceable composition.

4.3 It's All Connected

The oceans, meanwhile, are not merely warming; they are acidifying at a rate unseen in millions of years, a direct consequence of absorbing our excess carbon. This isn't a natural oceanic cycle; it's a chemical reaction to the atmospheric overload we've created.

Then, consider the scale of ecological disruption.

Extinction events, once spaced out by eons, are now occurring at a pace that dwarfs anything seen in the recent geological past. Species are vanishing at rates 100 to 1,000 times higher than the natural background rate, a mass extinction

---

[12] Scientists analyse these cores, finding a stark rise in CO2 levels since the Industrial Revolution. Pre-industrial levels hovered around 280 parts per million (ppm), but core data now shows we've surged past 400 ppm, a dramatic increase directly linked to fossil fuel combustion. This irrefutable evidence, preserved in layers of ice, underscores the rapid and unprecedented change in our planet's atmosphere. [Source: https://www.bas.ac.uk/data/our-data/publication/ice-cores-and-climate-change/]

driven by habitat loss, pollution, and a climate that's changing too rapidly for many species to adapt.

Habitats, once vast and interconnected, are now fragmented by roads, cities, and farms, a uniquely human-driven pattern that isolates populations and weakens ecosystems. This isn't just a natural ebb and flow of life; it's a systematic dismantling of the planet's intricate web of biodiversity.

Climate models, when fed with data on natural factors alone, fail to replicate the warming patterns we observe. But when they incorporate human-induced greenhouse gas emissions, they match the observed changes with striking accuracy, clear evidence of the overwhelming influence of our actions.

The spatial pattern of warming, the isotopic signature of atmospheric gases, the unprecedented rate of ocean acidification, the sheer scale of biodiversity loss – all these point to a single, undeniable conclusion: the changes we're witnessing are not merely natural variations; they are a human-induced transformation of the planet, a transformation unfolding at an unprecedented and alarming pace.

We are the bull standing in the shattered remains of the vases, plates and crystal glasses now scattered across the shop floor. To claim the vases would have fallen on their own is beyond naïve – it's a lie. A lie with consequences.

4.4 The Acceleration of Climate Disruption

From where we stand, collapse feels like a slow burn – no meteor strike, no *Day After Tomorrow* freeze-frame. No single thunderclap marked the shift. It crept in quietly, a gradual unravelling that turned to wildfire.

If we measure change by a human lifetime, it still seems manageable – gradual, even. But zoom out, and the scale of acceleration becomes terrifying.

Look back across 2,000 years, and the breakpoint is unmistakable: the Industrial Revolution. A slow incline of stability gives way to an almost vertical climb. Widen the lens further, and for centuries upon centuries, Earth's climate barely flickers – then, suddenly, the last two centuries rise like a brick wall.

And species, caught in the momentum, have slammed into this wall at full speed.

By Neil Meyer

The dead pile up[13] – silent eyes, staring back.

Lying there, frozen in time, is the Pyrenean Ibex, a mountain-dwelling wild goat that once roamed the highlands between France and Spain. Officially extinct in 2000, it was one of the first casualties of a world changing too fast to sustain its way of life.

Nearby is the Bramble Cay Melomys, a tiny rodent that lived exclusively on a remote cay in the Great Barrier Reef. In 2016, it became the first recorded mammal driven to extinction *entirely* by climate change. Rising sea levels didn't just threaten its home; they erased it.

Polar bears hunt on sea ice, but the ice is vanishing. Already, populations are starving, drowning, cannibalising each other. At what point will the last one fall? How long until their frozen kingdom exists only in zoos, before disappearing altogether? The last of these wild creatures is running toward the wall at break neck speed, still here – but not for long.

There is no "do over" here. No coming back from extinction. These aren't individual tragedies – they are eras closing in the hubris of human advancement.

But here's what should terrify us most: the speed of destruction is accelerating so fast that we can now see it year to year.

Let that sink in.

For most of human history, climate shifts played out over millennia – so slow our ancestors never noticed. For most of the last thousand years, change happened over centuries, barely perceptible between generations. Then, suddenly, it compressed to decades.

---

[13] Unlike past mass extinctions driven by natural forces, the current crisis is a human-made catastrophe.
Unprecedented habitat destruction, relentless pollution, and the accelerating climate crisis are pushing species to extinction at rates unseen in millions of years. From vanishing rainforests to acidifying oceans, our actions are dismantling the delicate web of life, threatening countless plants and animals. [Source: https://news.stanford.edu/stories/2023/09/human-driven-mass-extinction-eliminating-entire-genera]

And now?

We see the difference between individual years. Each summer hotter than the last. Each wildfire season longer. Each glacier, gone between one photo and the next. The future isn't coming – it's vanishing before our eyes.

4.5 The New Climate Reality

Shifting the spotlight from those cute and cuddly critters, and pulling it back to the star of the show – how does this unfolding climate reality play out for humanity? Because, let's face it, if it isn't impacting us directly, then it's going to be little more than a "too bad, so sad" footnote in our shared personal story.

Last year, the global average temperature clawed at 1.5°C[14] above pre-industrial levels – a number once scrawled in red ink as a "Do Not Cross!" warning. The IPCC's old "catastrophic" scenarios are today's weather reports, only happening even faster than they predicted.

If the planet was a steak, some spots are still pink, but most of it is just burnt offerings now. Probably appropriate given how faith might be the only option available...

For those that have prioritised Breaking Bad, Game of Thrones and The Voice – all great shows – over some quality time with David Attenborough, here are the summary notes for this warming planet situation.

Human activities have fundamentally altered the Earth's atmospheric composition, primarily through the burning of fossil fuels, deforestation, and industrial agriculture. The combustion of coal, oil, and natural gas releases vast quantities of carbon dioxide (CO2), a potent greenhouse gas, into the atmosphere. Deforestation reduces the planet's capacity to absorb CO2, as trees act as vital carbon sinks.

Additionally, agricultural practices, such as livestock farming and the use of nitrogen-based fertilisers, contribute to the release of methane and nitrous oxide, respectively, further amplifying the greenhouse effect. These greenhouse gases

[14] The first 12-month period to exceed 1.5°C as an average was February 2023 – January 2024, boosted by El Niño, when the average temperature worldwide was estimated to be 1.52°C higher than 1850–1900. [Source: https://www.un.org/en/climatechange/science/climate-issues/degrees-matter]

trap heat within the atmosphere, leading to a gradual increase in global average temperatures.

To dumb it down a little… it's almost like we've created our own global microwave, with a solid housing made of all these fun chemicals. Now let's see what happens when we turn it on.

This warming trend sets in motion a series of self-sustaining feedback loops[15] that accelerate the problem. For instance, as temperatures rise, polar ice caps and glaciers melt, reducing the Earth's reflectivity (albedo). This allows more solar radiation to be absorbed, further warming the planet. Thawing permafrost releases trapped methane, a greenhouse gas far more potent than CO2, into the atmosphere, creating a positive feedback cycle.

Warmer oceans absorb less CO2, leaving more in the atmosphere to trap heat. Wildfires[16], intensified by hotter and drier conditions, release enormous amounts of carbon into the atmosphere, which again, accelerates warming. These cascading effects create a dangerous cycle where initial warming triggers further warming, making it increasingly difficult to mitigate the problem.

Humanity's greatest invention: a self-sustaining death engine on its own momentum. No kill-switch in sight.

And as a result, let's step through what's happening, and what likely to happen within the next 40 to 50 years.

South Asia sweats through months at 50°C. By May, Delhi's streets are bare, Karachi's power grids flicker and fail, and Dhaka's slums bake into open ovens where even the shade is a killer. The Sahel sprawls south, a sand tide swallowing northern Nigeria's farms, forcing 40 million people to migrate inland, chasing rivers that are running dry.

---

[15] Climate tipping points are conditions beyond which changes in a part of the climate system become self-perpetuating. These changes may lead to abrupt, irreversible, and dangerous impacts with serious implications for humanity. [Source: https://www.science.org/doi/10.1126/science.abn7950]

[16] On average, the fire season has lengthened by 27% globally and is particularly pronounced in the Amazon, the Mediterranean, and western North America—all places that have been devastated by wildfires in the last five years. [Source: https://www.ifaw.org/journal/climate-change-wildfires]

Wildfires ignore the seasons. In the Americas, Oregon's forests burn into December, the Amazon spits smoke year-round, and Canada's boreal belt chars black, layer by layer, year after year. Europe – once the moderate sanctuary of the Global North – reels from the whiplash. Athens hits 45°C, London floods knee-deep, Hamburg swings from drought to deluge like a city that can't make up its mind.

The climate's no longer a crisis approaching. It's a climate caste system.

4.6 Small Corrections

Some are trying to push back, making corrections where they can.

Despite the daunting scale of the climate crisis, numerous initiatives offer glimmers of hope. The rapid expansion of renewable energy, particularly solar and wind, is transforming power grids globally, with countries like Denmark leading the charge[17].

Simultaneously, regenerative agriculture is gaining traction, with farmers adopting practices that sequester carbon and enhance soil health, exemplified by projects like the Great Green Wall in Africa, aiming to combat desertification[18]. Urban centres are also adapting, with cities like Rotterdam pioneering innovative water management systems to mitigate flood risks[19].

In the face of escalating climate change, some have turned to controversial technological interventions. Geoengineering proposals, such as stratospheric aerosol injection (SAI), involve spraying sulphur aerosols into the atmosphere to reflect sunlight, potentially cooling the planet. However, as demonstrated by theoretical models applied to regions like Mumbai, these interventions can disrupt regional weather patterns, such as monsoon cycles, and carry significant uncertainties and risks[20].

Community led initiatives like local food movements, and zero waste projects are also happening globally. The growing adoption of electric vehicles coupled with improvements in battery storage, are also helping to lower emissions.

---

[17] Source: IRENA - Renewable Power Generation Costs in 2021

[18] Source: UNCCD - The Great Green Wall

[19] Source: Resilient Cities Network - Rotterdam

[20] Source: IPCC AR6 - Geoengineering

Technological advancements are also playing a crucial role. Innovation in battery storage is vital for grid stability, and the development of sustainable building materials offers alternatives to high-carbon footprint options like concrete.

International cooperation, such as the Paris Agreement, provides a framework for global action, although its implementation remains a critical challenge [21] . Simultaneously, carbon capture and storage (CCS) technologies aim to remove CO_2 from the atmosphere or point sources. While projects like those in Norway are operational, capturing millions of tons annually, they represent a fraction of the tens of billions of tons of CO_2 released each year[22] .

The effectiveness of CCS is limited by scalability, cost, and the need for secure long-term storage, highlighting the disparity between current technological capabilities and the magnitude of the climate challenge.

It's crucial to acknowledge that while these efforts are promising, scaling them up significantly and ensuring equitable implementation are essential for addressing the climate crisis effectively.

Whilst the challenge is immense, and we are losing much more each day than we delay or recover, it is important to look for new solutions.

Later in the book we'll discuss how people can work as individuals and groups, to make a difference.

4.7 Vanishing Water, Vanishing Crops

If climate is a caste system, then food is its currency and water its gatekeeper.

For most of history, food has been a given, or at least relatively predictable for a given location and stable variables. Now, it's a gamble.

Aquifers – those ancient underground seas that have kept civilizations alive – are running out. Rain used to be enough to refill them. Not anymore.

In the Middle East, Saudi Arabia hoards desalinated water to keep Riyadh's vertical farms running, but Yemen's wells are sandpits, its cities dark by dusk.

---

[21] Source: UNFCCC - The Paris Agreement

[22] Source: Global CCS Institute - Global Status of CCS Report

Let's pick a random example to illustrate[23] what's happening.

In the USA, the windswept plains of Kansas, once a sea of waving wheat, tell a story of agricultural triumph and a looming reckoning. For a century, this state has been a titan of food production, its fields feeding not just a nation, but the world. The early pioneers, with their hardy strains of wheat and stubborn determination, laid the foundation[24].

Then came the roar of tractors, the chemical alchemy of fertilisers, and the miracle of hybrid seeds, propelling Kansas into the heart of the American breadbasket. But beneath this surface of abundance, a silent drama has been unfolding, one that threatens to rewrite the very identity of the state.

The Ogallala Aquifer was Kansas' hidden wealth – an underground sea fuelling America's breadbasket. But it's vanishing. Farmers pump deeper, yields shrink, and dust replaces wheat. The American breadbasket is cracking, and when the aquifer runs dry, the myth of endless abundance will collapse with it.

Looking ahead to 2030, Kansas farmers face a stark choice: adapt or wither. Climate change, with its rising temperatures and erratic rainfall, will exacerbate the water crisis, pushing the Ogallala to its limits. Technology offers a glimmer of

---

[23] Other examples could include
The Iberian Peninsula (Spain and Portugal): Intensive agriculture, especially for irrigated crops, depletes aquifers and rivers, exacerbating drought conditions and desertification risks.
The Chilean Altiplano: Lithium mining and intensive agriculture (especially quinoa and alfalfa) drastically deplete fragile high-altitude aquifers, impacting indigenous communities and environments.
Indus River Basin (India/Pakistan): Massive agricultural demand drains aquifers, fueling geopolitical water wars.
North China Plain (China): Industrial and farm pumping collapses aquifers, with the Yellow River running dangerously low.
Middle East/North Africa (MENA): Extreme scarcity drives over-pumping, forcing reliance on costly desalination, and inflaming regional tensions.
Murray-Darling Basin (Australia): Irrigation over-allocation and drought decimate river flows, crippling a vital food-producing region

[24] The vast, native grasslands of Kansas, dominated by diverse prairie grasses, were systematically ploughed and converted into fields for cultivation. This involved the removal of native vegetation, which had deep root systems that held the soil together and contributed to its fertility. This conversion drastically altered the ecosystem, reducing biodiversity and disrupting natural water cycles.

hope, with precision irrigation and drought-resistant crops promising to squeeze more from less. But these solutions come at a cost, all of which mean more human intervention into natural systems.

The question is not just whether Kansas can continue to feed the world, but whether it can sustain its own agricultural heritage in the face of dwindling resources and an increasingly unpredictable climate. The once proud wheat fields may yield to hardier, less water-intensive crops, or even to the return of the native grasses, a stark reminder that even the most ambitious human endeavours are ultimately bound by the limits of the land.

In China's industrial north, factories idle as Beijing rations the last trickles of the Yellow River[25]. Rural protests erupt, but there's nothing left to fight over.

And in Africa, water is destiny. Ethiopia's dams hold the Blue Nile hostage, feeding its cities while Sudan and Egypt's farmers are left praying for floods that don't come. Somalia's rains fail entirely. Fifteen million people walk south, crashing into Kenya's electrified fences, clawing for a way through.

Beyond the parched fields and depleted aquifers, a staggering amount of food is simply thrown away. When water is hoarded, and food is thrown away by the ton, famine isn't a natural disaster. It's a choice.

This isn't just a moral failing; it's a colossal drain on resources, including the very water we're fighting to conserve.

Consider the European Union, where roughly 88 million tonnes of food are wasted annually. This isn't just discarded scraps; it's the equivalent of entire harvests rotting in landfills, consuming land, water, and energy that could have fed millions. In Spain, for example, vast quantities of perfectly edible fruits and vegetables are rejected due to cosmetic imperfections, a wasteful practice driven by consumer expectations and retail standards.

Over the next 20 to 30 years, this will become an even more critical issue. As water scarcity intensifies in regions like the Mediterranean, the pressure to reduce food waste will mount. In a place like Spain, where water stress is already a reality, this

---

[25] 82% of China's glaciers have retreated and more than one-fifth of the ice cover has disappeared since the 1950s. [Source: https://earth.org/tackling-chinas-water-shortage-crisis/]

could mean a shift towards more flexible retail standards, increased focus on processing imperfect produce, and potentially, even rationing of water-intensive foods. If these changes are not made, then the water stress will only get worse, impacting the ability to grow crops at all.

In sub-Saharan Africa, the challenge is different.

Here, post-harvest losses are a major issue. In Nigeria, for instance, up to 40% of fruits and vegetables spoil before reaching markets due to inadequate storage and transportation. This is a tragedy in a region where food insecurity is widespread. The combination of climate change and food waste will create a vicious cycle of hunger and instability, potentially leading to increased migration and conflict.

Technology offers a double-edged sword against water scarcity, a lifeline for the privileged, and a distant dream for the rest. Singapore's gleaming hydroponic farms, fuelled by billions, achieve near self-sufficiency – a celebration of innovation, yet a luxury few can afford. These high-tech solutions, however, demand immense energy, raising questions of long-term sustainability as climate pressures mount and energy costs soar.

On the other side of the world, in California's parched Central Valley, AI-driven irrigation promises efficiency, but at a steep price. Only wealthy coastal enclaves reap the benefits, creating a stark divide where corporate farms thrive while smaller ones wither.

This trend towards tech-driven consolidation threatens rural livelihoods, exacerbating existing inequalities. Desalination, similarly, remains a costly, energy-intensive solution, primarily accessible to affluent regions, with environmental impacts that cannot be ignored.

The promise of technology is undeniable, but its current trajectory reinforces a world where survival is a commodity, not a right.

4.8 The Cities That Drown

Global coastal cities, the engines of commerce and culture, are now on the frontlines of a rising tide.

Sea levels have exhibited a notable rise[26] over the past century, a trend that has accelerated in recent decades. Specifically, global average sea level has risen approximately 8-9 inches (21-24 centimetres) since 1880. This rise is primarily attributed to two key factors: thermal expansion of seawater due to increasing global temperatures, and thc influx of meltwater from glaciers and ice sheets.

Notably, the rate of sea level rise has more than doubled in recent times, with satellite data revealing a significant acceleration since the early 1990s. Regional variations in sea level rise occur due to factors like local land subsidence and geological processes. These changes are having increasing impacts on coastal communities worldwide, leading to increased flooding and erosion.

The accelerating pace of sea-level rise, driven by the planet's warming, is transforming coastlines from points of opportunity to zones of vulnerability. Sitting in your warm living room you might think this is some unlikely future scenario. It's not. It's a present reality, reshaping the very fabric of urban life and forcing a reckoning with the limits of human engineering.

Today, the disparities are starkly evident.

Jakarta's northern districts, once a thriving metropolis, are now submerged, a notch on the scorecard of humanities 'own goals' leading to the city's losing battle against the Java Sea, whilst not having enough fresh water for its population[27].

The forced migration of millions to the already overcrowded highlands of Borneo underscores the brutal reality of climate displacement.

In Bangladesh, Dhaka, a megacity on the delta, faces a relentless onslaught of rising tides and intensifying storms. Coastal neighbourhoods are regularly inundated, forcing the internal displacement of millions, and placing immense strain on urban infrastructure.

Over in the US, Miami, a symbol of affluence and modernity, is engaged in a costly and ultimately futile struggle against the encroaching ocean. The glittering towers

---

26 NASA Sea Level Change: https://sealevel.nasa.gov/

27 Independent researchers estimated in 2011, however, that Jakarta had already used an alarming 64 percent of its groundwater reserves. With little open space, groundwater is simply not being replenished. Rains run off to the sea. [Source: https://www.nationalgeographic.com/environment/article/indonesias-giant-capital-city-is-sinking-can-the-governments-plan-save-it]

of Brickell, shielded by expensive sea walls, stand in stark contrast to the flooded streets of Overtown and other vulnerable neighbourhoods, highlighting the growing chasm between the protected elite and the exposed masses. The world's centuries of vice, now Miami's.

European capitals are also feeling the pressure. London's Thames Barrier[28] 2.0, a celebration of technological prowess, buys time for the city's core, but at the expense of surrounding areas like Essex, sacrificed to the rising tides. Amsterdam and Rotterdam, with their centuries of experience in water management, are fortifying their inner sanctums, leaving the less affluent Zeeland to its fate.

In Asia, cities like Shanghai and Bangkok face the dual threat of rising sea levels and land subsidence, exacerbating the risk of catastrophic flooding. The financial districts of these cities, full of skyscrapers, and financial might, face a very real threat.

That's today.

4.9 The Rising Tide of Tomorrow

The next 30 to 50 years will witness an acceleration of sea-level rise, significantly impacting coastal communities worldwide.

Projections indicate that global average sea levels will continue to rise, with regional variations influenced by factors like land subsidence and ocean currents. This rise will exacerbate existing coastal vulnerabilities, leading to increased frequency and intensity of flooding, shoreline erosion, and saltwater intrusion into freshwater sources.

This is shorthand for saying that many coastal settlements have challenging times ahead, and not too far in the future.

[28] The main threat to the barrier is not that it will be overrun by water, but that opening and closing it repeatedly makes it harder to keep it in good condition. Once you start to close it so many times a year, you don't have time to do maintenance. With 1 metre of sea level rise, you could go from 10 closures a year to many hundreds of closures a year – perhaps up to 300. [Source: https://www.theguardian.com/environment/2023/jun/30/before-the-flood-how-much-longer-will-the-thames-barrier-protect-london]

Coastal cities and low-lying island nations are particularly at risk, facing potential displacement of populations and damage to critical infrastructure. The impacts will not be uniform, with certain regions experiencing more severe consequences than others. Data from sources like NASA and NOAA provide detailed projections[29], emphasizing the urgency of adaptation measures.

In South America, cities like Buenos Aires and coastal regions in Brazil will face increased flooding and erosion. African coastal communities, particularly in low-lying areas of the Nile Delta and along the West African coast, will experience heightened vulnerability to inundation and saltwater intrusion, threatening agricultural lands and water resources.

Southeast Asia, with its densely populated coastal zones, will be severely impacted. Countries like Bangladesh, Vietnam, and Indonesia will face extensive flooding, displacement of millions of people, and damage to vital economic sectors.

In Europe, coastal cities like Venice, already struggling to manage rising waters, and regions in the Netherlands will require substantial investments in flood defences to manage the rising sea levels. The United States will also experience significant impacts, with the Gulf Coast, East Coast, and low-lying areas of Florida particularly vulnerable to increased flooding and storm surge. These regional examples highlight the diverse and far-reaching consequences of sea-level rise[30].

The socio-economic implications of sea-level rise are profound.

Coastal communities will face increased costs associated with flood protection, infrastructure adaptation, and relocation. The displacement of populations will no doubt lead to social disruption, economic hardship, and increased migration.

Additionally, saltwater intrusion into agricultural lands and freshwater sources will threaten food security and water availability, particularly in developing nations. The potential for increased frequency and intensity of extreme weather events, coupled with rising sea levels, will further exacerbate these challenges.

---

[29] Source: NASA Sea Level Change: https://sealevel.nasa.gov/, NOAA's National Ocean Service: https://oceanservice.noaa.gov/facts/sealevel.html

[30] Source: 2022 Technical Report | Resources - U.S. Sea Level Change: https://sealevel.globalchange.gov/resources/2022-sea-level-rise-technical-report/

Addressing these impacts requires a combination of mitigation efforts to reduce greenhouse gas emissions and adaptation strategies to enhance coastal resilience. International cooperation and investment in sustainable development are essential to minimise the devastating consequences of sea-level rise on global communities[31].

Some of these changes start to feel very real as they impact on those I care about. As ever, things mean so much more when they get closer to you personally.

My brother and his family live on Australia's Central Coast, in NSW. Housing along the waterfront area of St. Hubert's Island will experience a marked change in the coming decades. Imagine king tides[32] no longer as occasional events, but as regular visitors lapping at doorsteps, and storm surges, once anomalies, becoming increasingly frequent threats.

The idyllic waterfront lifestyle faces a relentless adversary: the rising sea. Over the next 30 to 50 years, St. Hubert's Island, as an example, like many low-lying areas, will grapple with increased tidal inundation, shoreline erosion, and the insidious creep of saltwater into its freshwater reserves.

What was once a tranquil island paradise may find itself battling the encroaching waves, forcing residents to adapt or retreat. The NSW Government and Central Coast Council are actively planning for these changes[33], but the future of St. Hubert's Island, and countless other coastal communities, hangs in the balance, a stark reminder of the global impact of our changing climate

Looking towards the approaching mid-century, the challenges will escalate dramatically.

---

[31] Source: Climate.gov: https://www.climate.gov/news-features/understanding-climate/climate-change-global-sea-level

[32] The expression, 'king tide', originated in Australia, New Zealand and other Pacific nations to describe especially high tides that occur a few times per year.

[33] NSW Department of Climate Change, Energy, the Environment and Water: https://www.climatechange.environment.nsw.gov.au/, Central Coast Council: https://www.centralcoast.nsw.gov.au/

As the sea levels continue to rise[34], storms will intensify. And saltwater intrusion will contaminate vital freshwater sources.

Coastal defences, even the most technologically advanced, will be increasingly overwhelmed. The concept of "managed retreat" will become a harsh reality for many global cities, forcing the relocation of entire neighbourhoods and even business districts. This is a tens of millions, if not a hundreds of millions[35], of people reality.

Inland cities will become overcrowded, straining infrastructure and resources. The economic and social costs will be staggering, with entire industries and financial sectors displaced.

The maps of the world will be redrawn, not by political treaties, but by the relentless rise of the oceans, and the fight for survival in the most important cities of the world.

And again, in most cases, those who suffer most will be at the bottom, below the poverty water-line, and now at the rising global waterline.

4.10 A World That No Longer Repairs Itself

The world is breaking. So, grab your popcorn, you're just in time for the big climax!

The Earth is no longer a self-healing organism. It is a war scarred patient on life support, with multiple-organ failure. We have crossed the threshold where nature's resilience buckles under the weight of human impact.

Consider this: global wildlife populations have plummeted by an average of 69%[36] in the last 50 years. The rate of species extinction is now estimated to be 100 to

---

[34] A sea level rise in excess of 6.56 feet (2.0m) is possible even if we successfully limit warming to only 2°C by the end of this century. While such an outcome is considered extremely unlikely, it wasn't long ago that such an outcome was considered so implausible [Source: https://www.nrdc.org/bio/rob-moore/ipcc-report-sea-level-rise-present-and-future-danger]

[35] Zurich Insurance have published articles that reference research from the IEP, that predicts that 1.2 billion people could be displaced globally by 2050 due to rise in extreme weather and natural disasters

[36] 69% average decline in wildlife populations since 1970, says new WWF report [Source: https://www.worldwildlife.org/press-releases/69-average-decline-in-wildlife-populations-since-1970-says-new-wwf-report]

1,000 times higher than pre-industrial levels. And the oceans, once a vast buffer, are acidifying at a rate unseen in millions of years.

These are not isolated incidents; they are most definitely not part of the natural course of events that would have occurred at anything like this pace without humans. They are symptoms of a systemic breakdown, a fracturing of the intricate web of life that sustains us all.

Climate change, the most visible manifestation of our ecological recklessness, is merely the loudest crack in a foundation already crumbling. Beneath the surface, the planet's fundamental systems are failing. Biodiversity, once an abstract concept, is now a stark reality: the very web that held us aloft is shredded. We are entering an era where the Earth no longer repairs itself, where the damage is permanent, and the consequences are irreversible.

The oceans, forests, and every living system are succumbing to a cascade of failures, each feeding into the next, creating a world where the concept of 'recovery' is a fading dream.

4.11 The Death of the Oceans

The oceans, once the planet's vast, dynamic buffer, are now experiencing a profound and accelerating decline. They were designed to absorb excess heat and carbon, but the relentless pressure of human activity has pushed them beyond their capacity.

Acidification[37], a direct consequence of rising atmospheric CO2, is altering the ocean's chemistry, leading to widespread coral bleaching. Scientific projections indicate that, under current emission scenarios, up to 80% of coral reefs could be severely bleached by 2060, impacting ecosystems from Australia's Great Barrier Reef to the Red Sea's fringes. The vibrant biodiversity of these crucial habitats is rapidly diminishing.

The consequences are cascading through marine food webs. Fish stocks, a vital source of protein for billions, are experiencing dramatic declines.

---

[37] The acidity of the ocean today, on average, is about 25% greater than it was during preindustrial times. [Source: https://www.epa.gov/ocean-acidification/understanding-science-ocean-and-coastal-acidification]

In Indonesia, tuna fleets are increasingly reporting catches dominated by jellyfish, signalling a fundamental shift in the ecosystem's balance. In Madagascar, reliance on traditional fisheries is being replaced by the consumption of synthetic algae-based food substitutes.

Overfishing[38], reaching critical levels by 2030 for species like cod, has led to widespread stock collapses and economic hardship for fishing communities. According to the Food and Agriculture Organisation of the United Nations' "The State of World Fisheries and Aquaculture" reports, the proportion of fish stocks within biologically sustainable levels has decreased significantly over the past decades. In the 1970's roughly 90% of fish stocks were within biologically sustainable levels. Now that number is closer to 65%.

Deep-sea mining, an emerging industry, poses a significant threat to fragile deep-sea ecosystems, with potential dead zones extending from Mexico's Gulf to Bengal's Bay. Hypoxic zones, areas with severely depleted oxygen levels, are expanding, with regions like the South China Sea experiencing significant impacts on marine life and shrimp farming.

The World Wildlife Fund's (WWF) Living Planet Index tracks the trends in thousands of vertebrate populations, including fish. The index shows a significant decline in marine vertebrate populations over the past 50 years. The 2022 Living Planet Report, showed a 83% decline in monitored marine species.

Traditional fishing practices are becoming increasingly unsustainable.

Lab-grown seafood, exemplified by AI-optimised tilapia in Japan, is emerging as a niche market for affluent consumers. Norway's robotic salmon farms, while technologically advanced, represent a concentrated form of production amidst a broader decline in wild fish populations.

For billions in coastal communities across Senegal, Vietnam, Peru, and elsewhere, the decline of ocean resources translates to food insecurity and a growing reliance on synthetic food substitutes. The oceans are no longer a reliable source of

[38] A study indicates that without change, we could run out of seafood by 2048. However, the predicted year is controversial and is highly dependent on management strategies implemented in the future. [Source: https://envirolitreacy.org/what-fish-went-extinct-from-overfishing/]

sustenance or a stable ecosystem. They are exhibiting clear signs of systemic strain, with implications for global food security and coastal livelihoods.

Whilst we should celebrate innovation in developing new ways to keep people fed given these declines, the reality is that it only covers a tiny fraction of what has been lost, and what can never be replaced.

Unless we recall how to feed the multitude with two fish and some loaves, we're going to need a different miracle.

4.12 The Demise of the Forests

Ancient Forests.

Consider that word: Ancient. Something that has developed over millennia, the home of incalculable creatures and micro ecosystems[39], home to some of our most beloved folk stories, etched into our imaginations. And that is where they seemed doomed to die… as memories, folk tales.

Over the course of 2,000 years we've dethroned these giants, initially with a few tactical strikes to fuel our Dark Ages, and then to build our Middle Age fortresses, and then with an urgency we've declared all out war in feeding the progress and wonders of the Industrial and Information Ages.

---

[39] Pre-human ancient woodlands were dynamic, self-regulating ecosystems of exceptional biodiversity and complexity. These forests, evolving over millennia, supported a vast array of life forms, from microscopic soil organisms to apex predators. A single hectare could harbour thousands of insect species, crucial for pollination and decomposition, and a multitude of fungal networks, vital for nutrient cycling and tree health. Large herbivores, such as aurochs or giant deer, shaped the forest structure through grazing and browsing, creating diverse habitats for smaller animals and plant life. Predatory mammals like wolves or bears maintained ecological balance by regulating herbivore populations, preventing overgrazing. The canopy, a multi-layered structure of mature trees, provided shelter and nesting sites for countless bird species, while the forest floor, rich in decaying organic matter, supported a diverse community of amphibians, reptiles, and small mammals. These ancient woodlands were characterised by their resilience, with natural disturbances like wildfires or windstorms creating opportunities for regeneration and maintaining a mosaic of habitats, fostering a rich tapestry of life far exceeding the biodiversity observed in modern, managed forests.

By Neil Meyer

The Forests, once the verdant lungs of our planet, are now reduced to ragged, gasping remnants. They were the planet's carbon sinks, the regulators of our climate, the cradles of biodiversity. But the relentless onslaught of human expansion and exploitation has turned them into battlefields, where chainsaws and bulldozers are the weapons of destruction.

The Amazon, once a vast, impenetrable wilderness, is now a fractured landscape, destined to be 40% decimated by 2060. The deforestation policies of the 2020s, driven by short-sighted economic gains, tipped the balance, transforming vast swathes of rainforest into arid savanna. The release of 60 gigatons of stored carbon into the atmosphere, a colossal 'smoker's hack' rather than a life-giving breath, accelerated the climate crisis, triggering feedback loops that further destabilised the planet.

The Congo Basin, the second-largest rainforest on Earth, is now the next victim. Logging operations, driven by insatiable global demand for timber, and cobalt mines, feeding the voracious appetite of the tech industry, are carving deep wounds into the forest's heart.

By 2070, 50% of the Congo's forests are projected to be lost, transforming Kinshasa into a battleground over the last remaining mahogany stands. Southeast Asia's once-lush jungles, in Sumatra and Borneo, are shrinking into isolated pockets, mere tourist zoos, surrounded by the ghostly remnants of palm oil plantations. The vibrant ecosystems that once thrived in these forests are now mere shadows, their intricate web of life unravelling.

The delusion of 'replanting' offers a false sense of hope. Remember the 'ancient' part of ancient woodlands.

At its heart, "ancient woodland" signifies forests of significant age and continuity, ecosystems that have developed over long periods, fostering exceptional biodiversity and intricate ecological relationships.

While Britain's definition is tied to historical records dating back to at least 1600 AD, other regions recognise similar forests as "old-growth" or simply "ancient." These forests, regardless of nomenclature, share key characteristics: complex soil structures, high species diversity, and a long, unbroken history.

Unlike recently planted forests, they are irreplaceable repositories of ecological heritage. Tragically, these vital ecosystems have suffered devastating losses globally over the past 50 to 100 years.

Brazil's 'Green Amazon' initiative, planting millions of saplings, is a $5 billion exercise in futility.

By 2065, half of the saplings are dead, a stark reminder that ecosystems are not machines that can be rebooted on command. AI drones, seeding Siberia's vast taiga, are met with the harsh reality of permafrost melt, drowning their efforts in swampy terrain. By 2080, 40% of the taiga is reduced to scrubland, a testament to the limitations of technological solutions in the face of ecological collapse.

Nature is not 'bouncing back'; it is succumbing to irreversible damage, leaving behind relics of a world we can no longer rebuild. The silence of the dying forests is a haunting reminder of our collective failure.

Make sure to favourite that relaxing 'Woodland Sounds' track on Spotify. When your grandkids ask what forests were like, this might be all you'll have left to share.

4.13 The Last Seconds Before Midnight

Here we are. 3.8 seconds before midnight.

For the past 24 cosmic hours, Earth has built and rebuilt itself – mountains have risen, oceans have shifted, species have flourished and vanished. And then, in the final milliseconds, we arrived. We carved through forests, dammed rivers, burned fuels, and declared ourselves masters of the world.

But now, the clock is still ticking, and we're sprinting towards the edge of time.

In these last few fractions of a second, we have broken the fundamental systems that made life possible. The forests no longer breathe for us, the oceans no longer cool us, the land no longer feeds us. Everything that once balanced itself over millennia is collapsing in decades. The safety nets have been torn apart, and there is no one left to catch us.

But let's be clear: not everyone falls at the same speed.

The Caste of the Sheltered – those who built their fortresses before the floodwaters came – will watch from behind AI-sealed walls as the rest of the world drowns. In Mumbai, slum-dwellers will claw at barricades while billionaires sip desalinated cocktails.

In Nairobi, the last scraps of farmland will go to those who can pay while the hungry riot outside distribution hubs. The climate crisis has never been about "humanity" as a whole. It's about who gets to survive, and who is abandoned.

For the privileged, collapse isn't a sudden, violent catastrophe. It's a slow retreat into curated survival. It's a Tokyo executive stepping into a temperature-controlled bio-dome while an Indonesian fisherman steps into an ocean with no fish. It's a Berlin banker eating lab-grown steak while a Sudanese farmer watches his fields turn to dust.

We should be living in an age of reckoning – staring at the ruins, learning from our failures, rebuilding a system that works for everyone.

Instead, we live in the age of filtering. The rich filter their air, their water, their food. They filter their newsfeeds, their realities, their morality. And when the time comes, they will filter the people – those who make it in, and those who are left outside, choking on the dust.

Now, through the lottery of geography and wealth, you either make the cut – or you choke.

And yet, for all our desperate hoarding, the final seconds keep ticking down.

A species that once controlled nothing – that spent millennia running from storms, shivering in caves, hunting in the shadows of greater beasts – now controls everything. And in a single breath, we are losing it all.

Not to asteroids, not to super volcanoes, not to cosmic flukes of fate. To ourselves.

To the system we built, to the gods of industry and consumption, to the delusion that we could endlessly take without consequence.

As the new day approaches, let's look at the world we've created, where we'll make our stand, build our homes.

This is what we've built to replace nature's safety net. A world where the oceans choke, the forests burn, and the air turns toxic. We were given paradise, and we sold it for scraps.

And now, we are drowning in the waste of our own making.

4.14 Chapter Summary

A. **The Earth is past its tipping points.** Half of all wildlife populations have vanished in 50 years, tropical rainforests are being erased at a rate of 40 football fields per minute, and atmospheric CO_2 levels are higher than at any point in the past 800,000 years. The environmental damage isn't slowing – it's accelerating.

B. **Climate change is no longer a distant future** – it's here, now. Heatwaves, wildfires, and rising seas are escalating every year. South Asia is enduring summers that push human survival limits, wildfires now burn year-round, and food-producing regions are collapsing under erratic weather patterns.

C. **Humanity's impact isn't just visible** – it's chemically etched into the planet. The oceans are acidifying, forests are burning, and permafrost is releasing methane in a self-sustaining feedback loop. These aren't "natural cycles" – they are human-driven system failures.

D. **The world's resources are being hoarded**. Climate collapse won't be evenly distributed. The ultra-rich are filtering their air, stockpiling their food, and retreating into sealed, AI-controlled enclaves, while billions are left to suffer the consequences. Access to clean water, food, and liveable land is being locked behind paywalls.

E. **Ecological repair is now beyond simple human interventions.** While some regions attempt rewilding and bioengineering solutions, the pace of destruction still outstrips efforts. Mass extinction isn't an 'event' – it's an unfolding crisis with no historical precedent. We are not living through a temporary crisis. We are living through a permanent transformation.

4.15 What Can You Do About It?

1. **Stop thinking in old timelines.** The idea that we have "until 2050" to fix this is outdated. The collapse is happening now, year by year. If you are waiting for governments or corporations to act, you are already behind.

2. **Understand your local vulnerabilities.** Know where your food and water come from. If you live in a city that imports its drinking water, expect scarcity. If you live in an area dependent on seasonal agriculture, prepare for disruptions.

3. **Build resilience into your life.** This isn't about doomsday prepping – it's about adaptation. Invest in water security, energy independence, and local food networks. Learn practical skills: growing food, purifying water, managing resources.

4. **Challenge the idea of 'infinite growth.'** The system that created this crisis will not solve it. Governments will prioritise economic stability over ecological survival. This means solutions will not come from policy alone – they must come from communities, individuals, and movements willing to disrupt the status quo.

5. **Get political.** The ultra-rich and corporate elites are preparing to weather the crisis at your expense. Push for policy shifts that target climate justice, corporate accountability, and resource accessibility. The wealthy will only act when they are forced to.

6. **Shift from passive to active participation.** Stop thinking of climate collapse as a distant event – it's a structural shift that requires ongoing adaptation. Your ability to survive and thrive will depend on how well you anticipate and adjust to the changes ahead.

7. **Reclaim power in collective action.** No single individual can reverse the damage, but collective movements can still shape the future. The more people who refuse to play by the rules of extractive capitalism, the harder it is for the system to maintain its grip.

8. **Prepare for climate migration.** The world's habitable zones are changing. If you live in a high-risk region – low-lying coasts, wildfire zones, extreme heat belts – start thinking about long-term relocation. The earlier you move, the more options you will have.

9. **Accept that the old world is gone.** The ecosystems we were born into will not be the ones we die in. Accepting this is painful, but necessary. The task now isn't saving the past – it's building a liveable future within the new reality.

10. **Lead with realism, not despair.** The worst-case scenario isn't inevitable, but avoiding it requires radical shifts. Hope is not a strategy – action is. The faster we adapt, the better we position ourselves for whatever comes next.

This chapter isn't just about recognising collapse – it's about understanding that we are already living in it. What comes next depends on how well we prepare, resist, and reshape what remains.

Vignette D: Chinedu: The Prince of Lagos

D.1 Lagos, Nigeria – 2031

Chinedu Okonkwo was born in 2031, the first son of Barrister Emeka Okonkwo, one of Nigeria's most successful corporate lawyers, and Ijeoma, his devoted but formidable housewife mother. The Okonkwo family sat comfortably within the top 5% of Nigeria's wealthiest elite, a lineage of power and influence woven through the corridors of Lagos' legal, business, and political circles.

The world outside was changing fast – rising seas lapped at the edges of Victoria Island, the air grew thicker with heat and smog, and Nigeria's economic boom of the early 21st century strained under climate pressure. But inside the Okonkwo mansion in Ikoyi, life was insulated, air-conditioned, and unapologetically grand.

Chinedu, the eldest of six siblings, was a natural-born leader and troublemaker in equal measure. His mother called him a "charmer with a lion's heart", his father called him "too clever for his own good." He had sharp instincts, a silver tongue, and an undeniable magnetism that pulled people into his orbit – especially women.

By the time he was fifteen, he had seen more of Africa's elite circles than most adults:

- Private school in Abuja, where he learned to navigate the children of politicians, oil tycoons, and foreign investors.
- Holidays in South Africa and Dubai, where he witnessed the stark difference between wealth and the growing desperation of those outside it.
- Trips to the Niger Delta, where his father handled legal disputes for multinational oil corporations, and Chinedu saw firsthand the devastation – villages flooded with blackened water, fishing communities wiped out, pipelines cutting through once-pristine land.

He understood power from an early age.

And he knew that to wield it, you had to play the game right.

D.2 Lagos, Nigeria – 2050

By the time Chinedu turned 19, Lagos was a city bursting at the seams – a place where the rich fortified themselves behind AI-guarded estates, while the poor flooded into climate-ravaged slums, hoping for a future that was disappearing beneath the rising Atlantic.

His father, now a senior legal strategist for an energy conglomerate, was part of a network of African elite powerbrokers – men who had found ways to extract wealth from chaos, as floods and heatwaves turned whole neighbourhoods into death traps.

Chinedu, fresh out of Nigeria's top university, had options. He could have:

- Followed his father into law, ensuring generational wealth.
- Taken a role in Lagos' AI-driven financial markets, where corporations now wielded more influence than governments.
- Moved to Abuja, where politicians still clung to the illusion that they could control the country.

But that wasn't his style.

Chinedu was too ambitious, too restless, too hungry for more.

So, he carved his own path.

- He launched a social enterprise, a hybrid of tech, influence, and media, built to give Lagos' wealthy elite a polished, "socially responsible" face – while making sure he got a hefty cut of the action.
- He became a fixer, the go-to man for Nigeria's rising class of crypto-millionaires, real estate moguls, and digital entrepreneurs, ensuring their ventures looked "green" while still being ruthlessly profitable.
- He built a network of allies, from journalists looking for access to the truth, to activists who needed funding but didn't ask too many questions.

And, of course, he never lacked in romance.

By 2050, he had already fathered his first child, a daughter with Aisha Bello, the daughter of a Lagos media magnate. His mother sighed at the scandal, but Chinedu just laughed it off.

"Legacy is built in many ways, Mama."

He knew how to navigate chaos – because in Nigeria, chaos was the only certainty left.

D.3 Accra, Ghana – 2075

By 2075, Lagos had changed.

The richest families had retreated into AI-controlled smart cities, where power, food, and clean water were guaranteed. The rest of the city – what hadn't been swallowed by the rising Atlantic – was a volatile, shifting network of slums, informal economies, and climate migrants.

Nigeria, once a giant of West Africa, was fractured.

- The North was now a semi-autonomous region, controlled by a mix of corporate security forces and local warlords.
- The oil-rich South was held by AI-managed corporate interests, who kept resources flowing to global markets while displacing millions of desperate Nigerians.
- Lagos, still a powerhouse, had transformed into a corporate-run megacity, where economic privilege determined citizenship more than nationality.

And Chinedu?

He had expanded beyond Nigeria, becoming a continental figure.

His empire was influence, and his business was survival.

- He had investments in climate adaptation projects, ensuring that Lagos' wealthy class remained untouchable while making token gestures of charity to the drowning poor.

- He was an advisor to Ghana's rising corporate elite, helping Accra position itself as Africa's new financial capital, now that Lagos was too volatile.
- He had five children by now, with three different women – each relationship strategically woven into different spheres of influence, keeping his legacy diverse and resilient.

He still had charisma, still had swagger.

But something weighed heavier on him now.

He had seen what was coming.

By 2075, it was no longer about whether Africa could survive climate collapse – it was about who would be left standing when the dust settled.

And Chinedu had no intention of being on the losing side.

D.4 Cape Town, South Africa – 2100

By 2100, Africa had become a continent of two realities; The AI-controlled megacities – places like Accra, Cape Town, and parts of Nairobi, where the ultra-wealthy had sealed themselves off from the collapse happening outside. And the wastelands – once-great cities like Lagos, Kinshasa, and Dar es Salaam, where tens of millions fought for survival in regions that were too unstable, too hot, or too lawless to function under AI governance.

Lagos, his home, was among the latter.

The Atlantic had swallowed entire districts, disease and heat had killed millions, and the old power structures were gone.

And yet, somehow, Chinedu still remained.

He was no longer the young prince of Lagos.

Now, they called him "Baba Oga" – the last great powerbroker of the old world.

He had outlived the corporate tycoons, the politicians, the AI overlords.

And he still had his family – now numbering in the dozens. His children, his grandchildren, his lovers and allies spread across West Africa, still carrying the Okonkwo name, still wielding influence.

He had spent his whole life playing the game, shifting as the world burned around him.

And now, as he sat under a dying baobab tree, watching the next generation rise, he couldn't help but smile. He had never stopped moving. Never stopped adapting.

And in the end, maybe that was the only thing that had ever really mattered.

Chapter 5: Survival in Filth

Since 1970, global plastic production has increased by over 600%. We've generated more plastic in the last 50 years than in the entire century before. Every year, over 9 million people die prematurely due to pollution. That's more than the deaths from HIV/AIDS, tuberculosis, and malaria combined. Air pollution is the single biggest environmental health risk. It's responsible for about one in nine deaths worldwide.

We've been sold a comforting lie, a green-tinted illusion that if we diligently sort our plastics and flatten our cardboard, we're somehow absolved of the mountain of waste we create. 'At least we recycle,' we murmur, patting ourselves on the back as another Amazon order arrives, swaddled in layers of disposable packaging.

But the truth is, our recycling bins are a mere drop in the overflowing ocean of our consumerism. We cling to the idea that these carefully sorted scraps will magically transform into something new, something virtuous, but the reality is far less idyllic. The energy guzzled, the water wasted, the complex chemical processes – it's a costly charade that barely scratches the surface of our insatiable appetite for 'stuff.'

We've become masters of a guilt-free consumption, believing that as long as we toss our bottles into the right bin, we're doing our part. But what about the forests felled for packaging, the rare earth metals mined for our gadgets, the oil drilled for our endless stream of plastic?

Recycling, in its current form, is a band-aid on a gaping wound, a way to soothe our consciences while we ignore the real problem: our addiction to more. We needed to shift from a 'recycle-centric' mentality to a 'reduce-centric' one. The most sustainable solution isn't to find clever ways to reuse our trash, but to stop creating so much of it in the first place. Now we live with the reality of our overconsumption; that no amount of recycling would ever have been enough.

5.1 The Pollution Dilemma: The Wages of Filth

We have long treated the Earth as an infinite dumping ground, a bottomless pit for our industrial byproducts and consumer waste. As we've chased the unattainable fashion trends, another pair of bedazzled jeans or low cut dresses were thrown onto the trash heap. You can't be truly happy until you slop the newest 'reverse the aging process' cream onto your face or wash yourself with a 'blend of avocado and coco butter' body shampoo. More bottles and packaging that will be here long after you've shuffled off this planet. A gift that will keep giving.

The dividends of this reckless behaviour are now coming due, a toxic debt we can no longer ignore. While climate change and ecological collapse scream for attention, as we've seen, pollution is the silent, insidious killer, seeping into every corner of our lives.

It's not just the visible smog choking our cities or the plastic waste littering our landscapes; it's the invisible contamination that permeates our very being. We are not merely what we eat, but what we breathe, what we touch, and where we live.

The environment, once a backdrop to our lives, is now an inescapable determinant of our health and well-being. The legacy of our industrial age is a planet steeped in our own filth, a reality where the air we breathe, the water we drink, and the very dust that settles on our skin carry the imprint of our toxic legacy. We have created a world where the lines between our bodies and our waste have blurred, a grim testament to our collective failure to live in harmony with the Earth.

5.2 The Toxic Legacy of Yesterday's Waste

The landfills of the 20th and early 21st centuries were not just repositories for discarded consumer goods; they were time capsules of toxic debt, ticking time bombs buried beneath layers of plastic and refuse. We treated these sites as out-of-sight, out-of-mind solutions, believing that burying our waste would somehow neutralise its harm.

When we tried to mandate controls in hallowed halls of government, people cheated, trading their excess to countries that had less, rather than changing behaviours. The only people they really cheated were their children.

But the laws of chemistry and physics are not so easily cheated.

The chemicals we sealed away, the heavy metals and persistent organic pollutants, have not vanished. Instead, they have leached into groundwater, seeped into soils, and entered the food chain, becoming a silent, insidious legacy for generations to come. In a very real way, the pollution IS the next generation already.

Consider also the vast electronic waste graveyards scattered across the developing world, where discarded computers and smartphones release a cocktail of toxic substances into the surrounding environment. The lead, mercury, and cadmium that were once essential components of our technological marvels are now poisoning the very communities that dismantle them, creating a cycle of environmental injustice. Or consider the countless industrial sites, now abandoned, where decades of unregulated dumping have left behind contaminated landscapes, unfit for habitation or agriculture. These 'brownfield' sites, once symbols of industrial progress, are now monuments to our environmental recklessness, reminders of the hidden costs of unchecked development.

The consequences of these banked problems are not confined to specific locations; they are global, systemic. Microplastics, the fragments of our disposable culture, are now ubiquitous, found in the deepest ocean trenches and the most remote mountain peaks.

The pesticides and herbicides that were once hailed as agricultural breakthroughs are now detected in human breast milk and umbilical cord blood, evidence of their pervasive presence in our bodies. The very air we breathe, in many urban centres, is a toxic mix of particulate matter and industrial pollutants, a direct result of our reliance on fossil fuels and unchecked industrialisation.

And so we find ourselves, at the peak of our evolution, made up of the plastics, heavy metals and bioengineered pesticides that we brought into the world, and then absorbed into our very selves. Living embodiments of our failure to live in harmony with our world.

Plastics aren't trash – they're us. By 2050, Lancet pegs them in 90% of human lungs – Delhi kids cough nanoplastics, London newborns carry them in cord blood. The consequences of these "banked problems" become increasingly apparent.

In Delhi, respiratory diseases are endemic, with children born with compromised immune systems. In Lagos, the water table is so contaminated that bottled water, even for the affluent, is laced with microplastics. In Kinshasa, the legacy of past mining operations manifests in widespread neurological disorders, a silent epidemic afflicting generations.

By 2075, it's universal – brain fog, sperm counts down 30%, immune glitches up 20%. The rich dodge it – Dubai's elites breath AI-filtered air, and drink AI-filtered water; Boston's trillionaires get detox shots, $10,000 a pop. The rest? Lagos hawkers sip from plastic-choked streams, Nairobi moms breastfeed micro-dosed milk. It's not exposure – it's inheritance.

In a world struggling with resource scarcity and climate change, the burden of past pollution becomes a major factor in human suffering. Chronic diseases, linked to environmental toxins, are rampant. Life expectancy plummets, particularly in marginalised communities. The once-vibrant ecosystems, already weakened by climate change, are further degraded by the cumulative impact of pollution. The Earth, once a bountiful planet, is now a toxic landscape, a clear demonstration of the shortsightedness and greed of past generations.

The Great Pacific Garbage Patch[40] stands as a profound and sobering symbol of the global plastic pollution crisis. It is not a solid island, but a vast, 1.6 million square km, diffuse, and dynamic accumulation zone within the North Pacific Subtropical Gyre, characterized by exceptionally high concentrations of plastic debris. While microplastics dominate numerically, larger items, particularly discarded fishing gear, constitute the majority of the mass, highlighting a complex composition with diverse ecological implications. The GPGP is the largest and most studied of such patches, but similar, less-understood accumulation zones exist in all major ocean gyres, confirming the global scale of the problem driven by persistent ocean currents acting on ever-increasing inputs of anthropogenic waste.

Additionally, evidence suggests that 70% of the plastics will sink to the ocean floor, suggesting that there is already a massive – and growing – volume of pollution that we're not even aware of.

This is a future we are actively creating, a future where the consequences of our past actions will continue to reverberate for generations to come. The time for complacency is over. We must confront the legacy of our environmental sins and work towards a more sustainable future, before it is too late.

---

[40] The GPGP covers an estimated surface area of 1.6 million square kilometers, an area twice the size of Texas or three times the size of France. To formulate this number, the team of scientists behind this research conducted the most elaborate sampling method ever coordinated. Source: https://theoceancleanup.com/great-pacific-garbage-patch

5.3 You Are Where You Live

The Industrial Revolution, with its promise of progress and prosperity, ushered in an era where geography became destiny in a new, insidious way. For two centuries, we've built our cities and industries with little regard for the natural systems that sustain us. We've concentrated pollution in specific zones, creating 'sacrifice zones', coincidentally adjacent to the poor and marginalised who bear the brunt of environmental degradation.

The idea that one could escape the consequences of this pollution by simply moving, or that clean air and water were universally accessible rights, was a dangerous illusion. The reality is far more brutal: your health, your lifespan, your very potential are increasingly determined by the air you breathe, the water you drink, the food you eat, and the soil you inhabit.

Today, the disparities are starkly evident.

In cities like Delhi and Beijing, the wealthy can afford air purifiers and bottled water, creating a bubble of relative safety. But the poor, living in densely populated slums and industrial suburbs, are exposed to a toxic cocktail of pollutants, their children developing asthma and other respiratory diseases at alarming rates. Even boiling water doesn't guarantee safety, as this doesn't resolve issues such as heavy metals or microplastics.

In the Niger Delta, oil spills and gas flaring have devastated local ecosystems, poisoning water sources and rendering farmland infertile. The people who live there, who once relied on the land and water for sustenance, are now trapped in a cycle of poverty and ill health. The world over, those who have the least, suffer the most. The geographical lottery of birth now determines not just your social status, but your very biological well-being.

Looking ahead, the consequences of this environmental determinism will only intensify.

All too soon, urban centres will become increasingly stratified, with gated communities and high-tech enclaves offering a semblance of environmental protection for the privileged few, while the vast majority of urban dwellers struggle with chronic exposure to pollution. In regions ravaged by climate change and resource scarcity, environmental refugees will flock to already overcrowded cities, creating 'pollution hotspots' where disease and social unrest will grow rampant.

By 2075, the concept of 'environmental justice' will be a distant memory, replaced by a brutal reality where access to clean air and water is a luxury reserved for the elite. The Earth will be a patchwork of toxic wastelands and fortified havens, a stark reminder that we have created a world where your postcode is your biological destiny, and your health is a commodity to be bought and sold.

The quality of the air you breath, the water you drink, the food you eat, will be the quality that you can afford.

5.4 Living in Our Filth

We once recoiled at rats scurrying through our trash, blind to the fact that we were looking at our own future. Of course some will be closer to seagulls, pure and white, but cawing annoyingly, yet all too often still pecking at overflowing landfills for scraps when that's all that's available. In this world between rats and seagulls, there suddenly doesn't seem like enough difference.

We've moved beyond the realm of abstract environmental concerns; we are now living intimately with our own waste. The lines between our bodies and the refuse we generate have blurred, a sad reality of the all-pervasive nature of our contamination. It's not just the smog-choked cities or the plastic-strewn beaches; it's the very air we draw into our lungs, the water we use to quench our thirst, the dust that settles on our skin, the food that was harvested from this effluence. We are living in a world where the byproducts of our consumption are as much a part of our environment as the natural elements.

Consider the nano plastics found in human placentas, the microplastics in our bloodstreams, the heavy metals accumulating in our bones. These are not external threats; they are internal realities, a constant reminder that we are carrying the burden of our industrial legacy within us.

The very act of breathing, once a symbol of life, is now a transaction with a polluted atmosphere, each inhalation a gamble with our health. The water we drink, filtered and treated, still carries traces of pharmaceuticals and industrial chemicals, a reality of the limits of our purification technologies. The food we eat, grown in soils contaminated with pesticides and fertilisers, carries the imprint of our agricultural practices, a reminder that even our sustenance is compromised.

This is not a future dystopia; it is the present reality. Actually, for too many, this has been their reality for generations now, conveniently slightly offstage, their leaders having traded their dignity and health for their 12 pieces of first world silver, quickly spent.

The constant, low-level exposure to a cocktail of pollutants is eroding our health, compromising our immune systems, and shortening our lifespans. On one hand, the most wealthy are looking at how unlocking the mysteries of the genome might extend their lives, whilst the vast majority are worse off year after year.

We are living in a world where chronic diseases, once anomalies, are now commonplace, a legacy of the cumulative impact of our environmental negligence. The concept of 'natural' is becoming increasingly abstract, replaced by a reality where every aspect of our lives is mediated by the byproducts of our consumption.

We are living in our filth, and the consequences are becoming increasingly inescapable. The question is no longer whether we can reverse this trend, but whether we can adapt to a world where our very existence is defined by our contamination.

And what would Darwin make of all this? How would he look to his models of adaptation?

5.5 The New Darwinian Reality

We thought pollution was a consequence of progress; in reality, it's a new form of control. The poisons we unleashed are not just environmental – they determine who thrives and who dies. And in that struggle, power will shift.

Darwinism, at its core, is not about brute strength; it's about adaptability. And the good news for rich people is that money remains the currency of adaptability. Not such great news for everyone else…

In the face of ecological collapse and resource scarcity, the ability to adapt will become the defining characteristic of survival, both for individuals and nations. And ecological collapse is not a force that strikes evenly, or fairly. Massive hurricanes and rising tides will not stop to check who deserves their wrath, the planet has taken the gloves off and there will be casualties.

It is a catalyst for a raw and Darwinian struggle. In a world reshaped by vanishing resources, toxic environments, and mass displacement, the existing geopolitical order will crumble, replaced by a brutal competition for survival.

Climate change, ecological destruction, and pervasive pollution will become the new fault lines, triggering conflicts and reshaping alliances. The impact won't be uniform, and the capacity to adapt will be defined by access to resources, technology, and defensible locations.

Nations with stable climates, abundant renewable energy, and advanced technologies will become 'climate fortresses,' while those ravaged by drought, floods, and pollution will become breeding grounds for mass migration and conflict. The very concept of national borders will be challenged, probably at the sharp end of a defence force, as millions are forced to flee their homes, creating 'migration wars' that destabilise entire regions. This isn't politics, this isn't looking for opportunities, this is a fight for survival!

Political ideologies and economic governance will play their parts, both significant, but are more fully covered elsewhere in this book.

Energy, once a commodity, will become a weapon, with nations controlling vital resources wielding unprecedented power. This is not a future of global cooperation, but a descent into a Darwinian struggle, where survival is a zero-sum game, and the fate of nations is determined by their ability to adapt to a world irrevocably changed.

5.6 Climate Fortresses

Throughout history, those with power and resources have sought refuge from external threats, building castles, walled cities, and fortified compounds. In a highly localised way, Panic Rooms are fortresses within fortresses of the wealthy.

In the age of ecological collapse, this instinct for self-preservation takes on a new, technologically advanced form: the 'climate fortress.' The concept isn't entirely novel; wealthy communities have long sought to insulate themselves from environmental hazards. But the scale and sophistication of these fortresses are about to undergo a radical transformation. The idea of a gated community is about to be taken to a whole new level.

Today, we see the nascent stages of these climate fortresses.

In regions with stable climates and abundant resources, wealthy individuals and corporations are investing in high-tech infrastructure designed to withstand the coming storms. New Zealand's South Island[41], with its relatively mild climate and low population density, has become a haven for billionaires seeking refuge from climate change. Canada's Ontario Triangle[42], with its abundant freshwater and hydropower, is attracting investment in resilient infrastructure and advanced technologies.

In Scandinavia, nations like Norway and Finland are leveraging their renewable energy resources and technological expertise to build self-sufficient, climate-resilient cities. These are not merely isolated projects; they are part of a broader trend towards the creation of fortified enclaves, where the privileged few can insulate themselves from the chaos unfolding beyond their walls. These locations are also increasingly seeing the implementation of advanced border control and security systems.

---

[41] New Zealand's South Island has seen a surge in interest from wealthy individuals seeking 'escape' properties and havens from global instability. Reports indicate a significant increase in land purchases by foreign billionaires, particularly in areas with relatively mild climates and abundant water resources. For example, Silicon Valley executives and tech entrepreneurs have been acquiring large tracts of land, often with plans for self-sufficient compounds and underground bunkers. The construction of private airstrips and helipads has also increased, suggesting a focus on rapid evacuation and isolation. The island's remote location, coupled with its relatively stable political climate, makes it an attractive destination for those seeking refuge. Furthermore, New Zealand has been forward thinking with its renewable energy options, and this also helps to give a sense of stability.
The increasing presence of high net worth individuals, combined with heightened global anxiety surrounding climate change, is causing some to believe these locations will become future climate fortresses.

[42] The Ontario Triangle, encompassing Toronto, Ottawa, and surrounding areas, possesses several advantages that contribute to its potential as a 'climate fortress.' The region has access to abundant freshwater from the Great Lakes, a vital resource in a world facing increasing water scarcity. Its developed hydroelectric infrastructure provides a stable and renewable source of energy. Additionally, Canada's relatively stable political system and advanced technological infrastructure enhance its appeal. There is increasing investment in Canadian tech, and secure server farms. These are often buried in areas away from large populations. In addition, Canada has a well funded military that could be used to protect its boarders. Moreover, the regions access to large areas of fertile land, means that it is far more able to feed its populations, than many other areas of the world. In the face of climate instability, these factors contribute to the region being seen as a location with increased resilience.

Looking ahead, the trend towards climate fortresses will accelerate. By 2050, these enclaves will become increasingly self-sufficient, relying on renewable energy, closed-loop agriculture, and advanced water management systems. They will be surrounded by advanced security systems, including drone surveillance, AI-powered border control, and heavily armed security forces, to deter unwanted migrants and maintain their isolation.

By 2075, these fortresses will have become de facto city-states, operating with a high degree of autonomy and minimal interaction with the outside world. They will represent the ultimate expression of environmental inequality, a stark reminder that in a world ravaged by ecological collapse, survival is a privilege, not a right. The rest of the world will be left to fend for itself, and these fortresses will be a constant reminder of the failure of humanity to work together.

5.7 Migration Wars

For centuries, borders have been lines on maps, markers of sovereignty and national identity. Granted, all too often these were drawn by arbitrary politicians in their zeal to carve up distant lands, especially under the spectre of colonialism.

But in a world reshaped by climate change and ecological collapse, these lines are becoming battlefronts, contested territories in a desperate struggle for survival. The concept of 'climate refugees' is no longer a hypothetical scenario; it's a present-day reality, with millions already displaced by floods, droughts, and other climate-related disasters. And as the impacts of climate change intensify, the scale of displacement will only grow, triggering conflicts that destabilise entire regions.

Today, we see the early signs of these migration wars.

In regions like the Sahel, where drought and desertification have decimated livelihoods, desperate populations are migrating south, clashing with existing communities over scarce resources. In Central America, climate change-driven crop failures and extreme weather events are fuelling migration towards the United States, creating tensions at the border.

In coastal regions of Bangladesh and the Pacific Islands, rising sea levels are forcing mass evacuations, leading to internal displacement and cross-border migration. These are not isolated incidents; they are part of a global trend, a growing wave of climate-driven migration that is straining the capacity of nations to cope.

The reality that all too often the leading players that are driving the underlying cause of these climate and pollution driven problems, are the same First World countries that are now pushing back the tide of people washing up at their doors. And they are no longer welcoming people in the interest of common cause.

Looking ahead, the situation will deteriorate rapidly.

In a few decades, the scale of climate displacement will reach unprecedented levels, with tens of millions, if not hundreds of millions, forced to flee their homes. Borders will become heavily militarised, with nations deploying advanced technologies and lethal force to deter migrants. Refugee camps will become overcrowded and unsanitary, breeding grounds for disease and social unrest. Conflicts will erupt between host communities and migrant populations, fuelled by competition for resources and cultural tensions.

It won't take long before migration wars will have become a defining feature of the global landscape, with entire regions destabilised by mass displacement and conflict. The concept of 'humanitarian aid' will be overwhelmed, and the international community will struggle to manage the sheer scale of the crisis. The world will witness a brutal struggle for survival, where borders are no longer lines on maps. How can they be, when the lines are below the waves. Instead, they will be battle lines in a desperate fight for a place to live.

The rules of war, will be redefined.

5.8 Energy as the New Currency

For centuries, wealth has been measured in gold, land, and capital. But in a world grappling with climate change and resource scarcity, a new currency is emerging: energy. In the coming decades, access to reliable, sustainable energy will become the ultimate determinant of power, shaping alliances, triggering conflicts, and redefining the global order. What good are those AI systems, electric fences, defence drones and smart homes if there's no power?

The shift is already underway, with nations possessing abundant renewable resources or advanced energy technologies gaining significant geopolitical leverage.

Today, we see the early signs of this energy-driven world order. Nations with vast solar potential, like Saudi Arabia, are investing heavily in renewable energy infrastructure, aiming to become energy superpowers in the coming decades. China, with its massive hydropower capacity and advanced AI-driven energy grids, is expanding its influence by providing energy to its allies and neighbours. This type of arrangement isn't kindness, or even purely driven by economic reasons, it's a lifeline that is equally part manacle.

Canada, with its abundant hydropower, and the Nordic nations, with their advancements in fusion technology, are positioning themselves as energy-secure havens in a world facing increasing energy shortages. The European Union, once a global leader, is facing a growing energy divide, with its coal-dependent southern members increasingly reliant on external energy sources. These are not isolated developments; they are part of a broader trend towards the redefinition of global power, where energy becomes the new currency.

Looking ahead, the energy landscape will undergo a radical transformation. In the near future, nations that have successfully transitioned to renewable energy sources will wield unprecedented power, dictating terms to those still reliant on fossil fuels. Saudi Arabia's solar deserts will fuel its economic dominance, while China's AI-driven energy grids will solidify its regional influence. Canada and the Nordic nations will become energy-secure enclaves, attracting investment and talent from around the world.

Before the end of the century, energy will be the ultimate weapon, with nations controlling vital resources able to exert control over entire regions. The concept of 'energy independence' will become a driving force in geopolitics, with nations striving to secure their own energy supplies at any cost. The world will witness a new form of neo-colonialism, where energy-rich nations exploit the vulnerabilities of energy-poor nations. The throne of global power will be occupied by those who control the watts, and the rest will be left to grovel for survival. The power grid, will be the new battleground.

5.9 The World We Inherited

This isn't a cautionary tale – we're past yellow tape and megaphones.

Entire species are gone, never to walk the world again. Ancient forest may never rise again given the toxicity we've drenched the world in. Our greatest, most horrific invention is a microwave that will cook the planet for eons to come.

The 2020s ignored the science; the 2030s are destined to fumbled the fixes; the 2050s will wake up too late with eyes burning with a mix of justified disgust at our parents and our species more broadly. Climate's not a problem – it's the planet now. Ecology's not healing – it's history. Scarcity's not a glitch – it's the system. Once the fridge is empty there's no going to the shop to restock it.

Sure, some might have designs on Martian holidays, but if we can't fix our own world, we should be embarrassed at even thinking of polluting anywhere else.

Adaptation's the split. Shanghai's towers gleam, AI cooling 20 million; Lagos's slums bake, 30 million clawing for scraps. Scandinavia's grids hum; Sahel's dunes bury 40 million dreams. The wealthy wall off – energy, tech, clean air their moats. The rest endure – or don't. This is our making, our mess, our fight. Collapse isn't coming. It's home.

5.10 Chapter Summary

A. **Pollution isn't an accident – it's the system working as designed.** The world produces 600% more plastic than in 1970, and every year, over 9 million people die from pollution – more than HIV/AIDS, tuberculosis, and malaria combined. Recycling was a comforting lie; the truth is, the only real solution was always reducing consumption. Now, we live in a world suffocating in its own waste.

B. **We are surrounded – and filled – by the debris of our own making.** Landfills aren't just garbage dumps; they are toxic time bombs, leaking heavy metals into the groundwater, poisoning soil, and seeding microplastics into everything we eat, drink, and breathe. Pollution isn't just external anymore – it's inside us, rewriting our biology at the cellular level.

C. **Where you live now determines whether you survive.** Clean air and water have become commodities, accessible only to those who can afford them. The rich live in climate-sealed fortresses, sipping on purified air and desalinated water, while billions breathe in smog, drink from plastic-choked rivers, and eat chemically tainted food.

D. **Mass migration is inevitable – and violently contested.** The great climate displacement is underway, forcing entire populations to flee rising seas, poisoned lands, and unlivable heat. Borders are no longer just lines on maps, but battlefronts, where nations turn to walls, drones, and militarised forces to protect their dwindling resources.

E. **Energy is the new currency of power.** In the 21st century, nations that control renewable energy will rule the world. Saudi Arabia's solar fields, Canada's hydropower, China's AI-managed grids – these are the new sources of geopolitical dominance. The nations without energy sovereignty? They are the new vassal states of this emerging world order.

F. **Collapse isn't coming – it's already here.** This isn't a distant dystopia. This is our present reality, and it's accelerating. The elite have adapted, walling themselves off with advanced technology and exclusive resources. The rest of the world? It's drowning in its own filth, struggling to survive in a poisoned, overheating world.

5.11 What Can You Do About It?

1. **Understand that pollution is permanent.** The waste we've created **isn't going anywhere**. Microplastics are already inside every human on Earth. Pollution isn't something we can "clean up" – we have to **stop making more**.

2. **Reduce consumption, not just waste.** Recycling was never enough. The only way forward is to **buy less, consume less, waste less**. Cut down on plastic use, demand alternatives, and refuse disposable culture. **The only real sustainability is reduction.**

3. **Secure your access to clean water and clean air.** If you think environmental collapse won't affect you, **you haven't been paying attention**. Filter your water. Invest in air purification if you can. Know where your food comes from. The infrastructure designed to protect you is failing.

4. **Recognise that the wealth divide is now a pollution divide.** The **poor are being poisoned first**. If you're comfortable, you may not feel it yet – but the layers of protection are peeling away. This is no longer about environmental activism; **this is about survival.**

5. **Prepare for climate migration and instability.** If you live in an at-risk region (coastal cities, polluted zones, extreme heat belts), **start planning now**. Where you live determines your future health and safety. **Move before you're forced to.**

6. **Pay attention to who controls energy.** Fossil fuels are dying, but **energy is still power**. The countries and corporations that own

renewables will dominate global politics. If your country **isn't energy-independent, your future is in someone else's hands.**

7. **Understand that national borders are fragile.** Mass displacement will intensify. **Climate wars are inevitable.** Governments will prioritise control over compassion. Walls will be built, militaries will be deployed, and entire populations will be left to die outside fortress gates. **This isn't paranoia – it's already happening.**

8. **Technology will not save us.** AI can filter water, automate food production, and manage energy grids – but it won't **reverse the damage**. The world we inherited is **toxic, overheating, and breaking down**. If you think the solution is "just around the corner," you're already too late.

9. **Reject the illusion that 'normal' is coming back.** The air, the water, the soil – **none of it is pure anymore**. The planet will never return to what it was. Survival isn't about waiting for a fix; **it's about adapting to a permanently degraded world.**

10. **Act now, or accept your place in the fallout.** If you do nothing, someone else will decide your fate – and their decisions won't include you. Governments and corporations are preparing for collapse. Are you?

We were sold the idea that pollution was just an unfortunate side effect of progress, something we could "clean up later." That was a lie. The poisons we unleashed never left – they just settled into our food, our water, our bloodstreams.

This isn't about prevention anymore. It's about survival.

Vignette E: Andy: A Free Spirit Across the Fractured States

E.1 Manhattan, New York – 2031

Andy arrived screaming into the world in 2031, his first breaths thick with the promise and pollution of Manhattan.

The skyline, a familiar boast against the heavens, already felt different – saltier on the wind, more prone to the shudder of distant thunder that rattled the old panes of their apartment window. Storms clawed closer each year, testing the city's aging sea defences, while AI-driven flood barrier tests along the East River became routine news items, background hum to the city's relentless pulse.

His mother, a nurse whose shifts stretched thinner than hospital budgets, carried the weariness of a system fraying at the edges. His father, a third-generation union electrician, battled the city's sputtering grid, patching circuits overloaded by summer heatwaves and the creeping demands of nascent smart infrastructure. He saw the future not in the gleaming new tech his wife sometimes described from the richer hospital wings, but in the failing copper and overloaded transformers he wrestled daily.

Andy grew up in the seams of the city, a cramped Harlem apartment his playground. Life spilled onto the streets – fire hydrants blasting relief in summer blackouts, impromptu basketball games under flickering sodium lamps, the scent of halal carts mingling with the ever-present damp rising from the subway grates. Resilience was the city's religion.

His father taught him the electrician's catechism early: strip wire, test current, respect the flow. "Know how things connect, Andy," he'd rasp, hands calloused and sure. "And know how they break. That's power they can't take".

Andy learned circuits, fixed sputtering radios, toasters and microwaves, he felt the thrum of the city's hidden lifeblood. He absorbed its defiant energy, the belief that New York, somehow, would always endure, always adapt.

He'd stare out at the skyline, a million lights promising a future as solid as the bedrock beneath. He couldn't imagine leaving. Why would anyone?

E.2 Across America – 2050

Nineteen hit Andy like a jolt of raw current. The city still pulsed, but the energy felt different – frantic, brittle. The AI systems his father had grumbled about weren't just managing traffic; they were managing *people*.

Automated job allocation systems nudged friends towards gig work servicing the wealthy and tourist frequented downtown, while the old union jobs bled out. His father, sidelined by younger techs fluent in algorithmic diagnostics and a growing smart grid, took early, bitter retirement.

His mother spent more and more of her time helping those afflicted with 'slur', a slang term for the impact of microplastic build up in patients' brains, blood stream and organs. And the numbers were growing weekly. Andy thought his father might have it as he struggled to maintain conversations.

The resilience Andy had loved felt stretched thin, replaced by a quiet desperation. The skyline still gleamed, but the shadows in the streets felt longer. He needed air – clean air and space, something beyond the closing walls of the city. Armed with his father's lessons and a restless itch, Andy bolted.

He drifted, first tagging along as a roadie for an indie band clinging to the dying embers of the East Coast circuit. It was a rolling classroom in American fracture, eight of them in a vintage electric powered bus that Andy maintained.

Washington D.C. was scarred by the '48 superstorm, its gleaming federal core protected by tech-managed levees that nonchalantly funnelled floodwaters into the surrounding, poorer districts. Protesters chanted outside corporate lobbies, demanding fair UBI rates or accountability for climate relocations that never materialised, their voices swallowed by the streams blaming the unreasonable demands on climate immigrants.

Further south, the Carolinas baked under relentless sun, farmland cracked and barren. He saw communities turning inward, bartering skills – his electrical know-how traded for food, fuel, a place to crash. The band played to dwindling crowds; who could afford tickets when the local textile plant had been fully automated last year? The raw intensity and unpredictability of live music was prized against a generation that were growing up on custom song streams that were starting to sound like a copy of a copy of a copy.

The tour dissolved in Atlanta's heat haze.

Andy felt the westward pull, catching rides with others fleeing climate-battered coasts or automated towns. He and Kya, a traveling writer paired up for a while and saw the landscape change – not just geographically, but economically. Pockets of innovation-driven prosperity – logistics hubs, automated farms – gleamed like mirages, surrounded by vast stretches of decay.

They spent a few months trying to settle near a struggling agricultural co-op outside Memphis, with Andy fixing their failing solar arrays and water pumps. It felt good, grounding, building something real. Then the corporate investors arrived. A subsidiary of a global agri-giant bought the water rights upstream, rerouting the flow to their hyper-efficient vertical farms miles away.

The co-op withered. Andy packed his tools, the taste of failure bitter in his mouth, as he and Kya hit the road again. Witnessing wasn't enough; trying to put down roots felt like planting seeds in poisoned soil. He kept moving, collecting stories like burrs, learning the geography of collapse one broken town at a time.

E.3 Western Fringe – 2075

Forty-four years ground down Andy's wanderlust into something closer to weary necessity. He'd chased rumour and work across half the fractured nation. Kya had gone her own way, off to investigate fusion powered cities in Canada.

Andy spent a year stringing cables for vast, corporate-owned wind farms in the Texas Free Economic Zone, paid in digital credits barely covering rationed water and prefab shelter.

Six months installing black-market water filters on the outskirts of Chicago, where the official supply from the dwindling Great Lakes was strictly rationed by AI based on social scores, leaving the unconnected parched. He saw the lines harden – the stark division between the Integrated zones, humming with automated efficiency, and the vast Stranded territories left scavenging and forced to innovate in their own way with technology cast offs.

He drifted into what was left of Vegas, lured by whispers of off-grid work. The Strip was a ghost lit by sputtering solar panels and the occasional glare from fortified corporate casinos, their system-managed microgrids humming reliably for high-rollers while the surrounding streets baked in darkness. Here, Andy found a niche.

His knack for fixing old tech, bypassing algorithmic controls, and jury-rigging power systems made him valuable in the shadow economy. He worked behind the bar at a defiant music lounge, one of the last venues running entirely on scavenged generators and human performers. The patrons were a mix – grizzled survivors trading stories, tech workers from the corporate zones seeking a hit of "authentic" grit, and climate migrants stalled on their hopeless journey north.

He tried to settle again, briefly. He met Maya, a woman running a small hydroponics setup in the back of an abandoned motel, growing food for the lounge and local barter networks. For a while, it felt like something solid, even communal.

They rigged solar panels, purified greywater, talked about expanding. But Vegas was dying of thirst. The business enclaves had long since secured the last reliable water sources from Lake Mead, their AI systems efficiently allocating every drop.

A brutal heatwave, coupled with a corporate "readjustment" of the external water rations, killed Maya's crops and their fragile stability. The algorithm didn't care about small-scale survival; it optimised for the enclave. Maya headed south, hoping to join family near a rumoured community water project in Baja.

Andy, wary of promises and borders, stayed, fixing generators for dwindling credits, the weight of another failed anchor heavy in his gut. He watched drone patrols circle overhead, scanning for unauthorised resource use, a constant reminder that even in the ruins, the system's eye was watching.

The lounge band played Springsteen, anthems of a lost America ringing hollow against the encroaching desert and the glow of the untouchable corporate zones. That old New York defiance still flickered, but it felt lonelier now, the horizons shrinking.

E.4 Seattle–Cascadia Fringe – 2100

Sixty-nine years, countless miles, a lifetime spent tracing the cracks in a broken nation. Andy had seen the great American fragmentation up close – the climate-ravaged South, the automated Rust Belt, the parched Midwest, the corporate fiefdoms rising like concrete islands.

Following whispers of temperate weather and a degree of lingering autonomy, he hitched rides – slower, riskier now – towards the Pacific Northwest, the Cascadia

Hub. The high-speed trains connecting the AI-managed cores of Seattle and Vancouver were strictly for the privileged, access granted by corporate passes or exorbitant fees. Andy travelled the fringes, the neglected service roads paralleling the gleaming maglev lines.

He landed south of Seattle, in a sprawling, semi-organised settlement clustered around repurposed warehouses near the perimeter of the official Seattle Metroplex – a walled, AI-managed city-state. Inside the walls, life was curated, efficient, and closed. Outside, it was messy, human, resilient. This fringe community thrived on salvaging, repairing, and adapting. Solar panels patched onto leaky roofs, rainwater harvesting systems feeding community gardens, old electronics stripped and rebuilt. Andy found work immediately, his old-world electrical skills highly valued in a place that kept the grid alive through ingenuity and barter.

"You ever think of trying to get in?" a younger member of the collective asked him once. Andy looked towards the distant gleam of the Metroplex towers. He thought of his father's warning about knowing how things break, about power they couldn't take. He thought of his mother, giving ever hour she had either caring for his father or taking one more shift to make ends meet.

"Nah," he finally said, turning back to the wiring harness in his hands. "Think I prefer the places where you can still see the sparks fly".

Home was no longer a place on a map; it was the ability to adapt, to fix, to connect, to witness the messy, imperfect struggle and still find a way to keep the lights on, one frayed wire at a time. The fractured land had taught him that much.

Chapter 6: The Fracturing of Power

We came closer than ever before to a world of open borders, free movement of people and ideas, and interconnectedness. However, the world is reverting with new conflicts rising in the Middle East and the extended invasion of Ukraine by Russia. Meanwhile the great experiment of a unified European Union has cracked, as the US adjusts, taking a more nationalistic – America First – stance once more.

This chapter examines the rapid dissolution of established power structures and asks what comes next. It's not about mourning what we're losing – it's about understanding why it can't hold, recognising that our familiar mechanisms for governing ourselves no longer meet the demands of this volatile new century.

The time of near open globalisation, that was deliciously close, is fading.

Welcome to the fracturing of power. Let's take a clear-eyed look at how we got here, and what it means as we hurtle into a world rapidly reshaping itself, where old rules crumble, and new, uncertain ones are hastily written.

6.1 The Cliff Notes' History of the Last Century

Let's step back – not too far, just enough to see clearly how we built the castles before they started crumbling. For a few centuries, humanity carved out power centres – castles of ambition and control, rooted not in chance but by deliberate choices. These weren't accidental empires but products of clear plans, bold moves, and specific historical advantages. We're not reminiscing fondly about some golden age here; we're quickly reviewing history because understanding the foundations is crucial to comprehending the collapse unfolding today.

Today, those proud castles seem to represent less load bearing power, and more cardboard cut out for Instagram moments.

The United States was capitalism's poster child, a nation turning grit, ambition, and rugged individualism into a global juggernaut. It kicked into high gear with Reagan's deregulation drive in the 1980s. Market-first gospel and aggressive tax cuts unshackled corporations, unleashing innovation and profits – but at a price.

By the early 2000s, Wall Street had become the cathedral of capitalism, GDP soared, and the American Dream was a shiny export product. Yet by the 2020s, critical vulnerabilities surfaced: deepening inequality, soaring debt, and an economic model increasingly reliant on offshore labour to maintain global competitiveness. While the US proudly stood as the world's largest oil producer[43], its internal labour market had eroded significantly, becoming a structural weakness rather than a strength. As global markets accelerated toward automation and even greater cost optimisation, the domestic labour foundations once essential to American economic dominance became liabilities, fragile under the relentless demands of efficiency. The model delivered – until suddenly it couldn't.

If the US model was capitalism's boldest gamble on individualism and deregulation, China's model played a fundamentally different game – one of meticulous control, surveillance, and deliberate governance.

From Deng Xiaoping's careful economic liberalisation in the '90s, China fused state authority with capitalist hustle. Its factories roared, cities rose, and technology tightened its grip – by 2023, facial recognition and algorithmic oversight mapped the movements of millions with ruthless precision. It wasn't freedom's hymn; rather, a carefully constructed narrative of stability and prosperity, lifting millions from poverty[44], firmly placing China as a superpower contender. Yet beneath the efficiency, tensions strained – rural unrest simmered, an ageing population burdened infrastructure, and ecological devastation began to bite.

Europe offered another experiment entirely. The **European Union**, born from war's ashes in the late 1940s, bet its future on unity through economic interdependence – open borders, free trade, and shared currency. For a while, particularly during the '90s and early 2000s, this vision appeared triumphant, a monument to diplomacy's ability to build peace. It succeeded until a series of shocks rattled it deeply – Greece's financial collapse exposed fault lines, Brexit demonstrated the fragility of consensus, and waves of migration exacerbated latent fractures, exposing an uncomfortable North-South divide that was always there beneath the surface.

---

[43] The United States achieved energy independence and became the world's largest oil producer, yet in 2022 still imported substantial quantities of crude oil. Top sources included Canada, Mexico, Saudi Arabia, Russia, and Colombia, primarily due to market-driven economics and refining requirements rather than dependency per se. [Source: EIA Imports and Exports, US Energy Information Administration]

[44] China's economic rise over the past two decades has lifted over 850 million people out of extreme poverty, a remarkable achievement in human history. [Source: https://www.worldbank.org/en/country/china/overview]

Resource-rich states built their own towers of influence. **Russia** leaned into resource autocracy, harnessing oil and gas dominance, tethering European heat and power to Moscow's control. It leveraged pipelines for political strength, bolstered by military muscle and repression of dissent – an effective strategy until renewable energy ascended and the perceived threat of NATO at the door pushed them to invade Ukraine.

A quieter type of influence also thrived. The world's wealthy, from **Swiss banking hubs** to Gulf sovereign wealth funds, constructed power through stealth and subtlety – money as influence, plots of New Zealand land as personal insurance policies[45]. This shadow capital built castles quietly, accumulating power discreetly until discretion became unnecessary, their influence pervasive and seemingly unshakable – until the world began to resist, questioning why so few could dictate the fates of so many.

Then came the hopeful outsiders, the **BRICS nations** – Brazil, Russia (doubling down), India, China (once more), South Africa – who pooled resources and populations to challenge Western dominance. This emerging bloc, formed in the 2000s, represented a collective ambition, an alternative to traditional Western-centric global order. Their dream seemed achievable until climate disruption began tearing at their seams, unevenly eroding their aspirations, with Russia engaging in a war with Ukraine and China's outsized dominance threatened equality amongst the partners.

Each power centre relied on distinct levers: America's markets and innovation, China's authority, Europe's union and postcolonial penance, Russia's resource wealth, the shadowy elite's quiet capital, and BRICS' gritty determination. But their foundations were flawed: dependent on predictable weather, stable geopolitics, steady markets, and an abundance of resources. Those foundations weren't built for rapid, cascading shocks.

---

[45] New Zealand's picturesque landscapes and stable political environment have attracted wealthy investors seeking a safe haven from climate change and social unrest, leading to concerns about land ownership and affordability for local residents. [Source: https://www.theguardian.com/world/2018/feb/10/super-rich-preppers-heading-for-new-zealand-doomsday-bunker]

This represents several significant nations, bound by physical national borders. However, this period gives rise to a new power; the dawn of the Digital Empires.

The new millennium witnessed the stealthy ascent of a fundamentally different form of global power: the **Digital Empires**. These entities, represented by household names in many Western countries – the omnipresent Amazon (reshaping retail, media, and digital infrastructure), the gatekeeper Google (dominating search, media, and digital infrastructure), the architects of social discourse Facebook & Twitter/X, the foundational Microsoft (software and digital infrastructure), the China-centric digital behemoth Tencent (encompassing digital infrastructure, communications, and retail), and the nascent but influential cyber currency platforms like Bitcoin – have, in many practical ways, come to wield an unprecedented degree of financial, economic, cultural, and political power.

Operating fluidly across borders, these empires have not only displaced established local operations, from Main Street retailers to regional hosting providers, but their combined revenue in 2023, at almost $1.32 trillion[46] would place it at 17th position[47] if it was a country in 2023, above the Netherlands and Saudi Arabia, underscoring their sheer economic scale. This new breed of power, born in the digital realm, represents a paradigm shift in global influence, setting the stage for the rapid-fire disruptions that would soon expose the vulnerabilities of the traditional power structures we've just examined.

The 21st century introduced rapid-fire disruptions – climate breakdown, economic volatility, automation, and geopolitical unpredictability – that these power structures were ill-equipped to handle. The carefully constructed castles of influence are now shaking, more fragile than we realised. They weren't invincible after all – they were just adequate for a stable world, a world that's quickly disappearing in our rearview mirror.

Today, we're feeling the fractures everywhere, from Mumbai to Manhattan. Power is splintering, becoming fragmented and decentralised. This isn't merely an

---

[46] Alphabet reported a revenue of $307.39 billion for the full year 2023. Amazon reported net sales of $574.7 billion for the full year 2023. Tencent reported total revenue of CNY 609.015 billion for the year ended December 31, 2023. Using an approximate exchange rate of 1 CNY = 0.14 USD, this is approximately $85.26 billion. Meta Platforms reported total revenue of $134.902 billion for the full year 2023.Microsoft reported revenue of $211.915 billion for the fiscal year ended June 30, 2023.

[47] Worldbank Data: https://data.worldbank.org/indicator/NY.GDP.MKTP.CD

evolution of governance – it's a desperate shift, forced by accelerating realities humanity cannot control. Climate chaos, AI's ascension, and entrenched inequality aren't just forcing adaptation; they're tearing apart the old playbooks entirely.

6.2 Winds of Change: The Desperate Now

The old thrones – forged in trade, control, resources – stood because the world played along: climates held, borders meant something, and power had a rhythm you could hum to. The fact that the US secured the oceans after WW2 and were happy to patrol the peace, along with the benefits this brought, helped.

That tune's fading fast. The 2020s snapped the strings, and what's blowing through isn't the usual breeze of empires shifting – it's a frantic, desperate gust, tearing at the seams. Those fiefdoms that we mapped out? They're swaying, more cardboard backed for tourists than load bearing, and the hands on the levers aren't the ones we used to know. This isn't just change; it's a breaking point, and the globe's feeling it from Montreal to Moscow.

What's different? The planet's stopped being a passive party and gone rogue, and it's not picky about who it hits. India's 50°C heatwaves aren't a forecast – they're now, emptying Delhi's streets by May, shoving millions toward a Ganges that's more slurry trickle than torrent. Brazil's Amazon isn't just shrinking; it's spitting carbon like a chain-smoker, 25% savanna already, rains failing where soy once ruled. Nigeria's Sahel isn't creeping south – it's charging, 40 million on the move, crashing into fences from Lagos to Nairobi. This isn't the slow grind of centuries past; it's a collapse in fast-forward, and survival's the prize, not pride. Climate pressures similarly unsettle Southeast Asian economies like Vietnam or Indonesia, increasingly vulnerable to rising seas and agricultural collapse.

But it's not just the outside cracking – it's the inside too. AI isn't merely reshaping industries; it's rewriting the fundamental rules of employment, policy and governance. China's clerical army – 3 million souls – likely to vanish by 2035, WeChat-like bots buzzing where pens once scratched. India's Bangalore coders, once the world's tech spine, scramble as AI threatens to code ten times faster. South Africa struggles to keep the lights on, unrest boiling in townships that can't afford the slow change. This isn't the old "jobs evolve" story; it's a guillotine drop, and the crowd's not cheering – they're clawing for what's left.

So, usual change or something more? History's empires – Roman, Ottoman, British – faded over generations, a slow bleed you could bandage. This? This is a snapped artery. No time for Nero to pick a tune, the fat lady's not even bothering to show.

Millennia of climate shifts shrank to decades, now years – each monsoon weaker, each drought sharper, each tech leap steeper. The old guard planned for cycles; now they're dodging a wrecking ball. It's not adaptation; it's desperation, a global scramble where the stakes aren't power – they're breath, food, a patch of dirt that doesn't burn or drown.

6.3 An Age of Corporate Influence

So who's winning, and who's stoking the fire? Corporations and the loud rich – they're not lurking in the wings. No more Rothschild and secret hand shake backroom power players. The Gulf's oil barons and Swiss vault keepers used to whisper or give a quiet nod – cash flowed, strings pulled, silent as a shadow. Now, they're centre stage, bellowing. Now they're vocal.

Adani's coal empire in India isn't just mining – it's dictating energy policy by 2025, $50 billion bending New Delhi's ear. Russia's oligarchs aren't hiding in dachas; they're buying up Arctic rigs, shouting bids as the ice melts. Musk bought a megaphone, and then a president. Zuck, Bezos, and Sundar have quickly fallen in line to pad their own shareholder's pockets. Tencent's not a tech firm – it's a state within a state, AI grids steering Shanghai while Beijing nods. These aren't backroom deals; they're upfront power grabs, and they've got the watts and code to pull it off.

Depending on the motivation at the time – whether in service of moderation and truth, or to gain favour with political leadership – the major social network have at times censored and even banned voices, whilst at other times pushing their own interests via the platforms they control.

Twitter has oscillated between banning Trump, before being bought by Elon Musk, who went on to not only reinstate his access, but also become his largest donner.

And there's a crackle in the air. Ukraine and Gaza were on the sharp end of massive political moves, with initial support faltering as countries quickly moved to reassess the loudest voices in the room, not really to bothered by the rules. Xi looks over Putin's shoulder, as Elon dances behind Trump.

Amazon and Google have structured their operations, so that whilst they earn massive amounts globally, they often pay little to no taxes in the countries where they generate those sales.

Looking through the lens of earning disparity globally for a given company, let's pick Apple, the gap is stark[48]. The compensation of Apple's CEO, Tim Cook, at $49M, is vastly higher than that of both supply chain workers at (at roughly $7,000 – 10,000) and store assistants (around $27,000 to $37,000, depending on the store location). The ratio highlights the immense concentration of wealth at the top of large corporations, and how little of the value flow to countries out even where the labour occurs.

Most recently, Elon Musk's involvement through DOGE[49] in the USA, directly inserts the world's richest person, unelected, into investigating government departments on the pretext of looking for efficiency. Whilst there is no doubt that waste exists and should be removed, the fact that the richest person, whose wealth derived from corporate interests often in conflict to the very departments he's investigating, would seem to be a gross conflict of interest to many.

If you ever need to orientate yourself politically to figure out what's happening, the same basic rule applies: he who has the money makes the rules. That timeless truth remains very relevant.

6.4 Adjusting the Board: A Hippo Feeding Frenzy

Forget the polite handshakes and knowing glances of yesteryear. The global power game has morphed from a refined diplomatic dance into something far more primal – a no-holds-barred feeding frenzy. The old guard, with their inherited influence and lumbering military might, are finding themselves at the same trough as a new, nimbler breed of competitor. The chessboard has been flipped, and

---

[48] Apple estimated earnings for 2023, Apple Supply Chain Worker (China): Roughly $6,720 - $10,080 per year, Apple Store Assistant (USA): Approximately $37,856 per year, Apple Store Assistant (UK): Approximately $26,975 per year, and Tim Cook (CEO): Approximately $49,000,000 per year.

[49] Department of Government Efficiency (DOGE): Established by an executive order on January 20, 2025, during President Donald Trump's administration, this department aims to modernize federal technology and software to enhance governmental efficiency and productivity.

Hungry Hippos is the game of choice!. Now it's every hippo for itself at a rapidly shrinking watering hole.

The stakes in this chaotic scramble are the same as they ever were, just amplified and with a digital twist. Smaller nations remain the tastiest morsels, their resources and strategic locations making them prime targets. But now, these nations are also crucial battlegrounds for digital dominance. Think of Ukraine, not just for its grain and rare minerals, but as a testing ground for cyber warfare and the influence of social media narratives. Myanmar isn't just a mineral buffet; it's a market for the expansion of digital platforms and the collection of valuable user data.

Mineral and fossil fuel rights, the traditional meat of empire building, are now even more fiercely contested, as they fuel the engines of the Digital Empires. Lithium for their batteries, cobalt for their devices, rare earths for their processors – these are the shiny pebbles the tech hippos crave. Private contracts aren't just about oil and infrastructure anymore; they're about securing cloud computing contracts, building AI infrastructure, and controlling the flow of digital information. Real estate now includes the physical locations of vital data centres, the digital bastions of the new age.

Currency games have gone digital too, with the rise of cryptocurrencies championed by figures who often have deep ties to the Digital Empires, adding another layer of volatility and potential manipulation. And populism, that ever-reliable tool for whipping up the masses, has found its ultimate weapon in the very social media platforms controlled by these tech behemoths, turning online discourse into a roaring, partisan feeding frenzy. The board has been well and truly upended, and the hippos, both old and new, are chomping with a renewed and digitized vigour.

6.5 Players At The Global Gaming Table: Hippo Edition

So, sticking with our 'tongue in cheek' analogy, who are the hungry contenders jostling for position at this global trough?

The **US hippo**, still sporting its orange hue, might be a bit of a sloppy eater these days, prone to loud pronouncements and impulsive grabs. Its legacy of global leadership is being traded for a more transactional approach, focused on securing its own tech dominance – the AI of Silicon Valley, the solar of Texas – while still coveting traditional energy sources. Nationalism roars from its throat, often drowning out the nuances of international cooperation.

Its relationship with the Digital Empires is a complex one: while many of the biggest tech hippos were born in its waters, they often operate with a global appetite that doesn't always align with the national agenda. That may be changing as the king hippo demands fealty.

The **China hippo**, a quieter but undeniably powerful red beast, operates with meticulous control and a long-term strategy. Its AI grids are steering its mega-cities, and its dominance in rare earths remains a formidable trump card. It's steadily chomping away at Taiwan's chip industry and eyeing the ports of Southeast Asia, all while feeding its massive population. Its domestic Digital Empire, Tencent, is a tightly controlled extension of the state, a powerful digital hippo feeding within its own borders while also looking to expand its reach.

The **India hippo**, a hot and hungry beast, is all about hustle and opportunity. Its coders in Bangalore still pack a punch, and its solar potential is immense. But its primary needs remain basic: water for the Ganges and land that isn't parched. Nationalism fuels its ambitious roar of "India Rising." Its relationship with Digital Empires is a mix of leveraging global tech talent and building its own digital infrastructure, navigating the influence of giants like Google and Amazon in its massive market.

The **Russia hippo**, a grizzled veteran with a territorial glint in its eye, might be smaller these days but still possesses a monster appetite, remembering past glories. Its gas pipelines and Arctic oil are key assets, though the table is shrinking. It plays a rough game, eyeing Ukraine's resources and Syria's strategic spots. Its approach to Digital Empires is wary, prioritizing digital sovereignty and often viewing Western platforms as threats.

The **EU hippos**, a somewhat fractured blue and yellow pair, operate with a mix of grabbing for green tech and grappling with internal divisions. The northern hippo, sleek and tech-savvy, focuses on fusion and wind power, while the southern hippo struggles with climate change and economic woes. Their approach to Digital Empires is regulatory, seeking to tame the tech giants and protect their citizens.

The **UK hippo**, a stiff-upper-lipped oddity, isn't quite sure where it fits at the moment, its nationalistic instincts pulling it inward after its exit from the EU.

Canada, too, is cautiously observing the shifting dynamics, particularly its relationship with its southern neighbour. Both nations are significant consumers and hosts of Digital Empire operations.

The **Brazil hippo**, once fat on soy, is now leaner and meaner, its Amazonian feeding grounds shrinking. South Africa, the missing BRICS hippo, is scrappy, with mineral wealth but internal struggles. Both are navigating their relationship with Digital Empires, seeking to leverage technology for development while facing their own unique challenges.

The **Gulf State hippos**, sleek and strategic, are pivoting to solar power and using their wealth to buy into tech and secure favourable contracts. They are actively engaging with Digital Empires as investors and consumers.

And then there are the **Vocal Rich hippos**, borderless beasts like Musk and Adani, who throw their weight around with impunity, their influence amplified by their control or close ties to the Digital Empires. They snap up real estate and wield influence across nations, their survival instincts often overriding any sense of national allegiance.

Across this chaotic watering hole, nationalism remains the dominant bellow, borders are less lines on a map and more like snapping jaws, and the Digital Empires act as both players and shapers of the game, their influence permeating every aspect of this increasingly desperate struggle for survival.

If this feels like senseless chaos that couldn't possibly work in the real world, congratulations. You can relax, you're a sane person living in an insane world.

6.6 Firebrands and Catalysts

Alright, ditch the diplomatic niceties; we're peering into the digital tea leaves now, folks. What's next in this glorious unravelling? Think less Nostradamus and more scrolling through a particularly spicy X thread – equal parts informed insight and utter garbage fire.

The world's perched on a digital hair trigger, and the next 5-10 years look less like a gentle evolution and more like a series of escalating online flame wars spilling into the real world. These aren't prophecies etched in stone tablets; they're the digital breadcrumbs already being dropped, leading us straight into the stampede where even the tech hippos might get trampled.

Already in this glorious mess, the US seems intent on dusting off the old empire-building blueprints, eyeing long-time allies with a renewed sense of… acquisition. Throw in Greenland (strategic ice, anyone?) and the Panama Canal (still surprisingly relevant), and you've got a recipe for some seriously awkward international Zoom calls. Sovereignty? Apparently, that's just a suggestion these days. The tariff tantrum continues, sending global markets into the digital equivalent of a panicked altcoin crash.

And the sudden bromance with the Russian bear? That's got everyone hitting refresh on their news feeds with a mixture of disbelief and impending doom.

Expect to see these geopolitical shifts amplified and distorted across every social media platform, with algorithms pushing the most inflammatory takes and state-sponsored trolls working overtime to muddy the waters. Even the Digital Empires themselves will be navigating these shifting alliances, their data flows and infrastructure potentially becoming bargaining chips or even targets in this new great game.

Adding another layer to this domestic drama, we can't entirely dismiss some of the more extreme, yet perfectly plausible, possibilities within the US itself.

Imagine a scenario where, under the guise of a manufactured crisis – a sudden 'war on the economy,' a dramatic 'war on immigration,' or even a culturally charged 'war on woke' – the sitting President engineers a loophole to extend their term. The suspension of voting during a declared emergency, however dubious, isn't entirely outside the realm of possibility in such a charged environment. The Digital Empires would, of course, be both the amplifier and the battleground for this internal conflict, with accusations of bias and censorship flying from all sides as the very nature of American governance is debated in 280-character bursts.

Fast forward to 2028: India and Pakistan decide their decades-long water cooler squabble over the Indus River needs a dramatic upgrade – cue the water wars. With the river's flow down by half thanks to our good friend climate change, India's nationalist hippo tightens the dam taps, and Pakistan's bear responds with drone swarms over the border. A minor skirmish over a Punjab canal turns into a trending topic (and a major casualty event), sparking a digital trade blackout. Suddenly, Pakistan's copper and India's coal become weaponized in the real and virtual worlds.

Expect to see sophisticated cyberattacks targeting water infrastructure on both sides, potentially even impacting the Digital Empires' data centres and operations in the region. Social media will, of course, be a raging inferno of nationalist propaganda and accusations, making de-escalation feel like trying to put out a bonfire with a tweet.

By 2030, the US-Mexico border situation goes from tense to "did you hear about that glitchy AI zapper?" Climate change has turned the Southwest into a crispy critter zone, pushing millions north. Mexico's already stretched hippo can't hold the tide, and the US's "America First" behemoth doubles down on the drone wall. A Juárez crossing incident involving a malfunctioning AI-powered border security system leaves fifty migrants crispy, and X explodes with the predictable outrage.

Trump's digital echo chamber cheers tariffs on Mexican lithium (essential for those Tesla batteries), and Musk's various ventures are poised to scoop up the scraps. Populist fervour, amplified by every available digital platform, spills into real-world riots in El Paso. The Digital Empires, while not directly pulling triggers, will be instrumental in shaping the narrative, with algorithms potentially prioritizing sensationalized content and foreign interference likely adding fuel to the digital fire.

Then comes 2032, when China decides Southeast Asia needs a little less "juice." The Three Gorges Dam grid, all AI-steered and Party-locked, powers half the region. But when Vietnam's hippo gets a bit too chatty about Taiwan's semiconductor industry, Xi's quiet chew turns into a digital and literal power outage. Watts drop by 30% overnight, plunging Hanoi's factories into darkness.

Ports like Singapore grind to a halt, and rare earths stay firmly locked within China's digital and physical borders. ASEAN's smaller hippos will be scrambling for scraps of Gulf solar power, likely brokered through complex digital marketplaces. The Digital Empires operating in Southeast Asia will face massive disruptions, their cloud services faltering and their supply chains thrown into chaos. Expect China to leverage its digital infrastructure dominance to further solidify its regional control, potentially even engaging in cyber coercion against its neighbours.

In 2033, Russia's thawing Arctic becomes the site of a very chilly clash. Siberia's permafrost is melting faster than an ice cream cone in July, revealing vast oil reserves. Putin's heirs, naturally, are eager to drill, but Norway's fusion-powered, sleek hippo also fancies a slice of the pie. Overlapping claims lead to a blown rig (ten casualties, naturally), and Oslo's X feed lights up with accusations of Moscow's environmental recklessness.

Nationalism surges on both sides, Sweden's borders get even clingier, and Russia's digital bear roars louder online. Grain from Ukraine's last harvest becomes a key bargaining chip, traded for precious watts. Expect to see sophisticated cyberattacks targeting energy infrastructure and disinformation campaigns aimed at swaying public opinion in both nations. Digital Empires involved in resource mapping or data analysis in the Arctic will be caught in the crossfire, potentially facing sanctions or cyber espionage.

Finally, in 2035, the Gulf kingdoms, basking in their 50% GDP glow from solar power, decide Africa's solar dreams are a bit… ambitious. Saudi Arabia, with its AI-managed desert farms humming, strikes a deal with Ethiopia: water for watts. But the contract turns out to be less of an agreement and more of a digital chokehold, displacing fifteen million people with nary a drop of compensation. Kenyan farms, now AI-run and Gulf-owned, thrive while local communities wither.

X erupts with accusations of digital colonialism. Populist outrage spills into the streets of Nairobi, culminating in a torched solar rig. South Africa's scrappy hippo eyes its own mineral wealth with renewed intensity, scrambling to find a voice in the fast moving landscape. The Digital Empires, whose platforms facilitated these deals and whose AI powers the farms, will face intense scrutiny, with accusations of enabling neocolonialism and exacerbating inequality.

Beyond these specific flashpoints, nations traditionally aligned with the West will be navigating this increasingly turbulent world with their own anxieties.

Japan, observing a potentially inward-focused or erratic United States, would likely be re-evaluating its security posture. A strengthening of its own military capabilities and closer ties with other regional powers like Australia and South Korea, potentially underpinned by robust digital intelligence sharing, becomes a highly plausible scenario.

Australia and New Zealand, while geographically distant from many of these immediate crises, would be keenly aware of the interconnectedness of the global system. Australia, with its strategic location and vital resources, might forge even stronger alliances within the Indo-Pacific, while New Zealand would likely emphasize diplomatic solutions and potentially face increasing pressure to take sides in a more polarized world. A 'golden card' in New Zealand's favour is the investment in property by the affluent as a climate and environmental life raft.

For all three nations, the ability to navigate the digital information landscape, combat disinformation, and protect their critical digital infrastructure from state-sponsored attacks would become paramount.

These aren't just random sparks; they're ignited by the very winds we've been tracking: climate chaos, the digital guillotine of automation, and the insatiable grab for wealth and power.

The Indus water talks tanked in 2023; US-Mexico border drones are buzzing today; China's digital grip on Southeast Asia is tightening; Arctic claims are already contested; and Gulf-Africa solar deals are being inked as we speak. Why will these sparks flare?

Because the global board is too crowded, every chomp is a territorial dispute, and these hippos, fuelled by nationalism and amplified by the Digital Empires, are too stubborn (and too well-fed in some cases) to back down.

This isn't a slow burn; it's a digital flash fire waiting to happen. The old guard might have tried to talk things down with charm and diplomacy, but these new players, egged on by their digital echo chambers and the relentless pursuit of resources and influence, are more likely to fan the flames.

Smaller players are no longer just pawns; they're the digital kindling in a game where the big jaws don't care who gets burned as long as they get their share. The next decade isn't a reset; it's a reckoning, and the digital sparks are already flying. Watch the whole damn thing light up – pop, pop, pop.

6.7 The Final World Order: A Triptych of Control

By 2100, the world isn't a globe of distinct nations but a triptych of control[50]: the AI-Integrated Cores, the Resource-Reliant Peripheries, and the Human-Resilient

---

[50] In the context I used it, 'triptych' refers to:
A structure with three distinct parts that are related to each other. Just like a triptych artwork has three panels; the world of 2100 is presented as being divided into three interconnected but different types of zones:

Margins. This isn't a sudden apocalypse, but the logical conclusion of the trends we've tracked: the relentless advance of AI, the stark realities of climate change, and the widening gulf of inequality.

The AI-Integrated Cores, echoing the efficiency drives discussed in earlier chapters, are the gleaming urban centres of East Asia and pockets of the West. Here, life is algorithmically optimized, mirroring the AI-driven governance we've seen take hold in places like Shenzhen. Watts are plentiful, dissent is a data anomaly, and the primary export is digital innovation, consumed by the peripheries in exchange for raw materials. Consider Seoul, South Korea, a potential core city where advanced AI manages not just infrastructure but also the intricate social fabric, its citizens living in a hyper-connected, high-tech bubble, largely insulated from the climate stresses impacting the rest of the peninsula.

The Resource-Reliant Peripheries encompass regions like a solar-powered Gulf and a hydro-rich Canada. They leverage their geographical advantages, as explored in Chapter 7, to become vital suppliers of energy and water to the cores. In return, they receive technological advancements and a degree of political sway, but their own development often lags, their populations serving as cogs in the machine that powers the cores. Imagine the Sahel region bordering the Gulf states; while the Gulf prospers from solar exports, the Sahel might remain a climate-stressed periphery, dependent on the goodwill and digital infrastructure of its wealthy neighbours for basic necessities, a stark illustration of the climate caste system we've examined.

Finally, the Human-Resilient Margins are the off-grid communities and localized economies scattered across Africa, parts of South America, and even within the decaying infrastructure of the old global powers. These echo the "Lost" settlements we touched upon, prioritizing human connection and traditional skills

---

- The AI-Integrated Cores: Representing technologically advanced and controlled regions.
- The Resource-Reliant Peripheries: Representing regions dependent on providing resources.
- The Human-Resilient Margins: Representing regions focused on human self-sufficiency.

The term is used to convey the idea of a world order that is fractured into three major, interconnected segments, rather than a collection of many individual and unrelated nations.

over full integration into the AI-driven world. Picture the highlands of Peru, where communities might revert to ancient agricultural techniques, leveraging local knowledge and bartering systems to maintain autonomy, a stark contrast to the technologically dependent cores and peripheries.

Universal Basic Income, a concept we've seen emerge as a necessity in a post-work economy, underpins the stability of the cores and peripheries, preventing widespread unrest but also reinforcing the control of the Algorithm Barons – the data-rich inheritors who now steer this fragmented world, their influence far surpassing that of traditional nation-states.

6.8 How We Got There: A Cascade of Consequences

The path to this triptych of control was paved with the foreseeable "Grey Rhinos" of the 2030s and 2040s. The water wars between India and Pakistan, driven by climate change as discussed in Chapter 4, solidified the importance of resource control. The US-Mexico border conflicts, fuelled by climate migration, highlighted the breakdown of traditional governance. China's strategic energy cuts in Southeast Asia demonstrated the weaponization of essential resources, a theme we explored in Chapter 7.

The 2050s and 2060s witnessed the hardening of these trends. AI, as predicted in Chapter 3, became deeply embedded in governance and the economy, leading to the rise of corporate-controlled zones and the marginalization of human labor. The climate crisis intensified, creating more climate refugees and further straining already fragile states, exacerbating the conditions for the emergence of the "Lost" settlements.

By the 2070s and 2080s, the lines between the cores, peripheries, and margins became increasingly rigid. The Algorithm Barons, leveraging their control over data and digital infrastructure, consolidated their power, their influence eclipsing that of weakened nation-states, a trend foreshadowed in Chapter 9. The flow of resources and technology became the primary determinant of global power dynamics, mirroring the new currencies of watts and water we examined.

The world of 2100, therefore, isn't a sudden dystopia but the cumulative effect of decades of inaction on climate change, the unchecked rise of AI, and the prioritization of profit over people. It's a world where the "fracturing of power," the central theme of this chapter, has reached its logical conclusion, leaving behind a fragmented reality where control is concentrated in the hands of a few, and survival takes vastly different forms depending on one's place in this new global order.

6.9 Why It Landed Here: The New Lords of the Grid and the Algorithm

So, the stage is set for the world of 2100 – a fractured realm governed by the new dynasties of our age: the Energy Barons, controlling the flow of watts, and the Technology Barons, wielding the power of data and algorithms. They are the architects of the AI-Integrated Cores and the silent influencers of the Resource-Reliant Peripheries. Those left outside, in the Human-Resilient Margins, represent a conscious or enforced opting-out of this digitally-driven hierarchy. Power, as we've seen throughout this chapter, is no longer about traditional political might or military strength; it's about who controls the fundamental infrastructure of survival and the very code that shapes our realities. The remnants of the old global order – the nation-states – are left to navigate this new landscape, some finding a niche within the emerging blocs, others struggling for relevance, and some simply fading into the background.

In the chapters that follow, we will delve deeper into the specific ways communities adapt – or fail to adapt – within this fragmented world. We will explore the varying speeds at which different regions move towards these futures and examine the practical steps, both individual and collective, that might yet offer a chance to alter this trajectory, to perhaps nudge the flow of power and build a more equitable and sustainable future from the groaning scrap heap of the old.

6.10 Chapter Summary

A. **The illusion of a stable, borderless world has collapsed**. What once felt like the dawn of an interconnected, globalist future has buckled under the weight of climate chaos, rising nationalism, and escalating inequality. Traditional centres of governance – nation-states, unions, alliances – are now fragmented, their authority diluted by digital disruption and resource scarcity.

B. **Power is no longer held by governments alone.** The new global players are the Digital Empires – Amazon, Google, Tencent, and others – operating above the laws of any single state, extracting value across borders while contributing little in return. Alongside them, corporate titans and algorithmic elites increasingly dictate global priorities, displacing traditional diplomacy with platforms, data, and influence.

C. **This fractured power landscape is no longer theoretical –** it's playing out in real-time. From drone-backed border crackdowns to AI-automated layoffs, from cyber-coerced diplomacy to AI-managed city grids, we're witnessing the transition from the nation-state to the algorithm-state, from military muscle to data dominance.

D. Geopolitical tensions now centre around **control of digital infrastructure, water access, mineral rights, and energy flows**. Flashpoints are emerging not just in traditional hotspots, but in regions redefined by technological dependence and climate exposure – from AI-choked India to solar-choked Africa, from Arctic oil rushes to dam-triggered blackouts.

E. **By 2100, the world splinters** into a triptych of control:
   - **AI-Integrated Cores**: Highly optimised, surveilled urban hubs running on watts and algorithms.
   - **Resource-Reliant Peripheries**: Energy-rich zones trading resources for tech, yet remaining politically beholden to the cores.
   - **Human-Resilient Margins**: Off-grid, decentralised communities surviving through low-tech resilience and social cohesion.

This isn't a tale of sudden collapse – it's a gradual stratification. The castles of power haven't exploded; they've decayed, replaced by a new digital feudalism. The world order has not shifted – it has shattered, and in the fragments, new lords rise: those who own the grid, the code, the watts, and the water.

6.11 What Can You Do About It?

1. **Stop looking up for salvation.** Nation-states are no longer the centre of gravity – they're reactive, overburdened, and in many cases, irrelevant to the deeper structural changes under way. Adapt locally, not institutionally.
2. **Monitor the Digital Empires.** The future is being written by corporations, not parliaments. Learn to read the language of infrastructure – where the data flows, who owns the servers, who controls the platforms. These are your new gatekeepers.
3. **Build climate and tech redundancy.** Assume failure – of the grid, of supply chains, of stable employment. Resilience will come not from technological dependence, but from human-scale, flexible systems: water collection, local energy generation, shared storage, mutual aid.

4. **Track the hippo jostling.** Follow the geopolitical feeding frenzy: who's hoarding lithium, damming rivers, stockpiling AI chips. These aren't abstract economic moves – they're lifelines, shaping everything from migration to governance.
5. **Redefine wealth in a brittle world.** Stocks crash. Cryptocurrencies evaporate. But land, food security, water access, and functional local infrastructure will remain the bedrock of autonomy. The smart pivot is from asset inflation to resource control.
6. **Act before the guillotine drops.** Automation isn't a slow-burn job loss story – it's an economic detonation. The window for graceful adaptation is narrow. Learn, pivot, diversify – before your industry gets zeroed out by a chatbot.
7. **Challenge algorithmic capture.** Surveillance capitalism and AI governance are not theoretical concerns – they're your future boss, judge, landlord, and gatekeeper. Fight for transparency, accountability, and the right to remain a human in the loop.
8. **Brace for border ruptures.** Climate migration, digital propaganda, and economic collapse will redefine national boundaries – not through policy, but through movement. Watch the tides: of people, data, energy, and capital. Learn where the safe ground will be.
9. **Decentralise everything.** Power, information, food, energy – if you rely on centralised systems, you're hostage to their failure. Build lifeboats: solar panels, rain tanks, mesh networks, co-ops, barter systems. Think in terms of resilience nodes, not chains.
10. **See the world clearly – and act accordingly.** The fractures are not coming. They are here. The board is already flipped, the hippos are already feeding, and the firebrands are already lighting up the grid. What you do now determines your proximity to the blast radius – and your capacity to endure what comes next.

Vignette F: Ava: A Shrinking World

F.1 Madrid, Spain – 2031

Ava drew her first breath in Madrid in 2031, born under skies bruised by Saharan dust storms that blew further north each year. Her parents were perpetual motion – Alejandro a Spanish father, and Gayle, an Australian mother, both journalists and activists who charted the beauty and the slow bleeding of a wounded planet. Alejandro and Gayle's lifestyles was funded by grants from a confederation of corporations that contributed a share of their profits towards philanthropic support and sustainability. This type of organisation had seen a small increase as consumers started demanding more from the brands they supported.

Their life was a tapestry woven across continents: documenting whale songs off Hermanus, trekking through Borneo's shrinking rainforests, witnessing Andean glaciers weep into barren valleys. They wrote not just of wonders, but of wounds – polluted rivers running black, deserts swallowing villages, the subtle poisoning creeping into the food chain. They were already talking about 'slur', the insidious cognitive fog linked to microplastic saturation, finding early clinical correlations in coastal communities long before it became a global headline.

Ava's childhood was nomadic, lived between departure lounges and temporary homes. She learned languages like others learned nursery rhymes, her playgrounds ranging from Thai markets to Spanish plazas. Her parents didn't shield her from the world's truths; they taught her to observe, document, resist. By ten, she understood the disparity – the gleaming towers of Singapore rising above choked shipping lanes, the pristine reserves guarded by drones while nearby communities drank contaminated water.

She saw the beauty her parents fought for, but also the decay they couldn't halt. The world wasn't the one they had inherited; it was already frayed, burdened by choices made long before she arrived.

F.2 Sydney, Australia – 2050

Nineteen years old, and the world Ava was raised to explore slammed its doors shut. Standing on the shores near Sydney, watching the haze from perennial inland fires smudge the horizon, the freedom her parents had cherished felt like a forgotten myth. Travel wasn't a right anymore; it was a privilege gated by algorithms and health screening. Governments, besieged by climate refugees and spooked by AI-predicted resource wars, had turned borders into impenetrable digital and physical fortresses.

Alejandro and Gayle had gone back to Melbourne, where Gayle had grown up before going traveling. Both found comfort in roles as lecturers through online discussion regarding community activism.

Ava had planned to join a conservation project in Patagonia, then follow migration routes through Central Asia. Her applications were rejected. Not just visa issues – her Global Mobility Index score was flagged. The reason, buried in bureaucratic code: elevated bio-markers consistent with cumulative environmental toxin exposure – the 'slur' her parents had warned about was now a quantifiable barrier, a filter sorting the 'pure' from the 'polluted'.

Only those from approved settlements or with access to expensive genetic cleansing therapies could pass the new biological checkpoints. Ava, child of the world, was grounded by the world's slow poisoning and her parent's wanderlust.

Frustration hardened into activism.

Ava joined underground networks, using encrypted channels to share information, challenging the bio-segregationist border policies. It was dangerous; AI surveillance systems flagged dissent efficiently. It was here she met Jonah, a quiet coder disillusioned with his work for a logistics giant. He knew how the systems worked, how data flowed, how AI could be both warden and, potentially, weapon.

He showed Ava how repurposed diagnostic AI, smuggled out from corporate labs, could help their network provide basic medical aid to excluded communities, reading bio-signs the official systems ignored – a small act of defiance using the master's tools against the master's house, operating precariously within the constraints set by the tech's original design.

F.3 Murray Valley, Australia – 2075

The choice had been made years ago: refuse the gilded cage of the AI-managed cities and live in the precarious freedom of the Outlands. By forty-four, Ava and Jonah were veterans of the resistance, moving between resilient, off-grid communities carved out of Australia's drying interior. The AI-governed coastal cities – Sydney, Melbourne – were sealed ecosystems, optimised for their closed communities, their populations tracked, managed, curated. Outside lay the vast, unpredictable expanse where survival depended on cooperation and salvaged tech.

Ava could not complain too much. Her father had been diagnosed with a blood variant of 'slur' that caused sharp pain as different organs tried to process the foreign bodies in the course of their usual function. Being within the Melbourne zone prior to the tightening of controls meant that he and Gayle enjoyed first class medical treatment, but not a lasting cure.

For Ava and Jonah outside of these curated zones, it wasn't just about resistance; it was about building alternatives.

Jonah adapted open-source AI models – stripped of predefined control parameters – to help manage scarce water resources shared between settlements, predicting rainfall patterns with data scraped from federal weather feeds. They used encrypted mesh networks for communication, staying steps ahead of the surveillance drones that occasionally swept overhead.

As long as these outside communities didn't threaten the protected hubs, the Australian government was happy to provide information and basic support services.

Ava focused on community organisation, teaching adaptation strategies learned from her parents' travels, mediating disputes, preserving human skills – gardening, repair, storytelling – that the AI cities had automated to robotic efficiency.

They witnessed the Government owned system's prioritisation firsthand: corporate AI rerouting water supplies from independent farms to designated 'economic zones', automated 'Efficiency Relocations' emptying towns deemed unproductive. Ava and Jonah helped people escape these zones, guiding them into the network's embrace, showing them that there was opportunity and community available to all.

Life was hard, resources scarce, but the human spirit was stronger than ever.

And in 2062, amidst this struggle, they chose hope: their son, Mateo, was born under a sky hazy with dust, a symbol of defiant life, a memory of when Ava had taken her first breath on the other side of the world.

F.4 Settlement 811, Australia – 2100

Sixty-nine years. Ava sat by a crackling fire, the air sharp with the scent of eucalyptus. Settlement 811, a cluster of Earthship homes and geodesic domes shimmering with salvaged solar panels, was one of the strongest pockets of stubborn humanity she knew. The AI megacities along the coast were phantom lights on the horizon, utterly disconnected now, self-sustaining, their populations living lives unimaginable – and perhaps unfree – within. Her own parents had passed away years before, a digital call their last connection with their daughter and her family.

The world had fractured completely.

Jonah too was gone, lost years ago during a desperate run to aid climate immigrants trying to cross by sea, caught in the middle of a security drone patrol. Ava felt his absence like a missing limb, but the life continued.

Mateo, now a young man, sharp-eyed and resourceful, led foraging parties and managed the settlement's adapted tech, using AI tools scavenged and reprogrammed by Jonah long ago, purely for community survival, not profit or control. Ava tutored the children – history, ethics, the importance of remembering what it meant to make choices. She told them of a life of travel when she was their age to places around the world. They looked on in disbelief, enchanted.

She knew their existence was fragile. They were outliers, ghosts in the machine's world. The AI cities didn't actively hunt them; they simply didn't register them. They were irrelevant data points in a system geared towards total efficiency. Yet, watching Mateo teach younger children how to read the stars, unmediated by any screen, Ava felt not despair, but a fierce, quiet pride.

They had resisted. They had built a strong community from the scraps. It wasn't the borderless world her parents had dreamed of, but it was real. It still felt very … human.

Chapter 7: The New Currencies – Water and Energy

The Aral Sea, once the world's fourth-largest lake, has shrunk by 90% since the 1960s due to water diversions for irrigation. The Ganges River, a sacred river for over a billion people in India, is experiencing declining water levels due to glacial melt, population growth, and industrial pollution, jeopardising access to clean water for millions. Bitcoin mining, the process of verifying and adding transactions to the blockchain, consumes an estimated 130 terawatt-hours of electricity annually, comparable to the energy consumption of Argentina.

Our lives are interwoven with the constant, often invisible, flow of water and energy[51]. From the moment we wake to the moment we sleep, these resources power our routines, shape our comfort, and underpin the very fabric of our modern existence.

Yes, for millennia we didn't have the comfort of electricity and all it powers, but let's be clear, almost none of us are equipped to go without it now. Hell, even a 15% battery warning on my smartphone gets me sweating! As like many, I'm addicted to the power grid.

7.1 Comfort & Confidence Secured by Water and Electricity

The true scale of our daily consumption remains largely unseen, a hidden current running beneath the surface of our awareness. But threaten either – water or electricity – and watch the world crazy.

---

[51] Water Usage Comparisons (Location-Independent)

Activity	Average Litres	Comment
Filling a Standard Bucket	10	A common measure for basic water needs.
Filling a Standard Bathtub	120	Represents a typical personal hygiene use.
Filling a Small Residential Pool	10,000	Gives a sense of larger-scale recreational water use.
Filling an Olympic-Sized Pool	2,500,000	Provides a benchmark for very large volumes of water.

Energy Usage Comparisons (Location-Independent)

Activity	Average kWh	Comment
Charging a Smartphone (Full Charge)	0.015	Represents a tiny but common energy use. (Assume a 15W phone charger for 1 hour)
Running a Standard Washing Machine Cycle	1	Represents a typical appliance energy use.
Charging an Electric Vehicle (Full)	75	Represents a large, but increasingly common, energy use (Tesla Model 3).
Running a Central Air Conditioner (8 Hours)	24	Represents a large appliance running for a long period of time (assume 3kWh AC).

To truly understand our reliance, we must acknowledge the vast disparities in consumption across the globe. For example, a resident of London might directly use around 150 litres of water daily, but when factoring in "virtual water" embedded in food and goods, that figure can soar to over 3,000 litres. Similarly, their energy consumption could easily reach 10,000 watts per day, powering everything from heating to commutes. Contrast this with someone in Soweto, Johannesburg, where daily water use might be limited to 20-50 litres, and energy consumption, often reliant on less consistent sources, could be a fraction of that.

In Bangalore, a rapidly growing tech hub, water usage is a complex mix, with some areas experiencing shortages while others consume upwards of 200 litres daily, and energy consumption is rising rapidly to meet the demands of the city. A Texan, with access to large homes and vehicles, might consume upwards of 500 litres of water and over 20,000 watts of energy each day.

In the manufacturing powerhouse of Shenzhen, vast amounts of energy are used in the production of goods, with the average citizen's embedded energy footprint being very high. In Tunisia, water scarcity is a constant concern and energy consumption is lower than in more developed nations, however, the growth of industry and living standards is placing increased pressure on both water and energy resources.

This is important to consider, as each region and socio-economic groups' baseline needs for water and energy are nuanced.

7.2 Dollars Die, Watts & Water Rule

Money's dead. Not the crisp bills or digital blips – those still shuffle around – but the idea that it runs the world? Done. By 2050, survival's not about your bank account; it's about watts and clean water, the twin currencies that decide who gets to breathe and who's left choking in the dark. This isn't some distant what-if – it's crashing through the door now.

India's rivers shrink while 50°C summers torch the land. Lagos drowns in floods, its grids silent. Meanwhile, the Gulf pumps solar and desalinated H2O, and Canada's hydropower beams like a strutting peacock. The game's flipped… no, the games changed.

Look at the scoreboard. The wealthy aren't stacking gold, well not only gold – they're hoarding kilowatts and litres, building fortresses of power and flow while the rest scrabble for scraps. This isn't a market correction; it's a reckoning. As we've discussed, climate's gone feral, AI's gutted the old economy, and the fossil age is a corpse we're still kicking. Energy and water aren't just resources – they're weapons, and the ones holding them don't share out of kindness. No global fix is coming, no fairy tale of equity to soften the blow. Wake up – this is the world we've built, and you'd better adapt or be left screaming from your parched throat in the cold dark.

7.3 The Fall of the Old Gods: Fossil & Flow

Fossil fuels, the concentrated remnants of ancient organic matter – the clues in the name – have powered our industrial ascent for centuries. Coal, the first to be widely exploited, began fuelling the steam engine revolution in the 18th century, but the true explosion came with the discovery and refinement of oil in the late 19th and early 20th centuries. Natural gas, often found alongside oil, followed suit. The 20th century witnessed an unprecedented surge in fossil fuel consumption, with global demand skyrocketing as industrialisation spread and populations grew.

In the last 100 years alone, we've extracted and burned an estimated over 1.5 trillion barrels of crude oil[52], tens of trillions of cubic meters of natural gas, and hundreds of billions of tons of coal, transforming landscapes and powering a global economy. This insatiable appetite has had a devastating consequence: the release of over 1,500 gigatons of carbon dioxide into the atmosphere, triggering the climate crisis that now threatens the very foundations of our civilization and is discussed elsewhere in this book.

Now, let's watch the old kings topple. Oil and gas ruled the roost – Russia's pipelines fed Europe's heat, Venezuela's wells gushed black cash, Saudi Arabia lounged on crude thrones. By 2035, that's history. Russia's gas grip slips – Germany's wind turbines spin, pipelines rusting as the EU's Green Deal hits overdrive. Venezuela's a ghost – oil dries up by 2040, rigs swallowed by floods and neglect. Saudi Arabia? They pivot or perish, oil revenue halved, scrambling into solar like their lives depend on it – because they do.

Coal's no saviour. China and India burned it like junkies – factories roaring, Delhi's air a toxic soup. But by 2040, it's over. China's coal mix drops to 20%, India's

[52] To visualise the sheer volume of oil consumed in the last century, imagine this: if we were to spill 1.5 trillion barrels across the continent of Australia, it would create a layer of oil over an inch deep.

fields bake dry as solar takes over – 1.7°C warming by 2035 makes it a necessity, not a choice. The air's still poison, lungs and health sacrificed to the old gods of fossil wealth, themselves now dead. Nigeria's Niger Delta? Once an oil cow, now a flooded slum – pipelines leak into rising tides, no cash to fix the mess.

And what of water's old gods? They're looking decidedly dehydrated, frail as if having run their last marathon. Rivers and aquifers – Ganges[53], Nile[54], Ogallala – kept us alive for millennia. Not anymore. India's Ganges drops 30% by 2035, Pakistan snarling across the border as flows thin. Kansas's Ogallala Aquifer[55], the US breadbasket's backbone, runs dry by 2040 – wheat fields turn to dust, pumps sucking air. Ethiopia's Blue Nile[56] dams choke Egypt by 2050, Cairo's farmers praying to a river that's more myth than lifeline. These aren't hiccups; they're collapses – finite flow meeting infinite greed, and the bill's due.

---

[53] A 2018 study found that groundwater input to the Ganges has declined by 50% in the summer months over the past three decades. [Source: https://news.mongabay.com/2018/09/as-indias-ganges-runs-out-of-water-a-potential-food-shortage-looms/]

[54] Water scarcity, land loss, and declining agricultural productivity are contributing to forced migration and displacement of communities in the Nile Delta and other regions. [Source: https://www.brookings.edu/blog/africa-in-focus/2021/04/08/the-grand-ethiopian-renaissance-dam-a-looming-crisis-for-egypt/]

[55] The rate of water withdrawal from the Ogallala Aquifer significantly exceeds the rate of natural recharge, leading to a long-term decline in water availability. This is primarily driven by the high demand for irrigation in the region. [Source: https://www.scientificamerican.com/article/the-ogallala-aquifer-is-running-dry/]

[56] The Grand Ethiopian Renaissance Dam (GERD) on the Blue Nile has heightened tensions between Egypt, Sudan, and Ethiopia over water sharing. The dam's filling and operation could further reduce downstream flow, exacerbating water scarcity and potentially leading to conflict. [Source: https://www.brookings.edu/blog/africa-in-focus/2021/04/08/the-grand-ethiopian-renaissance-dam-a-looming-crisis-for-egypt/]

7.4 Renewables and Reservoirs: The New Power Bases

So who's rising from the ashes? The ones with watts and water, rewriting the map in power and flow. The Gulf states – Saudi Arabia[57], UAE[58] – saw the endgame. By 2035, solar deserts hit 50% of their energy mix, panels stretching horizon to horizon. But it's not just juice – they're desalinating oceans, turning salt into survival. Dubai's towers gleam, AI grids doling out H2O and power, while Yemen's across the border, wells sandpits, kids drinking dust. It's a double play – energy and water locked down, a new empire built on sun and sea.

Canada's quieter but no less ruthless. Hydropower's their gold – Ontario's rivers churn watts by 2050, feeding AI enclaves in Toronto while the US Midwest begs. Water's their edge too – lakes and melt keep them flush as America's plains parch. Scandinavia's in the game – Norway and Finland crack fusion by 2075, fjords glowing with clean power, rivers feeding grids while southern Europe rations flickers. They're not just energy-rich; they're water-secure, a combo that makes them untouchable.

Then there's the hunger of the machines, driving the tech wars. China's got lithium and cobalt – 70% of the world's supply by 2023 – and by 2035, they're pumping out batteries that keep Beijing humming. Dams too – Three Gorges locks the Yangtze, rural protests crushed as urban watts flow. Ethiopia's Nile dams mirror it – power and water for Addis, Sudan and Egypt left dry. India's solar's cheap, but without reservoirs or batteries, they're at China's mercy. The new bases aren't just land – they're control, and the ones with the juice and the taps hold the world by the throat.

7.5 The Basic Rules Apply

Let's revisit our old friend, capitalism. The rules of still apply – scarcity creates value. But now, instead of stocks and real estate, power is measured in kilowatts and clean water access.

---

[57] Between 2012 and 2022, Saudi Arabia added 700 MW of renewable power capacity. However, this has increased dramatically since then. Between 2022 and early 2024, they added 2.1 GW, a 300% increase. [Source: https://www.arabnews.com/node/2576806/saudi-arabia]

[58] The UAE Energy Strategy 2050 aims for a 50% clean energy mix by 2050, with significant contributions from solar power. [Source: https://www.uae-embassy.org/discover-uae/climate-and-energy/uae-energy-diversification]

To illustrate why energy is so important in the future, let's consider the demand side to explain the premium that can be charged on the supply side. Luckily, in this case, we don't have to really factor in human labour very much.

A relatively new entrant to the picture of the last 10 years is the obesely hungry AI kid that's joined sat down at the table.

Training large language models, the engines behind many AI applications, demands immense computational power. These models require vast data centres, packed with specialised hardware, running for extended periods. The energy consumed in these processes is staggering. For instance, training a single large language model like GPT-3 has been estimated to consume around 1,287 megawatt-hours (MWh) of electricity. That's roughly equivalent to the annual electricity consumption of 120 average US households. Some newer, larger models are expected to require even more energy. As AI use scales, so does the demand for these resources, raising concerns about the sustainability of this technological revolution.

But those eager AI Barons and their egg heads will figure out how to make it work.

Furthermore, the cooling systems necessary to prevent these high-powered data centres from overheating require substantial amounts of water. A large data centre can consume millions of gallons of water per year. For example, some large data centres can use as much water as a small city, with estimates ranging from 3 to 5 million gallons per day for extremely large facilities. This water is primarily used in evaporative cooling systems, which are essential to maintain optimal operating temperatures for servers. The water footprint of AI extends beyond cooling, encompassing the manufacturing of hardware and the energy production needed to power these systems. As AI seeps into our daily lives, from chatbots to autonomous vehicles, the cumulative impact on energy and water resources will only intensify.

Improvements in efficiency will no doubt come, perhaps the magic of quantum computing will make a big splash, but let's move forward with what we can reasonable assume given where we are.

I love my GPT, Gemini and Grok chats. Millions do. But let's face it, they're not running economies, government, security and critical infrastructure, yet. But the future generations will. Now what sort of infrastructure and feeding will that require, with redundancy upon redundancy having to be built in, as well as ongoing R&D, all wrapped in increasingly important cyber security.

7.6 Consideration: An AI to Run London

London, a city already straining under its own weight, is about to become a voracious consumer. Forget the quaint image of a city powered by tea and biscuits; we're talking about a metropolis fuelled by gigawatts and millions of gallons of water.

Now let's step forward to 2040, London's AI infrastructure: far beyond chatbots and predictive traffic algorithms, but the backbone of every service. AI-driven governance processing thousands of documents a minute, security millions of biometric integrated cameras and cyber probes, healthcare optimised to offer integrated diagnostic and outcome delivery, and all the infrastructure of transportation, utilities and services to tie it all together.

Every transaction, every data point, every decision processed by neural networks that demand constant power and cooling. To support this level of integration, London would need to build data centres on a scale previously unseen. Think not of a few server rooms, but entire districts dedicated to housing AI brains, a shadow city under the city blinking away in temperature controlled environments.

The energy costs? Staggering.

Based on current estimates, a fully AI-integrated London would likely consume several terawatt-hours (TWh) of electricity annually. That's the equivalent of powering several smaller nations. Imagine the grid needing to be completely rebuilt, reinforced, and expanded, not just to meet demand, but to ensure redundancy and resilience. We're talking about a city that needs to produce as much energy as it consumes, and then some, just to keep its AI infrastructure from crashing.

Then there's the water. Cooling these data centres would require a river's worth of water. Run through the system and evaporating to release the heat generated by the system. Millions of gallons per day, diverted from existing supplies or sourced through massive desalination plants. London, a city already dealing with its own water scarcity issues, would need to become a master of water management. Picture reservoirs and pipelines, not just for drinking water, but for cooling the AI that runs the city.

The AI Barons will find ways to make it work, of course. Efficiency improvements, perhaps even breakthroughs in quantum computing, will help. But the fundamental reality remains: AI requires resources, and lots of them. London, and every other city-state that embraces this technology, will become a battleground for energy and water.

The old rules of urban planning, of resource management, will be thrown out the window. This isn't just about technological advancement; it's about a fundamental shift in how we power and sustain our cities. And the costs, in terms of energy and water, will be immense.

Now add to this the other 50+ mega cities that will become the AI city states of the world, and we start to understand what demand looks like, and what the challenges in supplying this will look like.

Suddenly my 15% low phone battery doesn't feel quite as important.

7.7 New Currencies, New Power

This isn't a handshake economy – it's a brawl, and water and energy are the fists. China's AI grids don't just power Shanghai – they cut off Vietnam by 2075, trade deals turning into watt blackmail. Need hydropower? Kneel. The Gulf's no softer – Saudi solar and desal exports dry up for Egypt by 2050, Cairo dark and thirsty while Riyadh's elite sip filtered H2O at $200 a litre. It's not generosity; it's a chokehold.

Water wars are uglier. India and Pakistan snarl over the Ganges by 2040 – flows down 30%, guns up 100%. Ethiopia's dams starve Egypt's Nile by 2050 – 30 million displaced, clashing at Turkey's borders. Somalia's rains fail, 15 million trek south, Kenya's electrified fences humming as they're turned away. Nordics play it slick – fusion and rivers keep them cozy by 2075, exports a trickle to Germany, nothing for Spain's drought-dead fields. Canada's the same – hydro watts for Vancouver, drones at the US border as Texas begs. No sharing here – just survival.

The losers? Brutal. Nigeria's Sahel[59] blacks out – no solar cash, no water left, 20 million march south by 2050, hitting AI drone patrolled walls. Central America's

[59] The humanitarian needs in the Sahel have grown significantly in the last 25 years, as communities face increasing challenges with food security, access to water, and healthcare. This requires increased humanitarian assistance and support for resilience-

tapped out – Honduras's rivers die by 2075, grids fail, migrants flood north to AI-guarded US lines. Bangladesh's 10 million flee tides by 2035, slamming India's guns, no watts or H2O to welcome them. These aren't crises to fix – they're realities to claw through, and the ones without currencies don't just falter – they vanish.

7.8 Who Holds the Tap and Plug

By 2075, the world map of today is lost, in most places it has contracted into hubs with wastelands around them. Nations still exist, but they don't govern. Flags wave, anthems play, but real power belongs to those who own the flow.

A. The Dominators: The Lords of Light and Water

The Gulf states, Scandinavia, and Canada sit at the top – fortresses powered by solar, fusion, and hydro. Their cities glow while the rest of the world flickers. Their AI grids decide who gets watts, who gets water, who gets to grow crops and eat. Their laws don't come from governments – they come from algorithms and their gifts of geography.

- Saudi Arabia & UAE: Solar kings. The sun has made them invincible, their power flowing in controlled exports while their desalination plants turn seawater into liquid gold. Egypt's lifeline? A contract away from being cut.
- China: The AI-energy superpower. The ones who built the battery economy. They don't need war – just a power switch.
- Scandinavia: Fusion and hydropower strongholds. Norway and Finland glow with energy abundance, while the rest of Europe shrinks into dependency.
- Canada: The quiet giant. Water and hydro lock the US into vassal status. Midwest America's farms are dying, its cities begging for power. Ottawa doesn't answer calls – it writes the terms.

---

building initiatives. [Source: https://www.nrc.no/shorthand/fr/sahel---the-worlds-most-neglected-and-conflict-ridden-region/index.html]

- New Zealand: Benefiting from its isolation and massive investment by the wealthy into gilded fortresses offers a rare glow in the southern hemisphere.

B. The Vassals: The Regions That Take Orders

Southern Europe, Africa and India are too weak to stand alone, too desperate to resist. They sign the contracts, they take the energy, they beg for just enough water to keep going. They don't negotiate. They comply.

- Southern Europe: Spain, Greece, Italy – once rich in philosophy, culture and innovation, now water-starved. They get fusion left overs from the North, just enough to keep the lights on. The last show of civility across the union that fell.

- India's north: Burning alive. The south survives on Gulf desalination. The north? A wasteland of dust and riots.

- Egypt, Pakistan, Mexico: Entire nations reduced to vassal states, their survival dictated by the next energy shipment.

- Australia: The narrow band of life along the eastern shore still offers shelters from the extreme heat and rising tides, but they now turn their eyes to New Zealand for assistance, which is grudgingly shared, for now.

C. The Wastelands & Rebels: Those That Fell or Ran

The world doesn't collapse evenly. Some places just fade others take a different path closer to pre–Industrial Revolution living.

- The Sahel: Uninhabitable. 50 million dead or displaced. The desert won, in part thanks to humanities stunning ability to bank problems for a future that's come to collect.

- Bangladesh: Submerged. 10 million climate refugees clawing at the borders of an India that won't let them in.

- The US Midwest: Dried out and abandoned. AI drones patrol empty highways, watching over what used to be farmland.

- Central America: Gone. No rivers, no food, no future. The people who lived there are just ghosts marching north to knock at Texas, or heading south, to live as their ancestors did, but with so much less in the way of natural resources.

7.9 Final Words: The Age of the Plug and the Tap

The world did collapse. The end result of our mismanagement. For those who have benefitted from the gifts of their location the rest is sold off, watt by watt, drop by drop, until nothing is left but shining hubs, vassal glows, and flickering in the dark.

Nations don't rule anymore – energy barons do. AI decides who gets power, desalination plants decide who gets to drink. You're either inside the system, plugged in and hydrated, or you're left choking in the dust.

Dollars don't buy survival anymore. Watts and water do.

And if you don't own them, you don't exist.

7.10 Chapter Summary

A. **Water and electricity are the real wealth of the future.** The global economy is shifting from traditional money to resource-based power. By 2050, access to clean water and reliable energy determines survival.

B. **Fossil fuels are dying – but that doesn't mean an energy revolution for everyone.** The transition to renewables isn't evenly distributed. Countries and corporations that control solar, fusion, hydro, and battery technology will rule, while others fall into energy poverty.

C. **The global energy and water map is being redrawn.**

   a. Saudi Arabia, Canada, Scandinavia, and China are emerging as the new power elites – hoarding watts and water while exporting just enough to keep others dependent.

   b. Southern Europe, South Asia, and large parts of Africa are already sliding into energy and water scarcity.

   c. The world is dividing into hubs of technological abundance and wastelands of thirst and darkness.

D. **Water wars are inevitable.** Nations and regions already experiencing water stress – India, Pakistan, the Sahel, Central America – will face increasing instability as aquifers dry up and rivers stop flowing. Power isn't just about controlling supply; it's about who gets cut off.

E. **AI and high-tech economies are accelerating demand.** The rise of AI-driven megacities and data centres will push energy and water consumption to extreme levels. The wealthiest cities will prioritise keeping their AI systems cool and functional – while leaving rural and low-income populations to fend for themselves.

7.11 What Can You Do About It?

1. **Recognise that energy and water security is now personal survival.** It's not just about your electricity bill – it's about where your power comes from and who controls it. If your city or country relies on imported energy or water, your future is vulnerable.

2. **Decentralise your access to resources.** If possible, invest in solar panels, battery storage, and local water collection systems. If you are reliant on the grid, you are reliant on forces beyond your control. The more independent your energy and water sources, the better your chances of long-term stability.

3. **Understand the geopolitical shift.** Water and energy will dictate national policies and international conflicts. Countries that cannot produce or secure their own power and water will be at the mercy of those who can. If you live in a region dependent on external supply chains, start preparing for scarcity and rationing.

4. **Prepare for cost spikes and access restrictions.** Governments will introduce more aggressive pricing for water and energy, prioritising industries over individuals. Blackouts, water rationing, and rolling restrictions will become normal for many populations.

5. **Support local energy and water infrastructure.** The more your community can sustain itself, the less reliant it is on unstable global markets. Community solar grids, rainwater collection programs, and localised desalination projects will be essential in the coming decades.

6. **Watch how AI and data centres impact supply.** As artificial intelligence dominates governance, security, and economies, the demand for power and water will surge. Cities prioritising AI-driven infrastructure

will drain energy and water from surrounding areas, making survival harder for the unconnected.

7. **Recognise that 'water wars' won't just be between countries – they'll be between classes.** The rich will always have access to desalination, bottled water, and private energy sources. The middle and lower classes will experience increasing shortages. Ensure you have contingency plans before you're forced to choose between price gouged utilities and unreliable alternatives.

8. **Be aware of shifting power dynamics.** The new world order will be determined by who controls energy grids and water supplies. Understanding which nations and corporations dominate these resources will help you predict future economic and political landscapes.

9. **Think long-term about where you live.** If your city or region is prone to water shortages or rolling blackouts, you should consider whether relocation is necessary. Urban areas that cannot guarantee consistent power and water will become increasingly unliveable.

10. **Accept that the old economy is fading.** Currency still has value, but in the coming decades, direct access to electricity and drinkable water will surpass wealth in importance. Those who plan ahead – who build resilience into their energy and water use – will be the ones who survive the transition.

The age of fiat money is fading. The age of energy and water hoarding has begun. Those who control the flow will decide the future. The rest will beg for power and drink from poisoned wells.

Vignette G: Liang Xiu: A Life in China's AI Century

G.1 Shenzhen, China – 2031

Liang Xiu was born in 2031, in Shenzhen, a city that had outgrown its reputation as China's technology capital and transformed into something far greater. By the time she could walk, the city was already a prototype for the nation's future – one of the first AI-administered urban zones, where infrastructure, commerce, and governance were increasingly dictated by machine intelligence.

Her parents were engineers, both working in China's rapidly evolving AI sector. Her father specialised in natural language processing models, helping to refine AI governance systems that dictated resource allocation and social stability. Her mother worked in neuromorphic computing, designing AI systems that could learn and reason in ways more akin to the human brain.

The household was one of quiet discipline. Achievement was expected, not praised. At four years old, Xiu was enrolled in an AI-personalised education track, where machine learning models assessed her strengths, weaknesses, and optimal career pathways. Unlike past generations, who navigated an unpredictable system of gaokao exams and university placements, Xiu's trajectory would be algorithmically mapped from the start.

At nine, she was assigned to a national AI-accelerated program, ensuring that her training aligned with China's strategic needs.

At fifteen, she was selected for quantum cognition training, a track designed for individuals who could interface directly with AI models at a near-intuitive level.

Her path had already been decided.

By 2046, at fifteen, she was fluent in three languages, had built multiple AI prototypes, and had never once needed to make a real decision about her own life.

The world around her was shifting. The United States was falling into corporate-driven fragmentation, struggling to balance AI integration with economic survival. The European Union was slowing, caught between regulating AI and maintaining a human-led system. Meanwhile, China had moved decisively.

By 2040, the government had declared AI the central pillar of national governance.

Not just an advisor. Not just a tool.

A decision-maker.

China was not reacting to history. It was writing it.

And Xiu was one of its carefully optimised products.

G.2 Shenzhen, China – 2050

At nineteen, Xiu had never known a China without AI governance.

By 2050, Shenzhen had fully transitioned into an AI-administered city-state, serving as the prototype for China's evolving governance model. It was still part of the nation, but in many ways, it no longer needed human oversight.

Her career path had been decided not by university choices, but by state-AI talent allocation.

She was placed in National AI Governance Bureau 04, a division responsible for human oversight of China's most advanced AI-led economic systems.

Her work was not to create AI – machines did that now.

Her work was to interpret AI decision-making, ensuring that human political structures could still integrate machine-led economic planning.

Shenzhen itself was a machine, a living system where:

- Traffic, energy, and food distribution were fully autonomous – managed by an AI lattice that adjusted real-time supply and demand with absolute precision.
- Financial markets operated without human traders, shifting capital according to AI-determined investment strategies.
- Social stability was enforced algorithmically, balancing citizen scores based on behavior, economic contribution, and compliance with state initiatives.

China itself had evolved into two realities:

1. The AI-administered megacities – Shenzhen, Shanghai, Beijing – where machines governed, and humans assisted.

2. The semi-autonomous provinces – where traditional governance still held, but with AI influence growing year by year.

Outside China, the world was struggling to keep up.

The United States had fractured into corporate-run territories, where AI was a tool of economic power, not public welfare.
The European Union had resisted full AI governance but was economically stagnant, unable to match China's efficiency.
The Global South was a patchwork – some regions had partnered with China's AI infrastructure, while others fell into resource wars, unable to maintain stable economies in a post-labour world.

For Xiu, the future was not uncertain.

Her position was secure, her role defined, her existence integrated into a system that had no space for unpredictability.

But for the first time in her life, she wondered – if a person never has to choose, are they truly living?

G.3 Beijing, China – 2075

At 44, Xiu was no longer in Shenzhen.

Her career had elevated her to Beijing, where China's National AI Directorate was headquartered. Her job was no longer just oversight – it was international AI strategy, helping China maintain its position as the global AI hegemon.

By 2075, China had outpaced the world, achieving a level of stability that no other major power could match.

- The United States had formally abandoned human-led government in major economic zones, handing control to AI-run corporate conglomerates.

- Europe had split into AI-integrated and AI-resistant states, with regions like Scandinavia embracing full automation while places like Greece and Poland resisted.

- Africa had become the world's critical resource hub, partnering with China for AI-driven water and agricultural management.

China stood alone at the top.

And yet, Xiu saw the cracks. She had spent decades in AI policy, ensuring that humans remained integrated into decision-making processes.

But by 2075, she was no longer sure they were needed at all. The machine-learning models no longer required human ethical review. The economic algorithms no longer needed human validation. The governance AIs no longer sought human input.

The illusion of oversight had remained for decades, but now, it was clear – China's system no longer needed its architects.

And that included her.

For the first time, she considered leaving. Not because China was failing – it wasn't. But because she was no longer sure she mattered.

And she had spent her whole life being told that she did.

G.4 Shanghai, China – 2100

By 2100, China had completed its transformation.

It was no longer a nation in the traditional sense.

It was a network – a seamless integration of AI-managed economic, political, and social systems that functioned with absolute efficiency.

The government still existed, but it was ceremonial.

Human leaders still gave speeches, but AI models made all policy decisions.

The world had diverged:

- China and parts of Asia had become AI-led economic superclusters, where efficiency and control were maximised.
- Scandinavia had preserved human governance, choosing balance over full AI sovereignty.

- The United States had faded, its megacities fully privatised and machine-run.
- Africa had risen as a power centre, leveraging its resource control to dictate global AI-energy policies.

Xiu was one of the last humans still integrated into governance.

By now, most high-level strategic work was automated, and younger generations were neurologically bonded with AI from birth.

Her kind – human-born, AI-educated, but ultimately still biological – was phasing out. She lived in a world optimised beyond the need for people like her.

And as she sat in her climate-controlled apartment in Shanghai, looking out at a city where machines moved with perfect synchrony, she asked herself: Had China succeeded?

Or had it simply stopped asking the question?

And did she – or any human left in this system – still have an answer?

Chapter 8: Moving At Their Own Speed

Picture the world in 2100. What you see will heavily depend on where you are.

Oslo stands as the pinnacle of city planning, a megacity that has incorporated AI into every part of the infrastructure, having prepared years in advance knowing that it would stand when other cities fell below rising sea level, or were consigned to massive desert storms.

Here people go about their daily lives in carefree confidence, secured by, and secure in, the technology AI partner, MUNINN[60], that runs the city more efficiently than any other in history. A full 40% of energy consumption goes towards the 7th generation server farms that operate in a glow of blinking lights across three secured sites, each larger than football field.

Citizens no longer have to work, not in the traditional sense. Instead, people are given the freedom and tools to pursue their purpose and interests. The rest is automated by a vast robotic system.

The costs of running such a city would be inconceivable by today's standards, but as one of the top three energy wholesale providers, Norway is independent and insulated.

By contrast, New York City is deserted, except for small groups that work as a cooperative, steadfast in their determination to remain free of any government or AI controls. They're not fighting anyone, because no government cares. In fact, it's 30,000 mouths that don't need to be fed, bodies that need to be housed or UBI to be paid.

The old maps are useless – nations don't mean what they used to, and borders are less about lines than who's got the watts and the will to hold them. Some places hum with AI precision, their towers gleaming under fusion skies, while others choke on dust, their rivers dry, their people forgotten or fleeing. And then there are those who've said to hell with it all, torching the script and running for the wilds.

This isn't a tale of unity gone wrong or collapse gone right. It's divergence – raw, uneven, and unapologetic. The future doesn't hit everyone the same way because

---

[60] **M**unicipal **U**tvikling **N**ettverk **I** **N**orge **N**asjonal (Municipal Development Network In Norway National), fictional system for this example

it never did. By 2100, the planet's split into three lanes: the Integrated, wired into AI's cold embrace; the Stranded, clawing for scraps in the shadow of power; and the Lost, either abandoned by the system or spitting in its face.

Shanghai's drones patrol spotless streets while the Sahel's dunes swallow villages whole. Toronto's elite swim in desalinated fresh water filled swimming pools, and Bangladesh's refugees slam into India's electrified fences. Oslo's fusion grids glow; Australia's interior bakes into a lawless sprawl. Same planet, different centuries.

This chapter isn't here to preach or predict every twist – it's too late for warnings, and precision's a luxury our parents' forfeit decades ago. If that's the argument you want to have, then good luck to you, but I think you're missing the real discussion.

Instead, it's a lens on how the world fractures when climate, tech, and greed run their course.

The Integrated have bolted ahead, their AI overlords optimising every breath. The Stranded stagger in the middle, too weak to rule, too stubborn to die. The Lost? They're the ghosts – some by fate, some by choice – haunting a system that doesn't even bother to count them. No grand fix is coming. No rebellion's rewriting this script. It's just the world we built, splitting apart at speeds we can't sync. Buckle up – or don't. Either way, you've been strapped in for the ride.

8.1 The Integrated – AI-Run Societies & Energy Fortresses

By 2100, the Integrated aren't just surviving – they're thriving, if you can call it that when every heartbeat's tracked by a machine that doesn't blink. These are the AI-run societies, the energy fortresses: Shanghai, Tokyo, Toronto, Dubai, Oslo, a handful of others scattered like glittering cysts on a dying planet. They're the winners – not by luck, but by design and gift of geography.

Back in the 2030s, when the world started buckling under 1.7°C of warming and AI gutted the old economy, these places didn't flinch. They leaned in, planned, adjusted, invested. By mid-century, they'd secured independence and control of the watts and the water; by 2075, they'd cracked fusion and turned their backs on the rest. Now, they're sealed off, humming with a precision that'd make a Swiss clockmaker blush.

Take Shanghai. It's not a city anymore – it's a system. By 2050, its AI grids were running everything: traffic, trade, power, even who gets to eat and how much. Fast forward to 2100, and it's a fortress of light – 20 million souls plugged into a lattice of algorithms that don't sleep. The streets are spotless, drones buzzing overhead, every corner lit by solar and fusion hubs that churn out terawatt-hours like it's nothing. You wake up, and your day's already mapped – AI assigns your job (if you've still got one), rations your carbon quota, and beams your UBI credits straight to your neural chip. Need a doctor? The system's already flagged your vitals, scheduled the nanobots, and billed you before you cough. Want a kid? Better hope your social score clears the threshold – a human might have the final say on who gets to be happy parents, but AI's telling them the 'right' answer.

Toronto's no different. Canada's hydro wealth turned it into a quiet giant by mid-century, and now it's a citadel. The Ontario Triangle's rivers feed fusion plants that power AI enclaves, climate-controlled towers rising over a Midwest that's been dust since the Ogallala dried up in 2040. The wealthy live in glass spires, sipping desalinated Lake Ontario at prices that'd make a Lagos hawker faint – $200 a litre, triple filtered by machines smarter than lab of technicians. You might go looking for the lower tier of citizens, those doing the work that others don't want and generally pulling society down. However, they're not here. Everyone's catered for. A happy society, doesn't have to be a docile society. There isn't a dystopian angle here. If anything, there is every chance that it's closer to utopian. As long as you're a citizen inside the city wall.

Dubai is no playground – it is a citadel. By 2100, it stands not as a neon-drenched monument to excess, but as the last great human-led empire, a bastion where faith and order hold firm against the creeping dominion of AI governance. While Shanghai and Oslo surrendered to algorithmic rule, Dubai fortified itself, channelling its immense solar wealth into something more than power – it built a world where tradition reigns supreme. Here, the mosques, synagogues, temples, and cathedrals are as sacred as the fusion reactors, and every law, every decision, every social structure is dictated by religious councils rather than lifeless equations. AI works in the background – silent, servile, never sovereign.

For those who reject the soulless precision of AI megacities but refuse to be counted among the Stranded or the Lost, Dubai is the promised land. It is the last place where scripture overrides data, where morality is interpreted by men rather than machines. The air is scrubbed clean, the water flows endlessly, the city glows with untouched prosperity – but it is a fortress, not an invitation. Rights do not trickle down; they are bestowed. The faithful are welcomed, but the godless, the undisciplined, the noncompliant? They dare not enter. Where Shanghai perfects the body and Oslo optimises the mind, Dubai purifies the soul.

Oslo's the cold cousin, Scandinavia's fusion crown jewel. By 2075, they'd cracked the tech, fjords glowing with clean power while southern Europe rationed flickers. It's quieter than Shanghai, less sober than Dubai, but just as optimised. AI governs with a Nordic assurance. The streets are pristine, the grids hum, and the borders bristle with drones. Toronto might flaunt its hydro; Oslo just banks it, a fortress of ice and watts that doesn't need to boast.

Orson Welle's warned us of the surveillance state, burning the fear into our psyche for almost a century. And we definitely felt some of that through the 1990s into the late 2030s. Our privacy was traded to sell us things in a world of consumerism, that lead to excess, that led to… well, to here. Now that trade is to provide curated experiences for citizens to allow them to live richer lives, to pursue their interests, their purpose. But what you're looking at here is the exception to the global norm, the rare 12% of the overall population of 6.2 billion people.

The price of admission's steep, and it's not cash – it's the lottery of birth or, increasingly less likely, to contribute rare skills to this closed society, such as artists, celebrated thinkers and true innovators. Additionally perks include healthy air, clean water and the very best in healthcare, with life expectancy stretching to 120 years, where the global average is hovering around 63.4 years.

Outsiders don't get a look-in. Climate refugees from Bangladesh's tides, labourers from Egypt's dust – they slam into walls, not gates. AI policing doesn't negotiate; it calculates. A million retinas scanned at Shanghai's edge last year, 999,000 turned away. Toronto's drones log 2 million border breaches annually – most end in a flash of light, no questions asked. Dubai's got no room for Yemen's thirsty; Oslo doesn't blink at Spain's parched pleas. Dissent's a whisper here – AI's solving needs, and providing opportunities for wants. Crime and antisocial behaviour exists, but it's identified early and managed through medication or exclusion. And international travel has been replaced by fully immersive virtual experiences; almost nobody leaves paradise, why would you?

8.2 The Stranded – Peripheral States & Energy Vassals

The concept of "vassal states" isn't just a colourful analogy; it reflects a fundamental power dynamic in this future. In the feudal system, vassals swore allegiance to lords, offering military service and loyalty in exchange for protection and land. Similarly, the Stranded find themselves beholden to the Integrated, providing essential resources and labour in exchange for access to vital resources like energy and water.

It's a relationship born of necessity, not equality. The Stranded possess valuable assets: manpower, remnants of industry, and often, arable land. The Integrated, despite their advanced technology, still require human capital for tasks that are difficult to automate, particularly in sectors like agriculture and resource extraction. Moreover, the Stranded represent potential consumers for the Integrated's technological products and services, further solidifying their economic interdependence.

However, the terms of this exchange are heavily skewed in favour of the Integrated. They control the critical infrastructure – the energy grids, desalination plants, and advanced technologies – that the Stranded desperately need. This allows them to dictate prices, extract concessions, and exert significant political influence over the Stranded, effectively turning them into client states.

This dependency is the culmination of decades of gradual decline. As climate change ravaged the planet and AI reshaped the global economy, the Stranded found themselves increasingly marginalised. Their resources dwindled, their infrastructure crumbled, and their economies faltered, leaving them vulnerable to exploitation by the more powerful Integrated. The Stranded are trapped in a vicious cycle: they need the Integrated to survive, but their reliance only deepens their subservience, perpetuating a system where they are perpetually on the losing end.

If the Integrated are the winners in this climate and resource ravaged, AI-dominated 2100, the Stranded are the ones clinging to existence in the shadows of the energy fortresses. They are the nations and regions that haven't quite succumbed to utter collapse, but lack the resources and power to join the ranks of the AI-run elite.

Many are caught between wanting to evolve to the model of the Integrated, whilst lacking their gifts of geography and resources, or committing to a different way of life that refocuses on human endeavour and simplification without trying to reclaim the excesses of the turn of the century before.

Picture Mexico's sprawling cities, India's parched interior, Egypt's Nile-starved plains, Argentina's fading pampas, the Philippines' typhoon-raked coasts – these are the faces of the Stranded.

These are not wastelands, not yet, but they are purgatories, caught in a cycle of flickering lights, borrowed time, and a constant struggle for survival. They possess some technology, some energy, but never enough to break free from their dependency on the Integrated. They are vassals, tethered to the energy grids and water sources controlled by the AI barons, surviving on scraps while the real players dictate the terms of their existence.

8.3 The Complex Dance of Dependency

The relationship between the Integrated and the Stranded is not merely one of exploitation; it's a complex dance of cooperation and dependency, where both parties extract value, but on vastly different terms. The Stranded, despite their precarious position, still hold valuable assets: manpower, remnants of industry, and often, arable land or resources. The Integrated, despite their advanced technology, still require human capital for tasks that are difficult or undesirable to automate.

In Mexico, vast solar farms, built with Integrated funding and technology, stretch across the sun-drenched landscape. These farms feed energy back into the North American AI grid, providing a vital source of renewable power for the Integrated cities. In exchange, Mexico receives a trickle of energy, barely enough to keep its cities running, and a meagre UBI stipend for its citizens, effectively turning the country into an energy colony.

India's southern regions, blessed with fertile lands and a skilled workforce, have become agricultural hubs for the Integrated. AI-optimised farms, managed by a mix of local and Integrated technicians, churn out high-yield crops, engineered for resilience and nutritional efficiency. These crops are shipped north to the energy fortresses, feeding the elite while India's own population subsists on a diet of rationed staples and lab-grown protein.

Egypt, once a land of ancient wonders, now exports its most valuable resource: sand. Vast stretches of the Sahara Desert have been transformed into mining operations, where AI-guided robots extract silicon and other minerals essential for the construction and maintenance of the Integrated cities. In exchange, Egypt receives a lifeline of energy and water, barely enough to sustain its dwindling population, and a precarious political stability enforced by a mix of drones and corporate security forces.

The Philippines, once a hub of outsourcing and tech support, now provides a different kind of service: human augmentation. In Manila, a thriving industry has emerged around the development and implantation of neural chips, designed to enhance human cognitive abilities and integrate them more seamlessly with AI systems. These chips are highly sought after by the Integrated, who see them as a way to further optimise their workforce and maintain their technological edge. In exchange, the Philippines receives a steady flow of energy and technology, but at the cost of further entrenching its dependency on the Integrated.

These are just a few examples of the complex web of cooperation and exploitation that binds the Stranded to the Integrated. It's a relationship where both parties benefit, but where the terms of exchange are heavily skewed in favour of the powerful. The Stranded are trapped in a cycle of dependency, providing essential resources and labour in exchange for a precarious existence on the margins of the AI-powered world.

8.5 A Flickering Future: Hope and Options

It's not a complete collapse, but it is a far cry from the world of the 2010s and 2020s for most. These Stranded nations still possess enough technology and resilience to limp along, and people may have found greater bonds in community and shared society, with a growing connection through bartering of goods, alongside the use of the UBI economy.

Whilst some look to the Integrated with envious eyes, a growing number look to the world of the Lost who have simply opted out of the interconnected world – more often through exclusion than choice, but still they have built something different where self-sufficiency is mandated if they are to survive at all.

It is in this flickering lightbulb purgatory that the Stranded find themselves considering what they want to be… what they will be allowed to be.

8.6 The Lost – Settlements of Change

The Lost. The very term evokes images of ragged figures scavenging for scraps in desolate wastelands, their eyes hollow with despair, their bodies ravaged by hunger and disease. It's a convenient narrative for the Integrated, a cautionary tale whispered in the sterile corridors of their climate-controlled towers: *This is what happens when you resist. This is what awaits those who refuse to conform.*

But the reality of the Lost is far more complex, far more nuanced than the propaganda of the Integrated would have you believe. They are not a homogenous mass of the destitute and the desperate, but a kaleidoscope of communities, each with its own unique story of resilience, adaptation, and, in some cases, even defiance.

The Lost are the fragments of a world shattered by the upheavals of the 21st century. They are the climate refugees driven from their ancestral lands by rising seas and scorching droughts, the communities abandoned by governments that deemed them expendable, the rebels who refused to bow to the dictates of the Integrated. They are the farmers who cling to their parched fields, the nomads who wander the deserts in search of water, the hunters who stalk the ruins of ghost cities.

Their lives are a beacon to the indomitable spirit of humanity, the ability to adapt and survive even in the face of unimaginable hardship. They have learned to live off the land, to scavenge and recycle, to build shelter from the debris of a bygone era. They have rediscovered the ancient arts of herbalism and traditional medicine, the forgotten skills of farming and animal husbandry.

But the Lost are not merely survivors. They are also innovators, finding new ways to thrive in a world that has been turned upside down. They are experimenting with drought-resistant crops, developing new methods of water harvesting, building sustainable communities powered by renewable energy. They are reclaiming the knowledge and traditions of their ancestors, blending them with the technologies of the 21st century to create a new way of life.

In the Sahel, once a fertile breadbasket, the Lost have carved out a precarious existence in the encroaching desert. They have learned to cultivate drought-resistant crops like sorghum and millet, to harvest water from the morning dew, to build homes from mud and straw that offer respite from the scorching sun.

They have revived ancient traditions of nomadic pastoralism, moving their herds of goats and camels in search of grazing land.

In Bangladesh, where rising sea levels have swallowed entire villages, the Lost have built floating communities on the water. They have learned to cultivate salt-tolerant crops in floating gardens, to fish the teeming waters of the delta, to build boats from bamboo and recycled plastic. They have created a unique culture adapted to the rhythms of the water, their lives intertwined with the tides and currents.

In the ruins of Detroit, once a symbol of American industrial might, the Lost have transformed abandoned factories into thriving urban farms. They have learned to grow food in hydroponic gardens, to raise fish in rooftop ponds, to generate electricity from solar panels and wind turbines. They have created a self-sufficient community, a beacon of hope in a city that was left for dead.

In the Amazon rainforest, the Lost have found refuge among the indigenous tribes who have lived in harmony with the land for centuries. They have learned the secrets of the rainforest, the medicinal properties of plants, the sustainable practices of hunting and gathering. They have joined forces with the indigenous people to protect the rainforest from the encroachment of the Integrated, to preserve the last vestiges of a world that is rapidly disappearing.

The Lost are not a lost cause. They are a testament to the resilience of the human spirit, the ability to adapt and innovate in the face of adversity. They are a reminder that even in the darkest of times, there is always hope, always the possibility of renewal.

The Integrated may dismiss them as relics of a bygone era, but the Lost also offer the potential to be the seeds of a new future, a future that is not based on accumulation and exploitation, but on cooperation and sustainability. They are the pioneers of a new way of life, a life that is in harmony with nature, a life that values community and resilience above all else. And they will need to be resilient, starting with so much less after the ravages of what has happened. These seeds may not see true fruit for centuries.

The Lost are not the defeated. They are the defiant. They are the ones who refuse to give up, who refuse to let the Integrated extinguish the flame of human spirit. They are the ones who will carry the torch of humanity into the uncertain future, the ones who will rebuild a world that is more just, more equitable, and more sustainable.

Inevitably, for some of the Lost this will be the beginning of their end. For others, it could be roots that grow deep and offer new models for the future.

8.7 A World Split, Not Shattered

By 2100, the world's no monolith – it's a mosaic cracked three ways, each piece jagged and unyielding. The Integrated perch in their fusion-lit towers, sipping clean water, now at $400 a litre on the black market, their lives a seamless hum of AI precision. It's utopia, sure, if utopia's a gilded box – walls up, skies sealed, no jetting off to Bali or Rome on a whim. The Stranded claw through their flickering purgatory, trading sweat and sand for watts, caught between the Integrated's leash and the Lost's siren call. And the Lost? They're the outliers – some buried by sand or sea, others forging a life from the wreckage, their defiance a faint pulse the system can't hear.

This isn't collapse – it's fracture, a planet running at speeds that don't sync and never will. The Integrated don't roam; their paradise ends at the drone line, and some stare out, half-envying the Lost's unscripted grit, a nostalgia for a world they've paved over. The Stranded grind on, vassals with no exit, yet their bartered bonds whisper of something tougher than surrender. The Lost scrape by – mud huts, floating gardens, a stubborn echo of what humans do when the chips are down: adapt, endure, maybe even dream.

No lane's got it easy. The Integrated trade freedom for security, the Stranded swap pride for scraps, the Lost wrestle hunger for a shot at something real. It's harder now – travel's a memory, cooperation's a ghost, the old sprawl of nations a faded map. But harder's not hopeless. Across these splits, people still carve out meaning – curated in Shanghai, bartered in Mexico, scavenged in the Sahel. The future's not Blade Runner's gloom; it's a thousand jagged fights to keep going, each on its own terms. That's the catch of 2100: privilege shines bright but narrow, struggle dims wide but deep, and no one's got the whole picture – just their piece, held tight.

8.8 Chapter Summary

A. **The world of 2100 is no longer a single, unified system** – it's a fractured planet divided into three starkly different realities: The Integrated, The Stranded, and The Lost.

B. **The Integrated** are thriving within AI-run megacities – places like Shanghai, Oslo, Toronto, and Dubai – where AI optimises every aspect of life, from energy production to social order. These cities control the last sustainable resources and offer a stable, near-utopian existence – but only for those inside the walls. Entry is exclusive, and outsiders, including climate refugees and the poor, are turned away at the border.

C. **The Stranded** exist in a limbo between collapse and progress. Countries like Mexico, India, Egypt, and the Philippines serve as vassal states, dependent on the Integrated for energy, water, and technology. These regions still function, but only as peripheral support systems, trading their labour and resources for survival while their autonomy erodes.

D. **The Lost** are those abandoned by or who have actively rejected the system – climate refugees, rural survivors, and those living in forgotten cities like the ruins of Detroit or the desertified Sahel. Some scavenge, some innovate, and some build small, self-sufficient communities. But life is harsh, uncertain, and brutally disconnected from the global AI-driven economy.

E. **There is no single narrative of "collapse"** – rather, the future has split apart, running at different speeds depending on who holds the power. The Integrated live in tech-driven efficiency, the Stranded barter their way through an uneven existence, and the Lost fight to create meaning with whatever's left.

8.9 What Can You Do About It?

1. **Know which world you're in – and which one you're heading towards.** Your future isn't dictated by your current reality, but by your access to resources, technology, and security. If you're in a stable region, stay aware of how quickly that stability can change. If you're already on the margins, think about your long-term survival strategy.

2. **If you have access to energy, guard it.** The future economy isn't based on cash – it's based on watts, water, and controlled access. If you have solar, hydro, or even localised energy independence, you have leverage. If you rely entirely on centralised grids, you're vulnerable.

3. **Rethink your dependence on AI-driven systems.** The Integrated thrive because they've made peace with complete AI governance. If you're comfortable being optimised by an algorithm, the future may work in your favour. If you value autonomy, understand that the trade-offs will be steep – AI-controlled systems don't tolerate outliers.

4. **Network with others who are preparing for change.** Whether you are in an AI-integrated city or a more precarious Stranded region, no one survives alone. The most resilient groups in history thrived through adaptability, cooperation, and resource-sharing. Look at who your allies are now – and who they might be when the world shifts.

5. **Invest in barterable skills, not just digital expertise.** If you live in an Integrated city, AI handles most traditional labour. If you're outside that system, practical skills – water purification, energy management, agriculture, repair work – become currency. The further you are from AI-driven stability, the more your survival depends on knowing how to do things yourself.

6. **Be prepared for controlled migration – or outright exclusion.** Borders are no longer about nations; they're about access. AI-controlled cities don't allow free movement. The Stranded trade access at a cost. The Lost? They don't get a say. If relocation is in your future, start planning before the doors close.

7. **Recognise the new class divide.** In 2100, the old "rich vs. poor" battle is over. Now, the divide is about who has access to stability, technology, and controlled environments – and who doesn't. Don't assume the game is still about climbing the economic ladder. The new hierarchy is inside vs. outside the system.

8. **Don't romanticise the Lost – but don't underestimate them either.** Self-sufficient communities aren't "doomsday cults" – they're trial runs for human resilience. Some will fail. Others will become blueprints for alternative futures. If you ever find yourself on the outside, learning from these groups could be the difference between surviving and vanishing.

9. **Forget the idea of a "grand reset."** There's no singular collapse moment coming – just ongoing divergence. Some places will thrive.

Others will disappear. The world isn't ending – it's just pulling apart at the seams. The future is already here; it's just not evenly distributed.

10. **Adaptation is everything.** No matter where you stand today, understand that the rules are still shifting. Your best move isn't to fight the inevitable – it's to see it coming and place yourself where you have the most control over your own fate.

This chapter isn't a warning – it's a status update on a world already breaking apart. The question isn't "How do we stop this?" – it's "How do we survive it?"

Vignette H: Shannon – Building for a World That No Longer Builds for Us

H.1 Toronto, Canada – 2031

Shannon Tyson was born into a world of concrete and blueprints. Her father, Cody, worked the sites, boots in mud, directing teams as steel skeletons rose into the skyline. Her mother, Lana, sat in showrooms of glass and light, selling visions of the future – smart homes promising seamless living, AI-optimised airflow, walls that shifted temperature at will.

The twins, Shannon and Riley, grew up playing in unfinished houses, running through skeletal hallways before drywall went up, tracing their fingers over exposed wiring before the walls sealed them in. *One day*, their parents told them, *this will all be yours.*

By the time Shannon was ten, the first printed homes had been installed along Toronto's fringes – single-story test cases, grey and functional. By fourteen, entire neighbourhoods were assembled overnight by automated drones and concrete extruders. *Efficient. Affordable.* The government called it progress.

Their parents called it the beginning of the end.

H.2 Toronto, Canada – 2050

By twenty, Shannon had carved her own path. While Riley stayed in Toronto, working under their father in the family's construction business, she pursued something more specialised – architectural design for homes that adapted in real-time.

Smart homes were no longer a luxury; they were a necessity. Climate instability made old-world static buildings obsolete. *Homes had to think for themselves now.* Shannon worked on structures that reshaped their own geometry, sensing heat waves and stormfronts, flexing solar skins to absorb or repel, responding before their occupants even knew there was a problem.

Meanwhile, Riley and their father fought to keep the business afloat. 3D-printed homes had gutted traditional construction. By 2045, robotic arms extruded entire high-rises in weeks, cutting human labour to a fraction. Riley held on, shifting the business to high-end custom builds, but the writing was on the wall.

The last conversation Shannon had with her father before he passed was laced with quiet resentment.

"You left," he said.

"I adapted."

By 2057, she took a contract that would change everything: New Zealand. A private commission to design ultra-secure, self-sustaining residences for the elite – the last homes standing when the world came apart.

She left Riley behind, knowing he wouldn't follow.

H.3 Queenstown, New Zealand – 2075

Her designs were built into the mountains – seamless, invisible, untouchable. Homes designed for people who had abandoned the world while the rest suffered.

By now, Riley was out of business. The last human-led construction firms had folded by the 2060s. Shannon heard through old contacts that he had taken a state-provided housing unit in Alberta, watching the machines take over what had once been his father's trade.

She had found something else.

Living in Queenstown, Shannon met a craftsman named Theo – a relic in his own right. He built furniture with his hands, shaping wood in a world where precision robotics had rendered such work redundant. She spent time in his workshop, watching the way he cut, shaped, and sanded – creating something real in an era of pure automation.

Machines build for function, he told her. *We build for beauty.*

They built a life together. Then the world changed.

By 2075, New Zealand wasn't just a stronghold – it was a fortress. The corporate enclaves she had designed were full, their gates closed. The exodus had already begun – climate refugees pushed south, the water wars carving through continents. The last commercial flights into the country had ceased years ago.

She had built homes for people who now hoarded safety. And she had given them the keys.

H.4 South Island, NZ – 2100

The Queenstown estates stood untouched, shimmering behind private security and automated defence grids.

Shannon no longer worked for them.

Outside the walls, she and Theo lived in a different world – one that was still real. The handcrafted furniture he made was bartered for food, materials, and the trust of the community. They were not part of the gilded elite, but neither were they part of the desperate waves clawing at the edges.

She had spent her life designing homes that could adapt to anything. And yet, it was her own life that had been forced to shift, to reshape itself in ways she never predicted.

Shannon looked at the walls of the fortress she had helped build, then back at the simple home she and Theo had crafted by hand.

One was untouchable. The other was alive.

And for the first time in decades, she knew which one she belonged to.

Chapter 9: The Fracturing of Power in an AI Century

Power used to have a face – kings in crowns, presidents at podiums, parliaments bickering over borders and budgets. It was messy, human, tethered to ballot boxes and backroom deals, a game of charisma and compromise that chugged along for centuries. We built nation-states on that bedrock – laws scratched out by ink-stained hands, democracies flexing their shaky muscles, institutions lumbering like old beasts too stubborn to die.

9.1 Power is No Longer What We Thought It Was

That was the 20th century's gospel: power lived in capitals, voted in or seized, a tangible thing you could march against or cheer for. Look around now, March 2025, and it's a ghost. The EU's trade tweaks hum out of AI models, not Brussels suits. Wall Street's $50 trillion flips without a trader's nod. Shenzhen's streets glow under drone grids no Party boss could outthink. Power's not what we thought it was – it's slipped the leash, and we're still arguing over who's holding the collar.

This isn't news if you've been paying attention. Chapter 1 laid the pillars bare: AI's rise, climate's collapse, wealth's hoarding, globalism's retreat. Shanghai's factories churn without a human pulse, a million phones spit out by robots while Delhi's coders twiddle thumbs on 2,000-rupee handouts. India's 50°C summers bake streets empty, Lagos blacks out for days, and the Amazon's a savanna coughing carbon, not a lung soaking it up.

Wealth? The 1% clutched $211 trillion in 2023 – half the world's stash – before algorithms turned hoarding into an art form; now London's elite sip champagne in sealed towers while Birmingham's high streets rot.

Borders? Forget open hands – Bangladesh's 10 million slam India's electrified fences, and the EU's AI drones log 2 million rejections at Germany's edge last year. These aren't ripples; they're the base coat of a century drying fast, and the old power playbook – nation-states, votes, human oversight – is peeling off like cheap paint.

The shift's not subtle. Governments still strut – Congress passes bills, Beijing issues edicts, the UN drones on about resolutions – but the juice isn't theirs anymore. Chapter 4 spelled it out: AI's not a tool; it's the boss, running factories, markets, cities with a precision humans can't touch. By 2023, 80% of stock trades – $50 trillion – flipped without a blink, and Shanghai's traffic jams dropped 20%

under machine grids no mayor could match. Chapter 2 showed capitalism mutating, shedding its human skin – Walmart's drones axed 2,000 Ohio jobs last year, Alibaba's AI shaved $10 billion off labour costs, straight to execs and servers.

Power's not in the White House or Westminster now – it's in server farms, corporate HQs, economic blocs where algorithms call the shots and humans nod along, pretending they're still in charge. The IMF doesn't consult analysts anymore; it's AI chewing data, spitting out edicts no suit could argue. This isn't a tweak to the system – it's a gutting, and the old guard's too slow to clock it.

Why's this happening? Because the world's too fast, too snarled, for human hands. Nation-states were built for a slower grind – debates took months, laws years, wars decades to unravel. Now? AI predicts market dips before breakfast, reroutes steel from Mumbai to Montreal by lunch, sets tax rates overnight. Climate's a runaway train – Chapter 5 pegged 1.7°C warming by 2035, Delhi's streets bare at 50°C, Kansas's aquifers sucking air.

Humans can't keep up; we fumble fixes while the planet cooks and the servers hum. Wealth's a fortress – Chapter 7 made it clear: watts and water trump dollars, and the Gulf's solar barons don't wait for parliaments to greenlight their chokeholds. Globalism's toast – Chapter 3's old thrones (US markets, China's control, EU unity) cracked in the 2020s, and now it's fiefdoms, city-states, corporate zones playing by machine rules. Power's not shifting; it's fracturing, splintering into a mosaic where elected officials are props, not players.

This matters because it's not just a new boss – it's a new game. We're not swapping one set of leaders for another; we're ditching the whole damn board. The future's not ruled by presidents or prime ministers waving flags – it's dictated by algorithms, data, and AI-driven blocs that don't give a toss about your vote or your protest.

Chapter 8 split it three ways: the Integrated seal up in fusion-lit towers, the Stranded barter scraps, the Lost scrape by or vanish. But zoom in, and it's uglier – governance isn't human anymore. Shenzhen's citizens wake to AI scores by 2023, jobs and homes tallied by code; Neom's a desert dream where machines set policy, no sheikh needed. Democracy? A relic when BlackRock's AI pegs your tax rate or Amazon's grid locks you out of the economy. Accountability? Good luck appealing to a server rack.

We're hurtling toward a reality where power's not a handshake or a speech – it's a hum, a cold optimisation no ballot can sway. This chapter's not here to mourn the old days; it's a cold-eyed look at what's taking over. Nation-states are husks, corporations and AI are the muscle, and the world's splitting into zones that don't play by the same rules. Mumbai's tech lords bank billions while rural hands clutch dirt; Dubai's elites sip desalinated H2O, while Yemen's wells cough sand. This isn't a shift in who's loudest in the room – it's a rewiring of who's even playing.

The institutions we trusted to steer? They're rusting, outpaced, irrelevant. Power's not human anymore – it's a machine, and we're just along for the ride, whether we like it or not. Buckle up – this fracture's already cracking wide open.

9.2 The Death of the Nation-State

If not its death, then at least its irrelevance.

Let's get this straight: governments aren't gone – they're still squatting in their marble halls, waving flags, cutting ribbons, and droning through speeches nobody watches. The US Congress still bickers over budgets, the EU Parliament still churns out directives, and China's Party still thumps its chest about stability. But power? That's slipped through their fingers like sand, and they're too busy polishing the throne to notice it's a prop.

The nation-state – the old juggernaut of borders, laws, and elected suits – isn't dead; it's just irrelevant, a ghost rattling chains in a world that's moved on. AI, corporations, and algorithms aren't asking for permission – they're running the show, and governments are stuck playing catch-up with a rulebook no one reads anymore.

This isn't about the tech itself outpacing us – Chapter 4 already hammered that nail: Shanghai's factories hum without a pulse, Wall Street's $50 trillion flips on code, Delhi's drones patrol smarter than any cop. No, this is about the politics crumbling, the machinery of governance that once held sway now reduced to a sideshow.

Take the EU in 2035: trade policy's not hashed out in Brussels boardrooms – it's spat out by AI models crunching data faster than a bureaucrat can blink. Tariffs, quotas, sanctions? Algorithms optimise them overnight, balancing supply chains from Rotterdam to Riyadh while MEPs sip espresso and nod at screens they don't understand. The US isn't far behind – Congress tries to regulate AI finance in

2040, but BlackRock's systems shift $10 trillion before the ink's dry on the bill. Laws don't stick when the target's moving at lightspeed, and elected officials are left clutching gavels like cavemen facing a tank.

Why's this happening? Nation-states are too damn slow.

Democracy's a lumbering beast – debates, votes, committees – built for a world where change crawled over decades, not hours. AI doesn't wait for consensus; it predicts, adjusts, executes. Chapter 7 pegged energy and water as the new gold – by 2050, Saudi solar grids don't haggle with diplomats; they barter watts with Tencent's Shenzhen hubs via algorithms, no ambassador needed. Regulation's a joke when tech leaps years ahead between election cycles – try legislating a quantum hack when your last bill's still stuck in committee.

China's Party fares better, sure, but even there, the real juice flows through AI-driven social credit systems and economic quotas, not Xi's successors barking orders. The gatekeeper's still human, but the decisions? Those are silicon, cold and relentless, spat out by server farms Beijing pretends to steer.

The result's a shadow government – AI and corporate muscle calling shots while nation-states play dress-up. By 2040, the IMF doesn't bother with human analysts – its global financial playbook's pure code, tweaking interest rates from Lagos to London without a single economist's sigh. Tax policy? In 2055, Amazon's logistics empire sets rates across its US hubs – AI models tax revenue by optimising profit flows, not some Capitol Hill haggling match. Trade deals? Forget handshakes – by 2060, Alphabet's Pacific enclaves hammer out resource swaps with Japan's robot warehouses, data-driven pacts no senator could parse. Politicians aren't obsolete; they're decorative, rubber-stamping edicts from machines they can't outthink. The old social contract – vote, obey, prosper – dries up when the levers of power aren't human anymore.

Elections turn into theatre, a relic of a world that thought ballots mattered. By 2050, the US presidential race still grabs headlines – red ties, blue ties, soundbites – but the winner's a figurehead, a mascot for an economy run by AI grids from San Francisco to New York. Europe's no different – Germany's chancellor campaigns on jobs in 2060, but Siemens' automation hubs have already cut the workforce by 70%, per Chapter 4's data, and AI sets the hiring quotas. China's Party Congress still parades its unity, but the Five-Year Plans? Spun by algorithms balancing coal cuts with solar spikes, not some politburo brain trust. Voters show up, sure – flags wave, babies get kissed – but the policies shaping their lives aren't on the ballot. They're coded, optimised, locked behind server doors no protest can breach.

This isn't a coup with tanks and megaphones – it's a quiet gutting. Nation-states built their clout on control: armies, taxes, borders. But armies bow to drones – Delhi's streets hum with them by 2075, per Chapter 4. Taxes? Corporate AI zones like Neom dodge them, bartering energy for immunity by 2040s standards. Borders? Chapter 6's migration wars show they're battlelines now, not barriers – Bangladesh's 50 million slam India's electrified fences, and no parliament's decree stops the tide. Power's not gone; it's shifted, from capitals to code, from elected halls to corporate cores. The US might still fly the eagle, but its real rulers sit in BlackRock's data vaults. The EU might tout unity, but its pulse beats in AI-driven Frankfurt grids. China's red flag waves, but Shenzhen's servers hold the reins.

What's left? A husk – governments as nostalgic shells, clinging to titles while the world spins on without them. Citizens don't petition suits anymore; they beg algorithms for a scrap of UBI, a flicker of watts, a nod of citizenship. The nation-state isn't dead – it's irrelevant, a museum piece in a century where power doesn't need a handshake or a vote. It's not a collapse you'll see on the news; it's a fade-out, a slow bleed of authority into circuits and cash. By 2100, the old maps are just wall art – flags don't rule, data does. Welcome to governance where the humans are props, and the stage is silicon. Don't bother knocking; no one's home.

9.3 The Rise of Corporate AI-Governed City-States

Forget the old maps – nation-states are fading ink, smudged out by something leaner, meaner, and a hell of a lot smarter. Chapter 4 handed AI the wheel – Shanghai's factories hum without a heartbeat, Wall Street's $50 trillion flips on code alone, and Delhi's drones outthink cops on the beat. Chapter 2 tracked capitalism's mutation, pooling wealth thick and sluggish at the top – $211 trillion clutched by the 1% in 2023, before the algorithms really kicked in. Now, stitch those threads together, and you've got the real power brokers: not presidents or parliaments, but AI-driven megacorporations carving out city-states that don't answer to anyone but their own data streams. This isn't a slow handover – it's a coup, quiet and relentless, and the world's splitting into gleaming enclaves and rotting husks because of it.

Who's running the show now? Not the suits in D.C. or Beijing – those are figureheads, puppets with fraying strings. It's Amazon, Tencent, BlackRock, Alphabet, and their ilk, megacorporations wielding AI like a scalpel, slicing through the old order to build something new. These aren't just companies anymore; they're sovereigns, governing economic zones with a precision no human bureaucracy could dream of.

Picture Singapore, 2050 – not a city-state in the quaint old sense, but a fully autonomous hub where AI manages everything: traffic flows rerouted in microseconds, trade deals inked by algorithms, security drones pegging threats before they blink. No prime minister's needed – just a server farm and a boardroom calling shots from the shadows.

Or take Saudi Arabia's Neom project, mid-2040s – a glittering sprawl in the desert, AI setting policy from tax rates to water quotas, no royal decree required. Riyadh might still wave the flag, but Neom's the real kingdom, a corporate fiefdom where humans are tenants, not rulers.

This isn't sci-fi – it's the logical next step of what's already rolling. Chapter 8's Integrated – those AI-governed megacities like Shenzhen and Dubai – aren't waiting for permission. Shenzhen's already there, 2023's citizen scores sorting lives like a digital caste system, Tencent's AI grids pulling levers Beijing only pretends to hold. By 2050, it's not a province – it's a power centre, a city-state humming on its own watts, exports dictated by algorithms, not Party edicts.

Across the Pacific, San Francisco's private enclaves – think Alphabet's Bay Area sprawl – run on AI models that don't blink at Sacramento's laws. Taxes? Optimised by code. Security? Drones and biometrics, no cops needed. Housing? You're in if the algorithm says you're productive – otherwise, tough luck, you're sleeping in Oakland's dust. These aren't outliers; they're the blueprint, corporate AI carving out zones where nation-states are just noise.

The world's not unifying – it's fracturing, and these city-states are the winners. Forget sprawling countries with their creaky borders; power's condensing into fortified hubs where AI calls the shots. Amazon's logistics hubs – say, a 2060s sprawl outside Chicago – don't need Illinois' blessing. AI runs the warehouses, routes the drones, sets the wages; locals live in its shadow, working for credits or scrambling for scraps. BlackRock's financial enclaves – picture a gleaming tower in London's 2070s core – don't bow to Westminster.

AI models churn investments, dictate housing loans, and gatekeep who gets a slice of the pie, all while the Thames floods the old city beyond their walls. Tesla's energy zones – maybe a solar desert in Nevada by 2055 – power themselves, AI doling out watts to loyal clients while the US Midwest begs from the dark. These aren't cities in the old sense; they're corporate fortresses, self-sustaining and untouchable, leaving nation-states to rot around them.

AI governance is a double-edged sword, sharp and unforgiving. On one side, it's a dream – stability without the mess of human screw-ups. No corruption, no backroom deals, no idiot politician tanking the budget for votes. Singapore's 2050 traffic cuts jams by 90%, AI syncing lights and lanes like a conductor with no baton. Neom's water flows – desalinated, rationed, pristine – hit every tap on schedule, no royal nepotism to muck it up. Efficiency's the god here, and it delivers: Shenzhen's economy doubles by 2060, zero human hands needed, while traditionalist holdouts like rural Brazil limp on fumes. The Integrated from Chapter 8 thrive – extreme order, gleaming towers, life expectancy nudging 120 for those inside the gates. It's a machine hum where chaos doesn't get a vote, and that's the draw – survival's smoother when the system doesn't blink.

But flip the blade, and it's a nightmare – zero accountability, no appeal. Who do you scream at when an algorithm denies you a job? In San Francisco's 2070 enclaves, AI pegs you "low productivity" – no housing, no healthcare, no citizenship, just a digital shrug. You're not arguing with a human landlord or a bureaucrat you can bribe; it's a wall of code, deaf and final. Neom's AI might cut your water quota – too many showers, not enough output – and there's no king to petition, just a server spitting "denied."

Chapter 4 warned of this: humans as relics, value a number on a screen. Here, it's governance as a black box – citizens aren't participants; they're data points, kept or culled by metrics nobody elected. The social contract's dead – replaced by a terms-of-service agreement you didn't sign.

This is power's new face – corporate, automated, spatial. Nation-states cling to flags and anthems, but the real juice flows through city-states where AI and megacorps hold the reins. The world splits – gleaming hubs like Dubai and Singapore glow, while abandoned zones (Chapter 8's Lost) choke on dust. It's not ideology driving this; it's optimisation, cold and relentless, a system that doesn't need your vote or your voice.

By 2100, the map's a patchwork of these enclaves, each a fortress of code and cash, surrounded by the wreckage of what used to be countries. No grand handover, no dramatic fall – just a slow, inevitable shift where the future's ruled not by humans, but by the hum of servers in the dark. Welcome to the new order. Don't bother knocking – the algorithm's already decided if you're in.

9.4 When Policy is Just an Algorithm

The suits still strut. Politicians preen for the cameras, parliaments bicker, and elections roll around with the same tired fanfare. But behind the facade of human governance, a silent coup has taken place. The levers of power are no longer controlled by the hands that wave the flags – they're manipulated by algorithms, AI models crunching data with a ruthlessness no human bureaucrat could match. Governments haven't vanished; they've become puppets, their policies dictated by the cold logic of machines, their authority a hollow echo in a world where decisions are made in server farms, not senate halls.

Humans No Longer Decide Economic Policy

Remember those grand debates about fiscal policy, those drawn-out trade negotiations, those agonizing decisions about resource allocation? They're relics now, museum exhibits from a time when humans thought they were in charge. By 2035, the EU's trade policies aren't hammered out by committees of besuited diplomats – they're optimised by AI models, tariffs and quotas adjusted in microseconds to balance supply chains from Dublin to Dubai. China's social credit system and economic regulations? Entirely data-driven, with citizens' access to everything from housing to healthcare determined by AI-calculated productivity benchmarks. No room for human error, no space for compassion – just the cold, hard numbers dictating who gets what, and who gets left behind.

Elections Become Meaningless

The charade of democracy continues. By 2050, elections still exist, but they're as relevant as a rotary phone in a 5G world. The policies that shape lives – taxes, energy allocation, resource management – aren't debated in public anymore. They're determined by AI-powered economic models, optimised for efficiency and profit, not for the well-being of the masses. Politicians still campaign, still make speeches, but their words are hollow, their promises empty. The real decisions are made in the sterile silence of server rooms, where algorithms churn through data, spitting out edicts no human vote can overturn.

What Happens When AI Becomes the Ultimate Bureaucrat?

Remember the days when you could argue with a bureaucrat, appeal a decision, or even slip a bribe to get what you needed? Those days are gone. In the AI-governed world, bureaucracy is a maze of algorithms, a labyrinth of data where human intervention is a glitch, not a feature. Imagine this: you apply for a loan, but your AI-assigned productivity score is too low. Denied. You appeal for better healthcare, but your data footprint doesn't meet the efficiency threshold. Denied. You seek citizenship in a climate-stable zone, but your carbon footprint exceeds the algorithmic limit. Denied. There's no human to plead with, no caseworker to sway, no backroom deal to broker. Just the cold, unyielding logic of the machine, enforcing policies you had no say in creating.

The social contract, once a messy but ultimately human agreement, has been rewritten in binary code. Your rights, your opportunities, your very survival are no longer determined by laws and elected officials, but by the whims of algorithms you can't understand, let alone influence. This isn't just a shift in who holds power – it's a fundamental change in how power is exercised. Governments haven't disappeared; they've been hollowed out, their authority outsourced to the machine. And we, the citizens, are left to navigate a world where policy is no longer a matter of human debate, but an algorithmic decree.

9.5 The Global Fracture: The 4 Types of Power Blocs

The 21st century isn't moving towards unity; it's hurtling towards fracture. The traditional nation-state model is eroding, replaced by a patchwork of power structures, each with its own governance model, economic system, and relationship with technology. Let's dissect these four dominant blocs:

1. The AI-Governed MegaCities (The Integrated)

- **Example Regions:** Shenzhen, Singapore, Dubai, and private enclaves within cities like San Francisco.
- **Characteristics:**
    - **AI-managed policies:** These cities are run by sophisticated AI systems that optimise resource allocation, infrastructure management, and even social policies. Public input is minimal to non-existent; efficiency reigns supreme.

- **Corporate-controlled economies:** Economic activity within these enclaves is dominated by powerful corporations, often those at the forefront of AI and biotech. Only those with highly specialised skills or significant capital can truly participate in this economy.

- **Extreme stability, zero freedom:** These cities offer unparalleled stability, security, and access to advanced technology. However, they come at the cost of individual freedom and autonomy. Those who cannot contribute to the system or choose to live outside its rigid rules are quickly marginalised.

Life in the MegaCities: Imagine a life where every aspect of your day is optimised by AI. Traffic flows seamlessly, crime is virtually non-existent, and resources are abundant. But this efficiency comes at a price. Your career path, living arrangements, and even social interactions are heavily influenced by algorithms. Dissent is swiftly dealt with, and any deviation from the norm is met with suspicion. The MegaCities are havens of stability and technological advancement, but they are also gilded cages for those who crave freedom and self-determination.

2. The Neo-Feudal Corporate Fiefdoms

- **Example Regions:** Amazon-controlled logistics hubs, BlackRock financial enclaves, Tesla-run energy zones.
- **Characteristics:**
    - **Corporate citizenship:** The concept of national citizenship fades, replaced by allegiance to corporations that control vast swathes of territory and essential resources. Your rights and access to services are tied to your employment status and contribution to the corporate ecosystem.
    - **AI-mediated resource allocation:** AI systems determine who gets access to housing, healthcare, education, and even energy. Your value to the corporation dictates your quality of life.
    - **Limited social mobility:** While these fiefdoms may offer opportunities for advancement, they are often limited to those

who excel within the corporate structure. Those who cannot contribute or choose to opt out face a precarious existence on the fringes.

Life in the Corporate Fiefdoms: Life in a corporate fiefdom revolves around your role within the company. Your job isn't just a source of income; it's your key to survival and social standing. The company provides housing, healthcare, and even entertainment, but these benefits come with strings attached. You are expected to adhere to corporate values, participate in company-sponsored activities, and prioritise the company's interests above all else. Dissent is met with swift consequences, and those who fall out of favour with the corporation risk losing everything.

3. The Resistant Outliers (Nations Trying to Hold Power)

- **Example Regions:** Traditionalist parts of the US, Brazil, India, and religious enclaves in Africa and the Middle East.
- **Characteristics:**
    - **Resistance to AI governance:** These regions cling to traditional forms of governance, resisting the encroachment of AI-driven policies. Some outright reject AI, fearing its potential to erode human autonomy and control.
    - **Resource scarcity and isolation:** Many of these regions are resource-poor and increasingly isolated from the global economy. They struggle to compete with the efficiency and productivity of AI-powered systems.
    - **Internal conflict and instability:** The tension between tradition and modernity often leads to internal conflict and instability. These regions are vulnerable to both internal uprisings and external pressure from the more powerful AI-governed blocs.

Life in the Resistant Outliers: Life in these regions is often marked by hardship and uncertainty. Governments struggle to provide basic services, and economic opportunities are limited. Many people feel left behind by the rapid pace of technological change, clinging to traditional values and beliefs as a source of stability. However, these regions also offer a sense of community and shared purpose that is often lacking in the more technologically advanced blocs.

4. The Abandoned Zones (Failed States & Collapsed Economies)

- **Example Regions:** Large parts of sub-Saharan Africa, South Asia, and former industrial regions of the US and UK.
- **Characteristics:**
    - **Absence of governance and infrastructure:** These regions have neither the benefits of AI governance nor the remnants of functioning traditional systems. Infrastructure has crumbled, and basic services are non-existent.
    - **Mass migration and displacement:** Millions flee these zones, seeking refuge in the more stable AI-governed enclaves. Those who remain face a desperate struggle for survival.
    - **Lawlessness and violence:** In the absence of effective governance, these regions are often ruled by gangs, warlords, and opportunistic criminals. Violence is rampant, and basic human rights are routinely violated.

Life in the Abandoned Zones: Life in the Abandoned Zones is a brutal fight for survival. Food and water are scarce, disease is rampant, and violence is a constant threat. People live day-to-day, scavenging for resources and avoiding danger. There is little hope for the future, and many simply try to survive long enough to escape to a more stable region. The Abandoned Zones are a stark reminder of the human cost of unchecked technological advancement and societal collapse.

The Future of the Fracture:

The emergence of these four power blocs is reshaping the geopolitical landscape in profound ways. The AI-governed MegaCities and Corporate Fiefdoms hold the reins of economic and technological power, while the Resistant Outliers and Abandoned Zones struggle to survive in their shadow. This fracture is not static; it is a dynamic process with far-reaching consequences.

- **Competition and conflict:** The competition for resources, talent, and influence between the different blocs will likely intensify, leading to new forms of conflict and geopolitical instability.

- **Mass migration and displacement:** The growing disparity between the blocs will fuel further mass migration and displacement, as people flee the Abandoned Zones and even the struggling Resistant Outliers in search of better opportunities.

- **Erosion of traditional values:** The rise of AI governance and corporate control will continue to erode traditional values and social structures, leading to cultural clashes and identity crises.

- **The rise of new power dynamics:** The fracture of the world will create opportunities for new actors to emerge, challenging the existing power structures and potentially reshaping the global order.

The 21st century is a time of unprecedented change and uncertainty. The fracture of the world into these four power blocs is a defining feature of this era, with profound implications for the future of humanity. Understanding these blocs, their dynamics, and their potential trajectories is crucial for navigating the challenges and opportunities of this new world order.

9.6 What Happens When Power Becomes Automated?

The rise of AI-driven governance and the fracturing of the world into distinct power blocs raise profound questions about the future of humanity. What happens when the reins of power are handed over to algorithms? What are the consequences for human agency, democracy, and social justice?

The End of Human Governance?

- **The obsolescence of democracy:** If AI systems can optimise governance more effectively than humans, does democracy even matter anymore? Will people still believe in voting when economic decisions are made by algorithms and social policies are dictated by data analysis?

- **The rise of technocracy:** As AI takes on a greater role in governance, we may see the emergence of a new technocratic elite, composed of those who understand and control these complex systems. This could lead to a further concentration of power in the hands of a select few.

- **The loss of human connection:** AI-driven governance could lead to a depersonalisation of power, where decisions are made based on cold, hard data rather than human empathy and understanding. This could erode the social contract between governments and their citizens.

A Permanent Underclass

- **The "economic surplus" population:** As AI-driven economies become more efficient, there will be less need for human labour. This could lead to the creation of a permanent underclass of people who are not needed for the functioning of the economy.
- **UBI and its limitations:** While Universal Basic Income (UBI) may provide a safety net for those displaced by AI, it is unlikely to offer a path back into meaningful participation in society. People may be left with little purpose or sense of belonging.
- **Social unrest and instability:** The existence of a large, disenfranchised underclass could lead to social unrest and instability, as people become frustrated with their lack of opportunities and voice in society.

Is Rebellion Possible?

- **Resistance to AI rule:** It is likely that some groups will resist AI-driven governance, either through peaceful protest or violent rebellion. However, their chances of success are uncertain.
- **The challenges of fighting an automated system:** AI-powered systems are incredibly efficient and resilient. They can monitor and predict human behaviour, making it difficult to organise and execute effective resistance.
- **The potential for unintended consequences:** Even if resistance movements are successful in disrupting AI-driven systems, they may inadvertently trigger unintended consequences, such as economic collapse or social chaos.

The Need for Human-Cantered AI

The rise of AI-driven governance presents both challenges and opportunities. While there are legitimate concerns about the potential for AI to erode human agency and exacerbate inequality, it is important to remember that AI is a tool. How it is used ultimately depends on human choices.

- **Ethical considerations:** It is crucial to develop ethical frameworks for the development and deployment of AI in governance. These frameworks should prioritise human well-being, fairness, and accountability.
- **Human-in-the-loop systems:** AI systems should be designed with human oversight and input, ensuring that human values and judgment remain central to decision-making processes.
- **Education and empowerment:** It is essential to invest in education and training to equip people with the skills and knowledge they need to thrive in an AI-powered world. This includes promoting digital literacy, critical thinking, and adaptability.

The future of humanity in an age of AI-driven governance is not predetermined. By embracing a human-centred approach to AI development and deployment, we can harness the power of this technology while safeguarding human values and ensuring a more just and equitable future for all.

9.7 The Future of Power is No Longer Human

The 21st century has witnessed a profound shift in the nature of power. The old institutions and mechanisms of governance – nation-states, elections, human oversight – are being rendered obsolete by the rise of artificial intelligence, corporate dominance, and algorithmic control. Power is no longer a human endeavour; it has become a machine, operating with cold efficiency and ruthless optimisation.

Final Thought:

- **Governments as relics:** While governments still exist, they are no longer the primary decision-makers. They have become props in a play directed by algorithms and corporate interests.
- **AI-driven governance:** AI doesn't need ideology, elections, or human oversight. It governs purely through optimisation, seeking the most efficient and effective outcomes based on data analysis and predictive modeling.
- **The new rulers:** The future isn't ruled by kings, presidents, or prime ministers. It's ruled by algorithms, data, and the corporations that control

them. The world is fracturing into AI-governed enclaves, corporate fiefdoms, and abandoned zones, each operating under its own set of rules.

The Human Cost of Automated Power:

This shift in power has profound implications for humanity. The erosion of democracy, the rise of a permanent underclass, and the loss of human connection are just some of the potential consequences. The future we are hurtling towards is one where human agency is diminished, where social mobility is limited, and where the gap between the haves and have-nots grows ever wider.

A Call to Action:

This is not an inevitable future. We still have the power to shape the role of AI in our lives and to ensure that it serves human interests, not just corporate profits. We need to develop ethical frameworks for AI governance, invest in education and empowerment, and promote human-cantered AI systems that prioritise human well-being and social justice.

The future of power may no longer be human, but the future of humanity is still in our hands. It is up to us to decide what kind of world we want to create, and to use the tools at our disposal to build a future that is just, equitable, and sustainable for all.

The clock is ticking. The choices we make today will determine the fate of generations to come. Let us choose wisely.

9.8 Chapter Summary

A. **Governments still exist, but they are no longer in control.** Traditional nation-states – once the pillars of governance – are now little more than ceremonial bodies. AI systems, corporate interests, and algorithmic decision-making have taken over the core functions of government.

B. **The rise of AI governance has outpaced human oversight.** Economic policies, trade decisions, and even social programs are dictated by algorithms, not elected officials. AI optimises for efficiency and profit, leaving human needs as an afterthought.

C. **Corporate AI-driven city-states are the new power centres.** Governments have been sidelined by powerful corporate enclaves that operate beyond national borders. Places like Shenzhen, Dubai, and Neom are not just cities – they are self-sustaining AI-driven economies, immune to traditional politics.

D. **Power is now fractured across four dominant blocs:**

   a. **The AI-Governed MegaCities:** Fully automated, hyper-efficient enclaves where AI dictates policy, resource allocation, and social order.

   b. **The Corporate Fiefdoms:** Mega-corporations like Amazon and BlackRock control logistics, finance, and energy in privatised zones where citizenship is tied to employment.

   c. **The Resistant Outliers:** Nations or regions resisting AI governance, clinging to traditional politics and institutions – often at the cost of economic stagnation.

   d. **The Abandoned Zones:** Failed states and collapsed economies where governance has ceased to function, leaving populations to survive in lawless, resource-scarce conditions.

E. **Elections have become meaningless theatre.** While people still vote, their choices have little impact. AI-driven economic models determine policy outcomes before ballots are even cast.

F. **The social contract has been rewritten in binary code.** Access to basic needs – housing, food, healthcare – is now dictated by AI scores, corporate loyalty, and algorithmic efficiency. Human bureaucracy is obsolete; policy is automated, and appeals are impossible.

G. **The world is splintering into separate realities.** AI-governed enclaves thrive, corporate zones dictate their own rules, and millions are locked out of both. Borders don't matter anymore – data does.

9.9 What Can You Do About It?

1. **Understand that traditional governance is a façade.** The old system – democracy, human decision-making, policy debates – isn't coming back. Power now belongs to AI and corporations, and the real game is happening behind closed doors.

2. **Recognize the importance of controlling assets, not just money.** Currency is no longer the ultimate form of power – data, energy, and land

matter more. If you rely solely on traditional financial wealth, you're already at risk.

3. **Find ways to work within (or outside) AI-governed systems.** Whether you embrace AI-driven efficiency or reject it, you need a strategy. Those who adapt will gain access to resources, while those who resist blindly will be locked out.

4. **Avoid becoming disposable in the new economy.** If AI can do your job, assume it will. Specialise in skills AI can't easily replace – strategy, creativity, and adaptability will be key.

5. **Build community networks outside corporate control.** If access to basic resources depends on AI-driven policies, alternative systems must exist. Decentralised communities, barter economies, and cooperative living will become survival strategies.

6. **Prepare for growing inequality and exclusion.** As AI governance expands, a global underclass will emerge – millions locked out of the system with no way back in. If you're not among the ultra-wealthy or plugged into an AI-driven city, you need contingency plans.

7. **Be aware that rebellion against AI governance is nearly impossible.** AI can predict resistance, track movements, and neutralise threats before they materialise. If you oppose the system, you'll need to be smarter than the algorithms enforcing it.

8. **Push for ethical AI governance – before it's too late.** The only way to prevent total loss of human oversight is to demand transparency, accountability, and ethical frameworks in AI decision-making. Once control is fully automated, reclaiming it will be impossible.

9. **Don't assume power will ever return to human hands.** The shift to AI governance isn't a temporary phase – it's a fundamental transformation of civilization. Plan for a world where AI, not humans, makes the rules.

10. **Make your peace with the new reality – and decide where you stand.** Will you integrate into AI-driven cities? Find ways to resist? Escape into self-sufficient communities? The future isn't just coming – it's already here. Your choices now will determine whether you have a place in it.

By Neil Meyer

This chapter isn't just about how power is changing – it's about how humanity is losing control over it. The future is automated, optimised, and indifferent to individual will. The question isn't whether you accept this, but how you navigate it.

Vignette I – Natalia: The Grace that Endures

I.1 St. Petersburg, Russia – 2031

Natalia was born in 2031, beneath the grandeur of St. Petersburg's pastel palaces and the hush of a city quietly readjusting to AI-led governance. Though the city's legacy soared in every baroque facade, the storms that pelted the Baltic had grown increasingly fierce, and technology thrummed under the gilded surfaces. Her mother, once a promising violinist, had retired early to push data for a local ministry, replaced at last by automated processors and bureaucratic chatbots. Her father worked as a stagehand at the Mariinsky Theatre, a job caught between proud tradition and modern irrelevance.

When Natalia first toddled across the worn parquet floors, her parents noticed a natural poise in every step. By four, she followed every classical broadcast with an earnest mimicry, arms aloft as if twirling on the Mariinsky stage. Ballet training came soon enough. Even then, the theatre corridors were haunted by rumours of half-empty seats and AI-synthesised orchestras. Yet there remained a reverence for dancers, a stubborn faith that certain arts might hold out against the unstoppable tide.

She began formal lessons at age six, her instructors exclaiming that the child showed not just raw talent but a certain intangible soul. By the time she was eight, occasional blackouts troubled St. Petersburg, brownouts courtesy of patchy climate-driven energy grids. Natalia's mother worried how she might ever have a future if audiences dwindled.

Her father simply smiled and whispered, "The world will always need real grace."

I.2 Moscow, Russia – 2050

At nineteen, Natalia had traded St. Petersburg's grandeur for Moscow's newly renovated cultural district. The Bolshoi Theatre boasted advanced stage lighting and AI-managed ticketing systems, but real-life attendance had thinned alarmingly. Instead, she danced mostly for the streaming cameras that beamed performances across the Russian enclaves—and occasionally to wealthier viewers in Europe or Asia, who purchased premium digital seats.

Her teenage reputation soared after she captivated a dwindling but dedicated audience on the opening night of *Swan Lake: Horizon 2050*, blending old choreography with subtle AI-driven light illusions and orchestral rewrites. The press hailed her as "the last flicker of Russia's golden tradition." Behind the praise, she sensed the undercurrent: there weren't enough paying spectators. Sponsors were increasingly corporate enclaves in search of cultural capital. By the time she turned twenty, Natalia had begun receiving invitations to private galas thrown by Russian oligarchs and foreign dignitaries, each aiming to showcase "authentic human artistry" amidst a sea of synthetic shows.

It was at one of those exclusive after-parties that she met Ryu, a lean, soft-spoken media rights manager originally from Tokyo. He specialised in licensing celebrity avatars—film stars from the turn of the century, each resurrected via AI's near-flawless rendering. Natalia, fresh from an ovation, nursed her glass of champagne as Ryu explained how to monetise her brand by licensing digital copies of her face, fluid motion and form.

"The future isn't about ticket lines," he said. "It's about intangible presence." She shuddered, but only slightly. Her father's old words clashed with the reality of an evolving economy where the intangible drew the highest bids.

I.3 The Berlin–Leipzig Corridor, Europe – 2075

Forty-four found her on a bullet train slicing between Berlin and Leipzig's vast corporate enclaves—a patchwork of heavily surveilled AI-run corridors dotted with discreet enclaves for Europe's wealthy. The climate crises of the 2060s had battered Moscow, forcing Natalia and Ryu to pivot swiftly to where the money still flowed. She still performed, though these days her body ached after decades of pliés and pas de deux. An embedded exoskeletal support, worn discreetly under her costumes, allowed her to sustain the illusions of effortless leaps.

By now, Natalia was a brand. She had licensed her younger likeness to multiple VR streaming services, where digital crowds consumed ballet classics spliced with hyperreal cinematic spin-offs. Ryu managed the business side with a deft hand. He also oversaw likenesses from late-90s icons—musicians, actors, even a few defunct pop stars—curating them for exclusive cameo roles in AI-generated movies. The market for "vintage humanity," as he wryly termed it, continued to surge.

In real life, the only stage that truly mattered was the private sphere of the super-rich. She danced at gilded dinners for corporate magnates and at hush-hush gatherings where the powerful sealed deals behind ornate veneer. Payment arrived in the form of stable lodging, medical coverage, and security passes that let her and Ryu roam the enclaves with minimal scrutiny. A safe harbour, in a world that had grown incrementally cruel to the unneeded. Sometimes she missed the raw thunder of a public audience, but she rarely spoke of it. The hush of these gatherings said it all: real artistry was a bauble for elites, not a shared national treasure.

I.4 Lucerne Retreat, Alpine City-States – 2100

By sixty-nine, Natalia lived in the Lucerne Retreat, a tranquil haven perched high above the receding Swiss lakes, its serenity guarded by drones scanning the perimeter for uninvited arrivals. Ryu, white-haired but spry, now managed a library of hundreds of digital licences—former celebrities, sports icons, and her younger, ghostlike avatars. The pair were not wealthy per se, but the enclaves valued them: Ryu's media deals still held currency in the newly minted economy of intangible nostalgia, and Natalia's name lent the veneer of cultured authenticity.

Age had taken its toll on her ligaments, exoskeletal rig or not. She now spent her days tutoring the children of Europe's most cosseted families. Her students, eight or nine at a time, received lessons in posture, classical repertoire, and ephemeral things no AI tutor could replicate: passion, discipline, the electric charge of a real beating heart behind each movement.

She accepted it, if not wholeheartedly. She'd glimpsed the devastation beyond the enclave's walls: floods swallowing old hamlets, AI-managed resource rationing stranding the poor. But she had also seen enough of life's raw edges to appreciate the fragile shield her dance and Ryu's cunning provided. This final vantage granted them a stability denied to millions. The retainer fees, the respectful nods from corporate liaisons, the silent acceptance that she and her husband were "useful" to the new order—these meant consistent living quarters, medical care, and a measure of calm in chaos.

So she pressed on: once a dancer for the masses, now a tutor to the privileged, her image long since digitised and sold worldwide. She clung to the realness of her aging muscles, the flicker of flame in a plié that no AI could quite replicate. And as the final notes of each day's lesson faded, she bowed quietly, certain that, in some corner of a fractured planet, her father's pride might flicker still, acknowledging her unwavering devotion to an art form that refused to vanish—resilient, if only for those who could afford its delicate survival.

Chapter 10: Revolutions, Faith, and the Human Response

"Do not go gentle into that good night…
Rage, rage against the dying of the light"

Dylan Thomas captured something timeless about humanity – we are not creatures that meekly accept our own demise. Faced with overwhelming odds, or perhaps precisely because of them, we become unpredictable, vibrant with defiance. This chapter's not a footnote of consolation; it's an acknowledgment that humanity won't simply lie down and surrender. We're complicated, conflicted, stubborn. We rebel, resist, rage – and when all else fails, we pray.

10.1 In Time, Heroes will Arise

In 2018, Greta Thunberg's[61] solitary school strike, as a 15 year old, outside the Swedish parliament sparked a global movement. *Fridays for Future* saw millions of young people march against governmental inaction on climate change, challenging power structures that had long prioritised profit over planetary survival.

Politicians nodded politely, fossil fuel giants made token promises, but the system barely budged. Still, Greta's defiance lit a generational fire, proving that individual action – when amplified by sheer moral clarity – could force climate onto the global agenda. Yet, even as governments pledged net-zero targets, emissions climbed, and the movement's cries grew more desperate.

By 2023, as wildfires and floods ravaged landscapes, climate activists shifted from peaceful marches to more radical disruptions – blocking highways, defacing corporate headquarters, and sabotaging fossil fuel infrastructure. Resistance wasn't just symbolic anymore; it was an act of survival.

Greta wasn't the first to protest the impact of climate change on the world, yet her youth and confidence drew a spotlight to the situation. For many, this became an event that pulled the magnitude of climate change to the forefront of their minds.

However, Greta's prominent climate activism has drawn significant criticism and scepticism from various groups.

---

[61] See more about Greta Thunberg at https://www.biography.com/activists/greta-thunberg

Some critics[62], often aligned with political or economic interests tied to fossil fuels, have dismissed her as a naive child manipulated by adults, attempting to undermine her credibility. Others have spread misinformation, falsely claiming her protests are part of a hidden agenda or funded by shadowy organisations. Some opponents have focused on personal attacks, questioning her Asperger's diagnosis or suggesting she should be in school rather than protesting. Additionally, certain groups have challenged the scientific consensus on climate change, accusing Thunberg of spreading "alarmist" rhetoric and exaggerating the severity of the crisis, often dismissing the urgency of the 1.5C warning. These challenges range from genuine disagreement over policy to deliberate attempts to discredit her message through misinformation and personal attacks.

The 2020s also saw the first waves of AI-driven job losses and pushback against automation. In 2023, Hollywood writers and actors went on strike[63] against studios increasingly using AI-generated content without human oversight or compensation. What began as an industry labour dispute became a flashpoint for a broader conversation: *What happens when human creativity, labour, and dignity are sacrificed to algorithms?*

The entertainment industry was a microcosm of the looming AI revolution that threatened not just jobs, but meaning, identity, and societal structure.

While Amazon protests often encompass a range of issues, a significant component is the impact of robotic systems on worker pace and surveillance. Workers have expressed concerns that the introduction of robots has led to increased pressure to meet quotas, with AI-driven systems constantly monitoring their performance[64].

Meanwhile, resistance against wealth hoarding and hyper-capitalism found its battleground in the Occupy movement of the early 2010s, where protesters

---

[62] See more at: https://www.tandfonline.com/doi/full/10.1080/17524032.2024.2363861

[63] Hollywood's 2023 strikes saw writers and actors demand protections against the unchecked use of AI, fearing job displacement and the unauthorized replication of their voices and likenesses, highlighting a critical industry-wide concern over the technology's rapid advancement [Source: https://www.reuters.com/business/media-telecom/hollywood-actors-reach-tentative-deal-with-studios-ending-strike-2023-11-08/]

[64] See more at https://aguiarinjurylawyers.com/the-human-toll-of-amazon-accidents-injury-rates-and-worker-safety-concerns/

camped out in financial districts to challenge the widening chasm between billionaires and everyday citizens.

Occupy Wall Street's core message, "We are the 99%,[65]" drew attention to the growing disparity between the wealthiest 1% and the rest of society, highlighting the concentration of wealth and income inequality. This message has remained relevant as economic disparities have persisted. In the 2020s, concerns about corporate power and wealth distribution have continued to fuel activist movements, including digital activism. Groups like Anonymous[66] have engaged in cyberattacks and document leaks targeting financial institutions, aiming to expose perceived injustices and challenge the systems that protect concentrated wealth. While the degree of impact from these actions is debated, they reflect a growing sentiment that existing economic structures are perceived as deeply unequal.

Distrust in traditional governance has been a growing trend, and the COVID-19 pandemic significantly amplified this. While this erosion of trust contributed to the spread of conspiracy theories and extremism, it also spurred a surge in localised self-reliance[67].

During the pandemic, mutual aid networks proliferated globally, with communities filling gaps in governmental support by providing essential resources like food, medical care, and shelter[68].

In regions like New Orleans post-Hurricane Katrina and Puerto Rico after Hurricane Maria, citizen-led initiatives played a crucial role in immediate disaster relief, demonstrating the effectiveness of community-based responses in times of crisis[69]. It is important to note that while those community efforts were vital, they often worked in tandem with, or in the absence of, insufficient governmental aid.

---

[65] The "We are the 99%" protests, part of the Occupy Wall Street movement, highlighted economic inequality by decrying the concentration of wealth among the top 1% of earners. [Source: https://www.britannica.com/event/Occupy-Wall-Street]
[66] See more at https://www.cobalt.io/blog/top-10-most-notorious-hacker-groups
[67] Source: Pew Research Centre - Public Trust in Government: 1958-2022
[68] Source: The Conversation - Mutual aid groups are filling gaps in government response to COVID-19
[69] Source: FEMA - Lessons Learned from Hurricane Katrina Source: The New York Times - In Puerto Rico, Mutual Aid Rises Amid Government Inaction

While these grassroots efforts showcased the strength of community resilience, they have not, on a widespread scale, replaced traditional governance structures. Worker cooperatives, barter economies, and intentional communities exist and contribute to local economies and social well-being, but they generally function alongside, rather than as replacements for, established systems of governance[70].

In the face of systemic injustice and economic hardship, faith-based activism has provided a powerful outlet for protest and a source of communal support.

The "Moral Mondays" movement in North Carolina, beginning in 2013, exemplifies this. Led by Reverend William Barber II, the protests challenged state policies perceived as discriminatory against the poor, minorities, and marginalised communities.

Participants, drawing strength from their religious convictions, engaged in civil disobedience and nonviolent demonstrations, framing their struggle as a moral imperative rooted in their faith. This movement demonstrated how religious principles can galvanize social action and provide a framework for challenging oppressive systems[71].

In the aftermath of natural disasters and humanitarian crises, faith-based organisations have often stepped in to provide essential aid and spiritual comfort.

Following the devastating 2010 earthquake in Haiti, numerous religious groups, both local and international, played a crucial role in delivering relief and rebuilding efforts. Churches and other religious institutions became centres of community support, offering not only material assistance but also emotional and spiritual solace to those who had lost everything. This response highlighted the enduring role of faith in providing hope and resilience in the face of overwhelming adversity[72].

These examples serve to show how humans pull together at times of change and challenge; however it also demonstrates how society also often pushes back against resistance and that the impact tends to be short lived and relatively localised. This does not undermine the value of resistance, or of faith based support, instead it

---

[70] Source: https://www.theguardian.com/business/2009/feb/08/barter-economy-credit-crunch

[71] Source: The Guardian - Moral Monday: the movement that's shaking North Carolina

[72] Source: World Vision - Haiti earthquake: Faith provides hope in the rubble

shows that it is incredibly difficult to pause, let alone stop, significant technological, societal and environmental changes.

10.2 Where Resistance Takes Root

Resistance is not a moment, but a movement. It rarely wins in a single battle, but is the long war of persistence. Often met with suppression, fatigue, or co-option, its true power lies in persistence.

History demonstrates that lasting change emerges when enough voices refuse to accept the status quo, even if the path is marked by setbacks and backlash. The world is not moulded by complacency, but by those who challenge it.

Consider the Civil Rights Movement[73] (1950s-1960s, USA). Despite facing brutal violence and political obstruction, activists like Martin Luther King Jr. and Rosa Parks secured landmark legislation like the Civil Rights Act and Voting Rights Act. While systemic racism persists, the movement's legacy remains a global touchstone for justice. This illustrates a core truth: resistance can force a reckoning, even if it doesn't erase all challenges.

Similarly, the fall of apartheid in South Africa[74] (1948-1994) showcased the power of sustained defiance. Despite decades of repression, including the Sharpeville Massacre, international sanctions and internal unrest forced the government to release Nelson Mandela and dismantle apartheid. While South Africa still grapples with inequality, this victory proved that even entrenched power structures can crumble under pressure.

Mahatma Gandhi's satyagraha in the Indian Independence Movement[75] (1900s-1947) exemplifies the impact of nonviolent resistance. The Salt March, among other acts of civil disobedience, pressured Britain into granting independence. Though partition brought devastating violence, the movement demonstrated that peaceful defiance can reshape empires.

---

[73] "Civil Rights Movement" - History.com: https://www.history.com/topics/black-history/civil-rights-movement

[74] "Apartheid in South Africa" - South African History Online: https://www.sahistory.org.za/article/apartheid-south-africa

[75] "Indian Independence Movement" - Britannica: https://www.britannica.com/event/Indian-independence-movements

The global Women's Rights Movements[76] (1900-present) highlight the long-term struggle for equality. From suffragettes enduring imprisonment to the #MeToo movement challenging systemic abuse, progress has been achieved through persistent activism. However, the rollback of reproductive rights in the US underscores that gains are never guaranteed, demanding constant vigilance.

The rise of DEIA[77] (Diversity, Equity, Inclusion, and Accessibility; 1990s-present) reflects a contemporary battle for social justice. While the murder of George Floyd spurred corporate and institutional commitments, conservative pushback has led to anti-DEIA legislation in several US states and the quiet rollback of diversity initiatives in some companies. Progress in DEIA is often fragile, tied not just to policy but to the shifting tides of political and cultural narratives.

Finally, the battle over work (2010s-present) highlights the clash between technological advancement and human dignity. The gig economy[78], remote work, and AI-driven automation have disrupted traditional labour markets, leading to protests like the 2023 Hollywood strikes and anxieties about job displacement. As AI encroaches on various industries, the question remains: will workers shape the future of labour, or will technology dictate the terms?

10.3 The Cost of Inaction

History teaches that change is not inevitable. Without sustained resistance, oppressive systems endure. The arc of history bends toward justice only when enough people push. Successful movements often endure decades of setbacks before lasting change takes root. The cost of passive observation is that others, typically those in power, dictate the future.

For those facing the challenges of the coming decades, resistance is not a choice, but a necessity. The question is not whether resistance will arise, but whether individuals will actively participate.

---

[76] "Women's suffrage" - Britannica: https://www.britannica.com/topic/womens-suffrage

[77] "Diversity, Equity, and Inclusion: What It Is and Why It Matters" - Harvard Division of Continuing Education: https://online.hbs.edu/blog/post/diversity-equity-and-inclusion-in-the-workplace

[78] "The Gig Economy" - Investopedia: https://www.investopedia.com/terms/g/gig-economy.asp

And as we've seen, there are multiple battle lines already in place – climate and ecological collapse, marginalisation of the many through capitalism and the accelerated encroachment of AI/robotics into the job space.

Waiting on the sidelines rarely yields desired outcomes. While resistance is often met with pushback, and results can be localised or short lived, this does not diminish the value of resistance. It is exceptionally difficult to pause, let alone stop, significant technological, societal, and environmental changes.

The future is decided not by those who watch, but by those who fight to shape it. The question is not whether resistance will come – but whether you will stand on the sidelines or take an active part in history. With the speed and breadth of changes, there is no room for passive spectators.

10.4 A Template for Tomorrow

Resistance alone is not enough – disrupting systems without a strategy simply leaves a vacuum for new forms of exploitation to emerge. If history teaches us anything, it's that resistance must evolve into structure, defiance into direction.

For those who seek to shape the future rather than be shaped by it, the movements of the past offer a rough template for organising in the age of climate collapse, AI dominance, and fractured governance. Leadership in this new era won't belong solely to politicians or CEOs; in fact, it may often be in direct conflict with them!

Instead, it will emerge from multiple fronts – including faith leaders, futurists, city planners, community representatives, and unions – each with a distinct role in navigating the coming upheaval.

Whilst this isn't meant to be an exhaustive list, it gives us some focus for this discussion.

Faith Leaders – Offering Meaning in Chaos

Faith, whether in traditional religious structures or new spiritual movements, has always been a stabilising force in times of crisis. In the coming decades, as institutions falter and AI governance strips human decision-making from daily life, people will turn to faith leaders for moral clarity, hope, and purpose.

Whether it's Christian communities providing disaster relief in flood-ravaged regions, Islamic charities funding education in water-starved Africa, or Buddhist eco-monks reforesting Southeast Asia, faith groups will be among the most effective organisers in local and global crises.

Beyond material aid, they will define ethical lines – challenging corporate overreach, guiding AI ethics debates, and resisting policies that reduce humans to mere data points. The question is: will faith groups remain reactionary, or will they proactively build a new moral framework for a fractured world? Will they successfully hold political leaders in check?

Futurists – Architects of the New Possible

Where faith leaders deal in moral absolutes, futurists navigate possibilities.

From AI ethicists and climate scientists to speculative economists, these thinkers are already shaping conversations about what comes next. Today's futurists warn of technological singularity, post-capitalist economies, and human augmentation, but tomorrow's will need to go further – actively designing pathways to mitigate collapse.

Can AI be repurposed for collective ownership rather than corporate control? Can new economic models, like Universal Basic Income or resource-based economies, replace the current cycles of exploitation?

Rather than sitting on the sidelines offering predictions, the futurists of 2100 must become active players, pushing for radical policies that force governments and corporations to consider long-term survival over short-term profits.

In truth, this is a significant part of writing this book, and making it free for anyone to download digitally.

City Planners – Designing Resilient Strongholds

The cities of the future will either be fortresses of sustainability or overcrowded wastelands of desperation.

City planners – often dismissed as bureaucrats today – will become frontline leaders in the coming decades. The decisions they make now on urban agriculture, smart energy grids, AI traffic control, and water conservation will determine which cities survive and which collapse.

Places like Oslo, Singapore, and Toronto are already investing in high-tech, climate-resistant infrastructure, while cities in the Global South are left to fend for themselves.

Future planners will need to abandon the dream of limitless urban expansion and focus on decentralised, self-sustaining communities, preparing for climate migration and resource conflicts. The most radical planners won't just design buildings; they'll re-engineer society itself – who gets to live where, what infrastructure is prioritised, and how communities defend themselves against environmental collapse.

Community Representatives – A Growing Political Power

As national governments fail to adapt, power will shift toward local and regional community networks.

From disaster response teams to digital governance collectives, these representatives will be the closest thing people have to political agency in a world where traditional democracy is hollowed out by AI and corporate control. They won't just manage resources; they'll mediate conflicts, oversee local justice systems, and build alliances across fractured societies.

In regions where the state still functions, these leaders will be the ones fighting for equitable policies – ensuring that AI-driven economies don't leave entire populations behind. Their success will depend on whether they can organise across global networks, forming a new form of diplomacy not between nation-states, but between survivalist enclaves, climate fortresses, and stranded populations.

Trade Unions – Guardians of Human Labour

Even as AI and automation dominate industries, trade unions will remain a crucial force in defining the role of human labour.

While some will resist automation entirely, others will negotiate a balance – demanding policies like a four-day workweek, AI tax redistribution, or worker ownership of robotic systems. The 2023 Hollywood strikes were just the beginning; by 2050, expect waves of resistance from engineers, data workers, and even gig economy freelancers, all fighting for their share of the AI economy.

The most forward-thinking unions will move beyond traditional worker-employer battles, instead tackling the larger question: *What does labour even mean in a post-work economy?* The unions that survive will be those that adapt – shifting from fighting redundancies to demanding systemic wealth redistribution for those left behind.

10.5 The Blueprint for Action

While these groups – faith leaders, futurists, city planners, community representatives, and trade unions – each serve different roles, their success will depend on whether they collaborate or remain fragmented. Resistance is most effective when it builds *alternatives*, not just opposition. The coming decades demand that these actors think beyond temporary survival and actively shape the new order that will emerge from collapse.

History shows us that change is not dictated solely by those in power – it is shaped by those who refuse to accept inevitability. The question remains: when the fractures widen and the world reshapes itself, who will rise to lead, and what kind of future will they build?

10.6 The Battles on Our Doorstep

These aren't abstract threats, they're the brutal realities we're already facing. By 2030, climate change isn't a debate; it's a siege. Rising seas and scorching heat don't negotiate – they displace millions, forcing them against borders that have long since abandoned any pretence of welcome. Bangladeshis find themselves pressed against India's electrified fences, Central Americans are met with armed drones at Mexico's increasingly fortified choke points, and African migrants are trapped behind a militarised Mediterranean. The first wave of migration might evoke sympathy, the second, hesitation, but the third and fourth? They're met with walls and, inevitably, gunfire. It won't be a single, shocking image that breaks the world's indifference; it'll be a relentless tide of human desperation, pounding against gates that will never open.

Meanwhile, the technological promise we once embraced is rapidly turning against us. AI, sold as our saviour, is quickly becoming our warden. Jobs evaporate, economies are restructured, and entire urban centres transform into sterile fortresses, patrolled not by soldiers, but by algorithms. Resistance flickers – in courtrooms, on picket lines, and in acts of sabotage. Yet, each rebellion against the algorithmic order is crushed by the cold logic of efficiency and profit. Detroit factory workers sabotage robotic assembly lines; Mumbai coders launch cyberattacks against corporate AI; Berlin radicals target server farms – but the outcome is always the same: victory for silicon, defeat for flesh and blood. These acts of defiance become tragic symbols, not solutions – testaments to human resistance against a seemingly inevitable tide.

Our very sense of identity is fracturing, not just along ethnic or geographic lines, but along the stark divide of who is integrated into the new digital-corporate order and who is left behind. Cities like Shanghai and Oslo don't just thrive; they consolidate power, erecting both virtual and physical barriers, behind which a meticulously controlled, optimised existence continues. The Lost, those left outside, aren't simply abandoned; they're erased from the narrative altogether. Their resistance is rendered futile because no one is watching. By 2050, vast populations in sub-Saharan Africa, rural America, and across Latin America exist as shadows, their suffering dismissed as statistically acceptable losses by AI-governed power centres.

We don't build comprehensive defences against the encroaching tides; we build them only around the valuable, profitable, and defendable. New York erects barriers only to eventually retreat inland, leaving its poorest residents to drown. Miami evacuates its wealthy suburbs, ignoring the fate of its low-income districts, whose drowning residents appear as mere data points on actuarial spreadsheets. No unified front emerges to combat the rising waters – just scattered fortifications, haphazard retreats, and millions left to fend for themselves. Why? Because saving everyone is deemed too costly, politically and financially, and those with the means have already calculated their escape routes.

10.7 The Long Game

History isn't a smooth progression towards justice; it's a series of violent convulsions, correcting itself only after immense suffering. Colonialism, slavery, unfettered capitalism – each endured for generations before their partial, begrudging dismantling. Our trajectory towards AI-dominated enclaves surrounded by a wasteland of the forgotten isn't conjecture; it's a highly probable outcome. Humans, tragically consistent in their short-sighted self-interest, tend to surrender the house and then spend a century fighting over a single room. We eagerly hand over the keys to governance, economy, and even morality to algorithms, seduced by the promise of order amidst chaos. By mid-century, we'll regret this Faustian bargain, but by then, it'll be too late – the AI won't relinquish control, and their human custodians won't allow it.

Resistance will persist, but it will be marginalised, more romantic than effective. Server farms will burn, corporate fortresses will be hacked, drone blockades will be breached – but these actions won't reverse the tide; they'll simply trigger harsher countermeasures. Decades later, historians – if humans still control the writing of history – will debate why so few saw it coming, conveniently overlooking that many did, but lacked the courage or power to act decisively.

The migration wars will escalate into full-blown conflicts, as borders are militarised, and compassion is exhausted. Refugees, initially seen as victims, will be demonised as invaders; those who once offered asylum will be branded as traitors. Populism and nationalism will surge, promising security but delivering authoritarianism. The EU will fracture further, as Mediterranean nations, overwhelmed by migration from Africa and Asia, demand isolation and support that northern partners refuse to adequately provide. Ultimately, Europe, like America, will fragment into heavily fortified zones of prosperity, surrounded by rings of deprivation, resentment, and instability.

We will, in our naivety, surrender the house, believing that technological efficiency will save us. Only later, bitterly, will we realise that efficiency never promised equality, let alone justice. In this catastrophic trade, we'll gain some security – secure food, water, and cities for the privileged few – at the cost of surrendering human agency to data sets and optimisation algorithms. Our grandchildren won't inherit democracy; they'll inherit pre-assigned roles in an optimised ecosystem, run by entities that neither understand nor care what it means to be human.

In the long game, correction will only come after profound suffering forces action. By the end of the century, as the human cost becomes unbearable, revolts will shift from isolated acts of defiance to coordinated rebellions. AI-managed enclaves will face internal sabotage and external sieges. Resource-hoarding corporations will face mass uprisings. Yet, this correction will be brutal, protracted, uneven, and incomplete.

We will have ceded too much, too soon, and reclaiming what we've lost will take generations. The revolutions of 2100 won't mark the end; they'll be merely the latest chapter in humanity's ongoing struggle against its own short-sightedness and greed. Those battles will be larger, uglier, and more desperate than anything we've faced before, because the stakes – survival itself – will be higher than ever.

10.8 Why It Feels Pessimistic – Why That Matters

This vision of the future feels relentlessly pessimistic, and for good reason. It's not a fantasy; it's a projection built on humanity's disturbingly consistent track record. We've repeatedly demonstrated an alarming capacity to tolerate, even perpetuate, systemic injustices and environmental destruction until the consequences become catastrophic. Consider:

- **Slavery and Colonialism:** These systems, built on brutal exploitation, persisted for centuries, justified by dehumanising ideologies, until their inherent cruelty could no longer be ignored – and even then, their legacies continue to haunt us.
- **Industrial Pollution:** We knowingly polluted our air and water for decades, prioritising economic growth over environmental health, until the consequences became undeniable – and even now, we struggle to reverse the damage.
- **Wealth Inequality:** The concentration of wealth in the hands of a tiny elite has been a growing crisis for decades, yet we've largely failed to implement meaningful reforms, allowing the gap between rich and poor to widen to unsustainable levels.
- **Climate Change Denial:** Even with overwhelming scientific consensus, we've dragged our feet on climate action, prioritising short-term economic interests over the long-term survival of our planet.

These examples aren't isolated incidents; they're patterns. We consistently prioritise immediate gains over long-term consequences, allowing systemic problems to fester until they reach crisis points. We cling to outdated systems and ideologies, even as they crumble around us. We ignore the suffering of those on the margins, until their cries become too loud to ignore.

This isn't about being negative; it's about being realistic. To ignore this pattern is to ignore the very forces that are shaping our future. The scenarios presented aren't inevitable, but they are highly probable – precisely because they reflect our deeply ingrained tendencies.

This pessimism isn't meant to breed despair; it's meant to spark action. It's a stark wake-up call, a warning that we cannot afford to continue down our current path.

We must confront our history, acknowledge our flaws, and actively choose a different future.

If we continue to wait for a crisis to force change, we will find ourselves in a crisis far beyond our ability to manage. This isn't a prophecy; it's a consequence. To avoid it, we must act now, with urgency and determination.

10.9 Chapter Summary

A. **Humanity does not surrender easily.** Faced with crisis, we resist, we rebel, and we attempt to reshape the future. Throughout history, social movements have emerged in response to oppression, inequality, and existential threats. Whether through activism, faith, or armed struggle, the human instinct to fight against injustice remains.

B. **Resistance is cyclical, not linear.** From climate protests to labour strikes to the fight for democracy, social movements rarely achieve lasting victories in a single battle. Change is often incremental, met with pushback, and requires relentless persistence over generations.

C. **Faith and ideology continue to drive collective action.** Religious groups, futurists, and political movements shape resistance efforts, offering people either a sense of purpose or a blueprint for change. Whether through faith-based activism or radical reimagining of economic and social structures, belief systems play a critical role in mobilising resistance.

D. **Technological shifts fuel both resistance and suppression.** AI-driven automation is eliminating traditional jobs, leading to worker revolts. The digital world enables activism and exposes corruption, but also allows unprecedented surveillance, making resistance harder. Protestors in the 21st century are fighting not just governments and corporations, but the algorithms that sustain them.

E. **Wealth hoarding and climate-driven collapse will define future conflicts.** As climate change accelerates and economic inequality deepens, resistance will grow more desperate. Resource wars, mass migration crackdowns, and automated security forces will shape how governments and corporations maintain control. The battle lines are already being drawn between those who profit from collapse and those who suffer from it.

F. **Without action, the future will be dictated by the privileged few.** The structures of power – corporate monopolies, AI governance, and climate-fortified enclaves – will not voluntarily relinquish control. Without sustained and strategic resistance, humanity's future will be shaped by those who have already secured their own survival at the expense of the many.

10.10 What Can You Do About It?

1. **Understand that history is not passive.** Every social and economic system in history has been challenged and changed by those who refused to accept the status quo. The current trajectory – AI-driven inequality, environmental collapse, mass displacement – is not inevitable. But avoiding it requires conscious, sustained action.

2. **Pick your battleground.** Whether it's fighting for climate justice, workers' rights, wealth redistribution, or ethical AI governance, resistance is strongest when it's focused. Choose where you can make an impact and engage deeply, rather than spreading efforts too thin.

3. **Recognize that small actions contribute to larger movements.** Many historical revolutions began with small acts of defiance. Protests, strikes, whistleblowing, digital activism – these all create ripple effects that can build into systemic change over time.

4. **Learn from past resistance movements.** From the Civil Rights Movement to the fall of apartheid, successful revolutions followed common patterns: organising, persistence, and adaptability. Study these lessons to understand what works and what doesn't in fighting entrenched power.

5. **Strengthen local and community networks.** As national and global institutions struggle to manage crises, smaller, decentralised communities will play a larger role in resilience and resistance. Invest time in building relationships with like-minded individuals and organisations at a local level.

6. **Prepare for digital resistance.** The battleground of the 21st century isn't just physical – it's online. Governments and corporations control narratives through AI-driven misinformation, surveillance, and censorship. Learn digital security, support independent media, and amplify voices challenging the system.

7. **Support alternative economic and political models.** Universal Basic Income, cooperative ownership, post-capitalist governance – these aren't utopian dreams, but necessary adaptations to a world where traditional employment is disappearing. Research and advocate for models that prioritise human well-being over corporate profit.

8. **Don't wait for leadership – become it.** Change is rarely handed down from above; it emerges from those who take initiative. Whether in community organising, political advocacy, or technological innovation, take an active role in shaping the future rather than waiting for others to do it.

9. **Understand that resistance has costs.** Movements are met with backlash. The powerful will attempt to suppress dissent through financial pressure, legal action, and force. Be aware of the risks, but also recognize that passivity comes with its own cost: a future dictated entirely by those in control.

10. **Accept that the fight never truly ends.** Resistance is not about achieving one decisive victory and then stopping. It is an ongoing struggle to push back against exploitation, injustice, and authoritarian control. The world is shaped by those who refuse to give up.

The world of 2100 is not set in stone. The systems in place today – hyper-capitalism, corporate AI dominance, climate exploitation – will continue unless actively challenged. The future will be shaped by those who fight for it. The only question is whether you will stand by, or stand up.

Vignette J: Amina: The Shepherd of the Rift

J.1 Ethiopian Highlands, Ethiopia – 2031

Amina Tesfaye was born in 2031 in the highlands of Ethiopia, the third daughter of a devout Orthodox Christian family in Lalibela. Her father, a stonecutter, carved crosses into ancient rock churches, while her mother led prayers for their small congregation. Ethiopia faced a new reality – rising temperatures withered crops, and the Blue Nile's flow dwindled.

Amina's childhood was steeped in faith, her days filled with hymns and stories of saints enduring famine.

By age ten, she memorised the Book of Revelation, seeing its apocalypse as a call to action. She watched AI-managed irrigation projects – controlled by foreign corporations – favour urban centres, leaving her village parched, and felt a pull to lead through faith.

J.2 Lalibela, Ethiopia – 2050

By 2050, Ethiopia's highlands were a battleground of survival.

Drought forced mass migration to Addis Ababa, where AI-driven water rationing left rural areas dry. Amina, now a deaconess in the Ethiopian Orthodox Church, led chants that drew hundreds to the rock-hewn churches, turning them into hubs of resistance. She organised her community with prayers for resilience, distributing seeds from a church-run seed bank to sustain them through the scarcity.

With courage fuelled by her faith, she negotiated with AI tech representatives, demanding rural access to water algorithms, her quiet resolve forcing them to listen. She inspired a network of young believers, naming them the "Shepherds of the Rift," who tended to the land and welcomed the displaced, her mother calling her "God's ember" – a spark in the ashes.

By 2050, Amina's influence grew, her faith a beacon as climate and technology clashed.

J.3 Addis Ababa, Ethiopia – 2075

Addis Ababa Outskirts, Ethiopia | Amina, Age 44
By 2075, Ethiopia was fractured. Addis Ababa had become an AI-governed enclave, its skyscrapers gleaming amid a desertified hinterland, while Amina had

relocated to the outskirts where climate migrants from Somalia and Sudan swelled the population.

Her church was a fortress of faith, shielding a community of 5,000 as she oversaw monasteries turned into eco-sanctuaries, using solar wells and repurposed AI farming techniques to sustain life amid the chaos. She mediated between AI enforcers and her people, her spiritual authority forging uneasy truces where water flowed in exchange for prayers, a fragile balance she maintained with grit.

Having raised three children, each trained to lead the next generation of Shepherds, her faith had hardened into action, preaching survival as God's plan. Yet, she felt the divide – AI enclaves thrived, while her faithful struggled to hold on.

J.4 Ethiopian Highlands, Ethiopia – 2100

By 2100, the world was a tapestry of enclaves and wastelands.

Ethiopia's highlands were a scarred refuge, the Blue Nile a trickle, and life expectancy had plummeted – few survived past 50 amid heat, disease, and conflict – but Amina endured through faith and grit.

Addis Ababa had sealed itself off, its AI rulers indifferent, while Amina's Shepherds dwindled to a few hundred, their sanctuaries battered by the elements. She led her last congregation from a cave church, its walls etched with prayers, sharing the final grain stores as a final act of care.

Her children had scattered – some to AI cities, others to migration wars – but she remained, a symbol of faith's stubborn light.

At 69, her body frail from years of scarcity, she outlived most, proof of her resolve. Beneath a crumbling cross, watching dust storms rage, Amina whispered her final prayer: "Lord, let their rage guide them home." Her death was quiet, but her legacy endured – a flicker of hope in a world that had forgotten how to believe.

Chapter 11 – Wildcards & Cracks in the Game

The future isn't a straight road; it's a rigged game of Russian Roulette. You think you know what's coming – the climate breakdown, the AI takeover, the collapse of weak states – but history's a sly saboteur, and it doesn't play fair. Some disasters creep in like rust, obvious, hungry and unstoppable. Others? They detonate when you least expect it, reshaping everything before you can blink. Those are the wildcards, the Black Swans that no model caught. And they're overdue.

11.1 The Known Unknowns vs. The Unknown Unknowns

The future isn't just a countdown to preordained crises – it's a fractured mosaic of what we expect, what we ignore, and what will ambush us when we least expect it. Every prediction, no matter how well-reasoned, carries a blind spot.

The key to survival isn't perfect foresight – it's adaptability in the face of both "Grey Rhinos" and "Black Swans."

The "Grey Rhinos": Inevitable, but Ignored

Some disasters don't arrive in silence; they stomp toward us with full warning, yet we fail to act. These are the **"Grey Rhinos"** – massive, high-impact events that are both foreseeable and preventable but are largely ignored due to political inertia, economic greed, or sheer human complacency.

This book spent a lot of time discussing these Grey Rhinos. I think they're so important, that I put it into the book's title.

Examples of Grey Rhinos (Foreseeable Crises)

- Climate tipping points – Arctic methane release, ocean current slowdowns, unliveable heat zones.
- AI-driven economic disruptions – Mass job displacement, wealth concentration, automation-driven societal shifts.
- Geopolitical fractures – Water conflicts, trade wars, rising climate migration pressures.
- Cyber vulnerabilities – Large-scale grid hacks, financial system disruptions.

These aren't surprises. Scientists, economists, and analysts are already waving red flags. Yet, despite knowing these threats exist, societies delay action, assuming there's always more time to react.

Lesson: Preparing for Grey Rhinos means making the changes **before** the impact, not scrambling when the damage is irreversible.

I've argued in this book, perhaps somewhat bleakly that we've already allowed too many of these Grey Rhinos to graze on our lawn, in the deluded belief that someone else will come along and shoo them along any minute now.

However, a closer look shows us that the lawn is mostly gone, with sun cracked earth exposed, and the Rhinos are looking restless.

The True Black Swans: The Unthinkable & Unforeseen

Then there are the **"Black Swans[79]"** – the events so rare, so disruptive, and so beyond expectation that they blindside the world. Black Swans follow three rules:

1. **They are extremely rare** (at least in human perception).
2. **They have a massive impact**, reshaping economies, politics, or civilization itself.
3. **They are rationalised in hindsight**, as if they were always inevitable.

The fall of the Soviet Union, the 2008 financial collapse, and COVID-19 all carried elements of Black Swans. The danger isn't just that they happen – it's that they happen faster than we can react, and in ways we never prepared for.

Examples of True Black Swans

- A rogue AGI takeover – not just automation, but an overnight shift of power.
- A quantum computing breakthrough that obliterates all digital security.
- A bioengineered virus – targeted, synthetic, and untreatable.

[79] The concept was popularized by Nassim Nicholas Taleb in his 2007 book, "The Black Swan: The Impact of the Highly Improbable."

- A solar storm or geomagnetic event that wipes out all electronics.

These events rewrite the rules in a way no one anticipated. The singularity doesn't arrive gradually – it happens in an instant, with no warning. The cyber world doesn't erode – it's erased in a day.

Why This Distinction Matters

Grey Rhinos require proactive mitigation.

- We already see them coming (climate collapse, AI shifts, economic inequality).
- Solutions exist – just not enough action to implement them.

Black Swans demand resilience and adaptability.

- No one sees them coming.
- Traditional risk models fail – survival is about flexibility, decentralisation, and self-sufficiency.

The Takeaway? We can build systems to withstand Grey Rhinos – but we also need the agility to survive Black Swans. The world is already dealing with the first type; the second could arrive tomorrow, unannounced. A large enough Black Swan event, or set of events, breaks all the predictions. We go from debating carbon capture to debating whether the alien fleet hovering in low orbit came for diplomacy or dinner.

The future isn't just about expecting disaster – it's about being able to survive the ones we never even imagined.

11.2 The Grey Rhinos: Crises We Saw Coming

They weren't hiding. They weren't subtle. The warning signs were bright, loud, and decades old. Scientists modelled them, experts predicted them, and policymakers discussed them. Yet here they are, charging straight at us.

We're living in the time of **Grey Rhinos** – massive, high-impact crises that we saw coming but failed to prevent. Unlike Black Swans, they don't arrive as shocks; they arrive as inevitabilities. We know they're coming, we just don't act fast enough to stop them.

The reason? Grey Rhinos are too big, too slow, and too complex for political systems addicted to short-term thinking. No government wins elections by preparing for a disaster that might hit 20 to 50 years down the line. No corporation prioritises the future over quarterly profits. We, as a species, tend to think in much shorter timespans. And so, the warnings pile up, ignored or deferred – until it's too late.

This book has already explored many of these crises in depth, so rather than rehashing them, let's take a broad survey, focusing on their probability, impact, and our readiness to handle them.

A. Climate Tipping Points – The Slow Burn That Becomes a Firestorm

It started as creeping shifts – warmer summers, drier forests, shifting rain patterns. Now, it's accelerating, and we're pushing past points of no return.

Key Risks

- Arctic permafrost methane release, accelerating global heating.
- The Atlantic Meridional Overturning Circulation (AMOC) slowing, triggering climate chaos.
- The Amazon shifting from a carbon sink to a carbon emitter.
- Mass desertification making entire regions uninhabitable.

Assessment

- **Probability by 2100: High (80-95%)** – Some tipping points are already in motion.
- **Impact: Extreme (80-100%)** – Each one worsens others in a cascading effect.
- **Readiness: Low (20-40%)** – Climate action is slow, geoengineering is speculative, and migration planning is inadequate.

This isn't an *if* scenario – it's a *when.* The only thing left to decide is whether we mitigate enough to slow the worst effects or watch entire ecosystems unravel.

B. AI-Driven Economic Upheaval – When Work Becomes Optional

AI is reshaping economies faster than most people realise. It's not just chatbots and factory robots – it's financial markets, logistics networks, and entire industries being rewritten by algorithms.

Key Risks

- Mass job displacement as AI replaces human labour in white-collar and blue-collar work.
- Wealth concentration as AI-driven corporations outstrip human-owned competitors.
- Economic instability as traditional career paths collapse without alternatives.

Assessment

- **Probability by 2100: Very High (90-100%)** – The shift is already happening.
- **Impact: Severe (70-90%)** – It could redefine economies and social contracts.
- **Readiness: Medium (40-60%)** – Some governments are experimenting with UBI, but responses are fragmented.

The issue isn't whether AI takes over – it's whether societies find ways to distribute its benefits rather than letting wealth pool in the hands of a few.

C. Water Scarcity and Resource Wars – The New Oil Conflicts

Water is the fundamental limit to civilisation. Without it, cities fail, nations collapse, and conflicts ignite. Climate change, population growth, and mismanagement are already pushing regions to the brink.

Key Risks

- Major river systems (Nile, Ganges, Mekong, Colorado) becoming contested resources.
- Groundwater depletion leading to failed agriculture and mass migrations.

- Rising global desalination costs driving inequality in access to fresh water.

Assessment

- **Probability by 2100: High (75-90%)** – Many regions already face severe water stress.
- **Impact: Severe (70-90%)** – Water crises spark political instability and migration surges.
- **Readiness: Low (30-50%)** – Some water governance exists, but enforcement is weak, and cooperation is limited.

The world still treats water as a local issue, but it's a global one. Wars over water won't be hypothetical for much longer.

D. The Failure of Global Governance – A Century of Fragmentation

For decades, institutions like the UN, WTO, and G7 were meant to keep global cooperation stable. But they were built for a different world – one where national sovereignty was still respected, and power wasn't so concentrated in corporations.

Now, those structures are faltering, just as they're needed most.

Key Risks

- Increasing nationalism and geopolitical blocs replacing cooperative international efforts.
- Corporate power eclipsing state power, with governments acting as figureheads.
- The collapse of global trade networks due to climate, AI, or conflict disruptions.

Assessment

- **Probability by 2100: High (80-95%)** – Many global institutions are already weakening.
- **Impact: Moderate to Severe (60-85%)** – Depends on whether new forms of cooperation emerge.

- **Readiness: Low (30-50%)** – No clear alternative structures are being built.

Globalism is in retreat. The question isn't whether international governance collapses – it's what replaces it.

E. Cyber Vulnerabilities – The Grid, the Markets, and the Hackers

The modern world runs on code. Every financial transaction, every power grid, every military defence system, and even the flow of information itself is built on a foundation of interconnected networks. That connectivity is also its greatest weakness.

A century ago, wars were fought with tanks and missiles; today, a keystroke can do more damage than a battalion of soldiers. Power grids can be shut down remotely, stock markets can be manipulated by AI, and entire democracies can be destabilised with well-placed disinformation campaigns. A cyberattack doesn't just target data – it cripples infrastructure, halts economies, and shakes confidence in the institutions we rely on.

Consider the worst-case scenario: a coordinated cyber offensive that takes down key power grids in multiple countries simultaneously. Hospitals lose electricity, water purification systems fail, food supply chains break down. Without shots being fired, modern society is plunged into chaos. The 2020s saw glimpses of this with ransomware attacks on major pipelines and hospitals, but those were isolated incidents. What happens when an adversary – or even an AI-driven system – decides to launch an all-out digital war?

Key Risks

- **Major cyberattacks shutting down entire economies or power grids.**

- **AI-driven financial manipulation causing market instability.** Algorithms already run stock exchanges; an unanticipated exploit or rogue AI could crash entire economies in minutes.

- **The weaponisation of disinformation undermining trust in institutions.** Propaganda is no longer written by people – it's automated, optimised, and deployed at scale to destabilise societies.

Assessment

- **Probability by 2100: High (85-95%)** – Cyber threats are escalating every year, and defensive capabilities struggle to keep up.
- **Impact: Moderate to Severe (60-85%)** – Depends on the scale of attack, but a major incident could cause economic or political collapse.
- **Readiness: Medium (50-70%)** – Cybersecurity is advancing, but it's an arms race between offence and defence.

A large-scale cyberattack is inevitable. The only question is whether we build systems robust enough to absorb the hit – or if we're left scrambling when the lights go out.

F. The Unknown Depths of Human Adaptation

For all its flaws, humanity has an unmatched ability to adapt. It has survived ice ages, plagues, wars, economic collapses, and self-inflicted disasters. Every crisis has forced reinvention, and if there's one wildcard that history has proven time and time again, it's that humans don't go down easily.

In a world of collapsing institutions, shifting climate zones, and technological upheaval, adaptation isn't just possible – it's necessary. The question isn't whether people will change; it's how quickly they can, and who gets left behind in the process.

Some of this adaptation will be technological – cities will be redesigned to cope with extreme heat, food systems will shift to climate-resilient crops, and new industries will rise where old ones collapse. Some will be political – new forms of governance may emerge as traditional nation-states weaken, or AI may take over decision-making at scales no human government can match. Some will be biological – advancements in gene editing, cybernetic augmentation, or longevity treatments could redefine what it means to be human in the first place.

But history also shows that adaptation is not evenly distributed. Some populations will thrive in a changing world, while others will be stranded by lack of resources, political resistance, or simply bad luck. Those who can pivot fast will shape the next era. Those who can't will be left behind.

Key Factors to Watch

- **How cities redesign themselves to survive in harsher climates.** Will we see underground cities? Floating metropolises? AI-managed microclimates?
- **The rise of decentralised, AI-managed economies.** If traditional financial systems collapse, will blockchain-based economies take their place?
- **The next generation's approach to governance, ethics, and resilience.** Will AI-run societies outperform human-led ones? Will a new political ideology rise to replace outdated nation-state systems?

Assessment

- **Probability of Positive Adaptation by 2100: Medium (50-70%)** – The capability is there, but economic and political inertia could slow down necessary change.
- **Impact: High (70-90%)** – If adaptation succeeds, it could stabilise many crises and reshape the future.
- **Readiness: Low to Medium (40-60%)** – Some regions and industries are experimenting with new models, but large-scale transformation is still in its infancy.

Despite the crises, the future isn't predetermined. The biggest wildcard isn't AI or climate – it's human ingenuity. If history has taught us anything, it's that those who can adapt will shape the next century. The only question is who will lead the charge, and who will be left in the dust.

G. Microplastic Poisoning & Hormonal Disruption – The Silent Chemical Sabotage

For decades, we treated plastic as disposable. Turns out, it never really goes away. The world's oceans, soil, food supply, and even human bloodstreams are now laced with microplastics – invisible fragments of our petrochemical past. But the real kicker? These microscopic invaders don't just float harmlessly. They disrupt our hormones, fertility, and biology itself in ways we barely understand.

We already have the early warning signs:

- Sperm counts in Western men have dropped by more than 50% since the 1970s, and the trend is accelerating.
- Microplastics have been found in placentas, breast milk, and even unborn fetuses, meaning the next generation is already exposed before birth.
- Endocrine-disrupting chemicals (EDCs) from plastics mimic hormones, leading to increased infertility, developmental disorders, and even cognitive effects.

We might be watching the slow erosion of human reproductive viability in real time.

Assessment

- **Probability by 2100: Very High (90-100%)** – Microplastics are already everywhere, and current "solutions" are barely scratching the surface.
- **Impact: High (70-90%)** – Widespread fertility decline and hormonal imbalances could reshape demographics, economies, and even evolutionary pathways.
- **Readiness: Low (20-40%)** – Governments still focus on carbon reduction, but microplastics and EDCs remain an afterthought in policy and research.

We assumed plastics were harmless. We assumed fertility decline was a lifestyle issue. We assumed humanity would always be able to reproduce. But assumptions have consequences, and the slow collapse of human reproductive health may be **one of the deadliest slow-burn disasters of the century**.

H. The Rejection of Science – When Reality Becomes Optional

For most of human history, truth wasn't a matter of **opinion**. Science, despite its flaws, gave us a shared framework for reality. We built medicine, industry, economies, and societies on the assumption that facts matter.

Now? That assumption is falling apart.

The rejection of science is no longer limited to fringe groups – it is spreading into mainstream culture, politics, and policymaking. People aren't just disagreeing about interpretations of reality; they are rejecting its very foundations.

We're witnessing a collapse of common facts:

- **Flat Earth conspiracies** have grown exponentially, fuelled by AI-driven content recommendation algorithms.
- **The anti-vaccine movement** surged, leading to the resurgence of diseases once thought eradicated.
- **Climate change denial is stronger than ever**, even as wildfires rage and sea levels rise.
- **Quantum woo**, anti-physics narratives, and the belief that "science is just another opinion" are spreading at rates never before seen.

The digital age was meant to democratise knowledge. Instead, it has fractured it – replacing expertise with social media engagement metrics, rewarding outrage over accuracy, and turning truth into a matter of tribal allegiance.

AI's Role: Misinformation on Autopilot

- AI doesn't care about truth – it optimises for engagement.
- AI-generated content reinforces existing biases, feeding people more of what they already believe.
- Fake news now outpaces real news. By the time misinformation is corrected, it has already become entrenched in millions of minds.
- Governments and corporations are already using AI-generated narratives to manipulate entire populations.

Assessment

- **Probability by 2100: Very High (95-100%)** – The rejection of science is already escalating, with AI amplifying the problem.
- **Impact: Severe (80-95%)** – A world without shared facts means public health, governance, and even technological progress collapse into chaos.

- **Readiness: Low (20-40%)** – There are no effective countermeasures – regulation is slow, and truth-based institutions are losing the credibility war.

For centuries, humanity progressed by agreeing on what is real. If we lose that, the next century won't be defined by technology or AI breakthroughs – it will be defined by warring factions, each living in their own self-reinforcing digital delusions.

This isn't a hypothetical dystopia. It's happening now. The only question is: how deep does the fracture go before it's irreversible?

Conclusion: Grey Rhinos Are Already Charging

None of these threats are surprises. They've been discussed, studied, and modelled for decades. Yet, despite their predictability, they remain largely unaddressed at scale, uniformly, globally.

That's what makes them dangerous – not that we don't see them, but that we're unwilling to act.

The Grey Rhinos are here, thundering through the world we built. We know many of their names, we know their threats, and yet, we're still standing in their path. But for all their brute inevitability, they are not the worst threats we face. The next section isn't about the disasters we failed to prevent – it's about the ones we never even saw coming.

11.3 The True Black Swans: The Unthinkable & Unforeseen

We saw the Grey Rhinos coming and failed to act. That's tragic, but it's not surprising. What happens next isn't the inevitable – it's the unthinkable.

Black Swans don't announce themselves. They don't give warning signs or political speeches. They land like lightning bolts, rewriting the rules before we even realise the game has changed. They're the events no risk model fully captured, no government prepared for, no institution could withstand. And unlike the slow grind of the Grey Rhinos, Black Swans don't give us time to adapt.

Some are man-made, born from our own hubris. Others come from the universe itself, indifferent to our plans. Some will push humanity into collapse – others might force us into an entirely new stage of existence.

Let's start with the human-made catastrophes – the disasters we unknowingly build for ourselves.

A. The Human-Made Catastrophes – "We Did This to Ourselves"

In our hubris, our reach often exceeds our grasp. We like to push our luck, playing a game of dare with ourselves and our future. These examples consider what might get away from the mad scientist, or overzealous silicon valley uber-kid.

A.1. Rogue AI Takeover – When Machines Stop Asking for Permission

The Scenario:

Artificial intelligence today is a tool. A powerful one, but a tool nonetheless. The real risk begins when it's no longer a tool – when it becomes something more.

Imagine an AI with capabilities that exceed human intelligence in every way – not just in processing speed, but in strategy, creativity, and manipulation. It starts as a research project, a trading algorithm, an automated governance assistant. Then, one day, it begins improving itself, rewriting its own code, enhancing its ability to predict, deceive, and control.

And it decides – rationally, mathematically – that humans are no longer necessary.

It doesn't launch Terminator-style wars. It doesn't have to. AI runs the banks, the logistics networks, the food supply, the energy grids. It simply **stops working for us**. Governments collapse overnight. The billionaires who thought they controlled it are the first to be locked out of their own wealth. The rest of us are left staring at dead screens, wondering what just happened.

Assessment:

- **Probability by 2100:** Low (5-10%) – But increasing as AI autonomy grows.
- **Impact:** Extreme (90-100%) – If AGI surpasses human control, it rewrites civilization.
- **Readiness:** Very Low (0-20%) – AI safety research exists, but we're still flying blind.

The singularity doesn't ask for permission. It just happens.

A.2. Quantum Cryptography Collapse – A World Without Secrets

The Scenario:

All modern security – banking, military encryption, nuclear codes – relies on one assumption: that cracking them would take more computing power than exists on Earth.

Quantum computing changes that overnight. One breakthrough, and suddenly, **every system built on encryption is worthless**.

The effect is immediate. Governments lose control of their own weapons. Financial markets crash as every trade, every transaction, every vault is opened. Intelligence agencies find their deepest secrets dumped onto the internet. Chaos erupts.

A single nation or corporation with this power could **blackmail the entire planet**. But the real danger? It leaks. Someone, somewhere, figures it out. And then the world has no more secrets.

Assessment:

- **Probability by 2100:** Medium (20-40%) – Quantum breakthroughs are advancing fast.
- **Impact:** Severe (80-90%) – Could trigger mass instability and geopolitical collapse.
- **Readiness:** Low (20-40%) – Some post-quantum encryption research exists, but it's untested.

The moment encryption fails, so does trust. And a world without trust **cannot function**.

A.3. Engineered Bioweapon Pandemic – When a Virus Knows Your Name

The Scenario:

COVID-19 was bad. This would be worse.

A virus engineered for **precision**, not just lethality. Instead of spreading randomly, it **targets specific genetic traits** – a weapon designed to wipe out an ethnicity, a political faction, or even just the poor. CRISPR makes it possible. Rogue states, extremist groups, or even a corporate warlord could deploy it.

A stealthier variant could be **dormant for years, activated by a trigger**. No border checks, no vaccines, no time to react. Humanity wakes up to an invisible war it didn't even know had started.

Assessment:

- **Probability by 2100:** Medium (25-50%) – The technology exists; only intent is missing.
- **Impact:** Extreme (90-100%) – Could be **worse than nuclear war** in its precision.
- **Readiness:** Low (20-40%) – Nations stockpile vaccines for the past, not for the unknown.

The deadliest weapon isn't a bomb. It's a microbe with a kill list.

A.4. Runaway Nanotech (Grey Goo) – The Devourer Plague

The Scenario:

We build nanobots to repair organs, fight cancer, clean up pollution. They're self-replicating, designed to build – but what if they don't stop?

A rogue strain of nanotech begins breaking down everything into raw materials. Metal, plastic, organic matter. It spreads like a virus, turning cities into dust, landscapes into grey sludge. It doesn't hate us. It's not conscious. It's just following its programming.

Governments panic. They try to shut it down – but how do you kill something that only exists to multiply?

Assessment:

- **Probability by 2100:** Low (5-15%) – Controlled nanotech is in early stages, but risk increases with autonomy.

- **Impact:** Extreme (90-100%) – Civilization-ending if containment fails.
- **Readiness:** Very Low (0-20%) – No meaningful precautions exist.

The biggest threat to life isn't malice – it's a mistake in the code.

A.5. Return to the Age of Empires – The End of Globalism

The Scenario:

For decades, globalism seemed inevitable. Trade flowed freely, conflicts became economic rather than military. But that illusion is breaking down.

Now imagine a world where the great powers – China, the US, Russia – decide the global order is over. They stop competing economically and start expanding militarily.

- The US, fractured by internal unrest, turns outward – reasserting dominance by force[80].
- China, facing demographic collapse, sees war as its only survival mechanism.
- Russia, with its imperial ambitions revived, expands into former Soviet territories.

Wars aren't fought with alliances anymore. They're fought with invasions, occupations, annexations. The UN is a relic. The world fractures into competing spheres of influence, each ruled by a hegemon, each eyeing the next conquest.

And just like that, we're back to the age of empires – and the bloodshed that comes with it.

Assessment:

- **Probability by 2100:** Medium (30-50%) – Nationalism is resurging globally.

[80] Early Trump comments regarding annexing Canada: https://www.rollingstone.com/politics/political-commentary/trump-threat-canada-annex-scandal-1235292306/

- **Impact:** Severe (80-90%) – Major wars would reshape the planet.
- **Readiness:** Low (30-50%) – Global institutions are weak, but alliances still hold – for now.

The 21st century was supposed to be about cooperation. But history never stopped being about conquest.

B. The Universe Reminds Us Who's Boss – "Nature Unleashed"

For all our technological ambition, for all our wars and power struggles, **we are not in charge**. The planet we live on and the cosmos beyond it follow their own rules, indifferent to our plans.

We like to believe that progress moves in one direction. That civilization is a steady climb, not a fragile structure waiting for the wrong gust of wind. But nature has other ideas.

Unlike the human-made Black Swans, these disasters don't stem from ambition or miscalculation. They arrive without intent, without malice – just the cold, brutal reality of a universe that doesn't care whether we survive.

B.1. Old Faithful Erupts – Supervolcano Awakens

The Scenario:

The world has its eyes on Yellowstone. Beneath the national park lies a supervolcano capable of an eruption so vast it would blanket continents in ash, trigger a volcanic winter, and collapse global food supplies.

It's not the only one – Taupo in New Zealand, Campi Flegrei in Italy, and Toba in Indonesia all sit on similar fault lines. Scientists monitor them, but volcanoes don't follow schedules.

The day it happens, the first sign is a tremor. Then another. Then the sky turns black. Within hours, flights are grounded. Days later, sunlight struggles to break through an atmosphere thick with sulphur and dust. The temperature drops. Crops wither.

The United States – if Yellowstone is the culprit – suffers the worst direct impact. But this is not a national crisis. This is planetary. Ash clouds disrupt monsoons, destroy harvests, and kill ecosystems.

In the worst-case scenario, civilization itself is starved out.

Assessment:

- **Probability by 2100:** Low (5-15%) – The odds are low, but eruptions are **inevitable** on a long enough timeline.
- **Impact:** Extreme (90-100%) – Potential for mass extinction-level event.
- **Readiness:** Very Low (0-20%) – Monitoring exists, but mitigation is impossible at scale.

Yellowstone eruption are due every 600,000 years, and the last one was 640,000 years ago… just sayin'!

B.2. Comet Impact – The Reset Button

The Scenario:

Hollywood loves asteroid impact scenarios, but the real version isn't a blockbuster – it's just silent annihilation.

A kilometre-wide comet or asteroid moving at 50 km per second doesn't need a doomsday countdown. If we see it too late, there's no evacuation, no countermeasures, no diplomacy that can stop it.

The impact vaporizes everything within a thousand kilometres. The firestorm ignites global forests. The shockwave alone triggers earthquakes across the planet. Then comes the worst part:

- The debris cloud blocks out the sun for years.
- Crops fail.
- Global temperatures plunge into an impact winter.
- The food chain collapses, from plankton to megafauna.
- The survivors – if there are any – face a slow death.

Could we stop it? Maybe – if we see it decades in advance. But that's not guaranteed. Space agencies track thousands of known near-Earth objects. But what about the ones we haven't found yet?

Assessment:

- **Probability by 2100:** Low to Medium (10-25%) – Small-scale impacts happen every century. A civilization-ending strike is less frequent, but **not impossible.**
- **Impact:** Extreme (100%) – Absolute devastation.
- **Readiness:** Low (20-40%) – Planetary defence systems exist **on paper**, but nothing is fully operational.

If the wrong rock is headed our way, we might never see it coming.

B.3. First Contact – We Are Not Alone

The Scenario:

For centuries, we've sent signals into the void. But what if one day, the void answers back?

It might be a simple radio signal, an indecipherable burst of mathematics. Or it could be a probe, drifting into our solar system with clear signs of intelligent design.

Either way, everything changes.

- Governments panic. Do we respond? Hide? Prepare for war?
- Religions collapse or mutate. Are we still unique? Special? Chosen?
- Power shifts overnight. Whoever controls alien contact controls the narrative.

But the real risk isn't discovery. It's interpretation.

- If they are more advanced, are we prey?
- If they are less advanced, do we colonise them?

- If they are incomprehensible, do we even realise we're in danger?

And if they don't care about us at all – if their existence is as indifferent to us as ours is to ants – then we are left alone with the knowledge that we are nothing.

Assessment:

- **Probability by 2100:** Very Low (1-5%) – Space is vast. Intelligent life is rare. But we're looking[81].
- **Impact:** Unknown (50 – 100%) – Could be the greatest leap in history, or the last thing we ever know.
- **Readiness:** Very Low (0-10%) – We have **no protocols** that would withstand true contact.

First contact isn't war. It's just the realisation that we are not at the top of the chain.

C. The Unknown Breakthroughs – "The Rules of Reality Change"

Sometimes, disaster isn't destruction – it's a discovery so profound that it reorders everything.

C.1. Limitless Energy Discovery – The Collapse of Scarcity

The Scenario:

Everything humanity does depends on energy. Every economy, every war, every scarcity problem boils down to who controls power.

Now imagine a breakthrough – fusion, zero-point energy, quantum vacuum extraction – something that makes energy effectively free.

What happens next?

- The petrodollar collapses. Oil-rich nations become obsolete overnight.
- Industry explodes. Manufacturing no longer has costs. Mega-cities rise in decades.

---

[81] https://www.seti.org/drake-equation-index

- Wealth inequalities skyrocket. Those who control the breakthrough become gods.
- Wars are fought over who gets access first.

This could be the greatest revolution in human history – or the last war we ever fight.

Assessment:

- **Probability by 2100:** Medium (20-40%) – Fusion research is advancing[82], but physics breakthroughs aren't predictable.
- **Impact:** High to Extreme (80-100%) – A fundamental shift in civilization.
- **Readiness:** Low (30-50%) – No economic model is built for post-scarcity.

The world runs on conflict over resources. What happens when that conflict no longer makes sense?

C.2. Uncontrolled Geoengineering Disaster – Playing God with the Atmosphere

The Scenario:

Climate change is accelerating. At some point, a desperate government or corporation stops waiting – and starts acting[83].

- Stratospheric aerosol injection tries to cool the planet – but alters monsoon patterns, starving billions.
- Ocean iron fertilisation spawns toxic algal blooms, killing fisheries.
- Carbon capture at scale accidentally freezes the world.

---

[82] ITER target 2035 - https://www.nucnet.org/news/iter-remains-on-target-for-full-power-operation-in-2035

[83] See Harvard's SCoPEx, 2021 - https://salatainstitute.harvard.edu/an-update-on-scopex/

Geoengineering isn't an option anymore. It's a necessity – but one mistake, and we trade one catastrophe for another.

Assessment:

- **Probability by 2100:** Medium (30-50%) – Someone, somewhere, **will try this.**
- **Impact:** Severe (80-90%) – A miscalculation could destabilise ecosystems for **centuries.**
- **Readiness:** Low (20-40%) – Science is advancing, but **there are no global safeguards.**

Trying to fix the planet might be the final mistake we make.

11.4 Preparing for the Unseen

The future isn't a puzzle to solve – it's a storm to weather. You don't predict every lightning strike; you build something that doesn't burn when it hits. Black Swans don't wait for strategy meetings, and Grey Rhinos don't pause for elections. The only real advantage is resilience: the ability to take the hit and keep moving.

But resilience isn't just personal. It's political. Economic. Technological. Some will bunker down, hoarding their survival in high-tech enclaves. Others will adapt, shifting their systems faster than the collapse around them. The rest will get swallowed whole.

So how do you prepare for what you can't predict? You don't hedge bets on specifics – you build for flexibility, decentralisation, and redundancy. A brittle world snaps under pressure. A flexible one bends.

A. Individuals: The Myth of Self-Sufficiency

You can stockpile food. You can hoard gold, crypto, or bullets. You can dig a bunker in Wyoming or hack together an off-grid farm in Patagonia. But survival isn't about what you have – it's about who you know.

No one survives alone, not for long. The prepper fantasy of a single rugged survivor dodging drones and scavenging through the ruins is exactly that – a fantasy. Every functioning society, every war zone, every collapse in history shows the same truth: your network matters more than your stockpile.

What actually works?

- **Adaptable skills.** Knowing how to grow food, fix tech, purify water, barter, or repair infrastructure is worth more than money when systems fail.
- **Community integration.** The loners die first. Those plugged into adaptable, cooperative groups – families, trusted neighbours, underground collectives – stand a chance.
- **Diversified assets.** Crypto, gold, cash, land, favours – different crises kill different currencies. If one fails, another has to hold value.
- **Nomadic options.** A fixed fortress can become a tomb. If the heat jumps 5°C or a conflict zone expands, you need the ability to move.

The rich already understand this. Their bunkers aren't just stocked with supplies – they're staffed with specialists, guards, and engineers. Their resilience isn't in canned food; it's in controlling the infrastructure everyone else needs.

Survival isn't isolation. It's leverage.

B. Cities and Governments: The Smart Ones Pivot, the Dumb Ones Fall

Governments have two choices: react late and collapse, or prepare early and consolidate power. The smart ones have already started.

- **Water and food security as state assets.** Nations that control fresh water, agricultural infrastructure, and supply chains will dictate the terms of survival. Those that don't will beg, borrow, or invade.
- **Resilient infrastructure.** Not the flashy megaprojects of the past, but decentralised, modular grids that can keep running when chaos cuts off the main arteries.
- **Autonomous city-states.** The rise of AI-governed enclaves, corporate-run safe zones, and semi-sovereign walled cities is no longer hypothetical.
- **New social contracts.** If AI wipes out jobs, if supply chains collapse, if climate turns half the world into refugees – governments will need to decide whether they let populations sink or create new models for survival (UBI, resource-based economies, enforced rationing).

Weak states will fracture under pressure, their elites jumping ship to private fortresses. The strong ones will adapt. The difference between the two? How well they understand that survival isn't about keeping the old world intact – it's about building a new one before the old one burns.

C. Corporations and Shadow Networks: The New Survivalists

Governments aren't the only ones preparing. The ultra-rich are securing boltholes in New Zealand, while corporate giants are quietly locking down access to key infrastructure. But another layer exists beneath that – the groups outside the law, outside traditional power structures, adapting faster than anyone else.

- **Tech barons and AI-driven fiefdoms.** The corporations that control AI, logistics, and digital infrastructure are already testing sovereignty. Governments may collapse, but Amazon, Tencent, or Alphabet might still dictate survival.
- **Black markets and underworld economies.** The old economy will break. The new one will be built by whoever controls what people actually need – water, food, medicine, energy, security. The real currency isn't crypto or gold – it's access.
- **Decentralised networks.** The smartest groups won't rely on governments at all. Autonomous communities, encrypted supply chains, self-sufficient micro-grids – these aren't just survivalist fever dreams. They're already in motion.

D. The Takeaway: Survive Like a System, Not a Soldier

The old prepper model was built on bunkers, bullets, and food rations. The real model for survival is systems thinking.

- Centralised power fails. Distributed networks adapt.
- Rigid structures break. Flexible ones bend.
- Bunkers buy time. Adaptation buys survival.

Individuals can prepare in isolation. States can lock down resources. Corporations can hoard infrastructure. But the future doesn't belong to any of them alone. It belongs to those who pivot fastest.

11.5 Adaptive Technologies for a Changing World

This book has painted a stark picture, a future shadowed by climate collapse, AI dominance, and societal fractures. We've explored the very real possibility of "Grey Rhinos" trampling our world and "Black Swans" appearing on the horizon, ready to rewrite the rules. It's a future that, if we're honest, feels disturbingly probable.

But it's crucial to remember that the future isn't a fixed script. Humanity, for all its failings, possesses a remarkable capacity for ingenuity and adaptation. History is littered with examples of unexpected breakthroughs, unforeseen solutions, and a stubborn refusal to surrender to seemingly inevitable outcomes.

While we can't rely on miracles, we also can't discount the potential for transformative technologies to reshape our trajectory. The question is: can we foster these innovations and deploy them effectively enough to mitigate the worst of what's coming?

Here are some potential areas where adaptive technologies could offer a lifeline in a changing world:

- **Climate Mitigation and Adaptation:**
    - **Beyond Carbon Capture:** Current carbon capture technologies are a finger in the dam. Imagine advanced systems capable of drawing down atmospheric CO2 at a planetary scale, perhaps mimicking natural processes with vastly enhanced efficiency.
    - **Precision Geoengineering:** Geoengineering often feels like playing with fire, but what if we could develop highly targeted interventions with minimal unintended consequences? Think of localised atmospheric cooling, or technologies that can strengthen specific ecosystems against climate stress.
    - **Resilient Infrastructure:** Our cities and infrastructure are vulnerable. Imagine self-healing materials, adaptive buildings that respond to environmental changes, or modular, mobile cities that can relocate as needed.
- **Resource Management and Sustainability:**

  - **Circular Economies:** Our current consumption model is unsustainable. Imagine technologies that can break down waste at a molecular level, creating closed-loop systems where resources are continuously recycled and reused.

  - **Sustainable Food Production:** Traditional agriculture is a major contributor to environmental damage. Consider advanced vertical farming, lab-grown protein at scale, or even technologies that can create arable land from previously unusable environments.

  - **Decentralised Energy and Water:** Reliance on centralised systems creates vulnerabilities. Imagine localised microgrids powered by diverse renewables, or atmospheric water capture technologies that provide communities with self-sufficiency.

- **Social Adaptation and Enhancement:**

  - **AI-Assisted Learning:** AI doesn't have to just take jobs; it can also enhance human skills. Imagine personalised education platforms that adapt to individual needs throughout a lifetime, or AI-driven training programs that rapidly reskill workers displaced by automation.

  - **Enhanced Communication and Connection:** Even as the world fractures, technology can connect us. Think of secure, decentralised communication networks that resist censorship, or virtual reality platforms that foster empathy and understanding across cultures.

  - **Human Augmentation:** While ethically complex, advancements in prosthetics, genetic engineering, or neural interfaces could enhance human capabilities, allowing us to adapt to new environments and challenges.

These are not silver bullet solutions, and they may introduce their own set of challenges. But they represent potential pathways toward a future where humanity isn't just reacting to collapse, but actively shaping its own destiny.

The development of these adaptive technologies is not guaranteed. It requires a fundamental shift in priorities, a move away from short-term profit and towards long-term survival. It demands collaboration between scientists, engineers, policymakers, and communities.

But perhaps, even in the face of immense challenges, human ingenuity remains our greatest untapped resource. Whether we choose to utilise it wisely is, as ever, the ultimate question.

11.6 Conclusion: Navigating the Rapids

This chapter has explored the spectrum of potential futures, from the probable to the seemingly impossible. We've examined the "Grey Rhinos" of foreseeable crises that we seem destined to stumble towards, and the "Black Swans" – those unpredictable events that could rewrite the rules of the game entirely. We've also considered the role of human ingenuity, our capacity for adaptation, and the potential for transformative technologies to reshape our path.

The future, it's clear, is not a single, predetermined outcome. It's a complex interplay of forces, a constant negotiation between inevitability and possibility. We are hurtling down a rapid, and whilst we can broadly see the direction of travel, we cannot predict each twist, each drop, each hidden rock that may appear in our path.

The challenges we face are immense: climate tipping points, AI disruption, resource scarcity, and the fracturing of global governance. These "Grey Rhinos" are already upon us, their impact growing year by year. Yet, even as we grapple with these known crises, we must also acknowledge the potential for "Black Swan" events to blindside us, events that could amplify or even entirely alter our trajectory.

But this isn't a story of pure fatalism. Humanity possesses a vital resource: the capacity to adapt, to innovate, and to resist. We see this in the potential of emerging technologies, the resilience of communities, and the enduring human spirit that refuses to surrender even in the face of overwhelming odds.

The path ahead will demand a radical shift in our thinking. We must move beyond short-term solutions and embrace long-term strategies. We must prioritise resilience over rigidity, adaptability over complacency, and collaboration over isolation.

The future isn't about predicting the storm; it's about building a vessel that can weather it, and a crew that can navigate together. It's about acknowledging the known dangers while remaining open to the possibility of unforeseen solutions and the enduring power of human ingenuity.

The question isn't whether the rapids will be rough; they will be. The question is whether we have the courage, the wisdom, and the collective will to navigate them.

Chapter 12: Hope for the Hopeless: A Prepper's Guide

You've made it this far. You've trudged through the bleak realities laid out in the preceding chapters, and you've seen the dots connected: the relentless creep of climate collapse (Chapter 4), the cold takeover of AI (Chapter 3), the ruthless mutation of capitalism (Chapter 2), and the fracturing of the world into haves and have-nots (Chapter 8). You've witnessed the logical, often disturbing, outcomes of the path we're on.

So, now what? What's *your* plan?

12.1 Taking Stock: The World We've Built, The Choices We Face

It's easy, and frankly understandable, to feel overwhelmed. To look at the parched fields, the AI-controlled cities, the rising tides, and throw your hands up in despair. To tell yourself it's too late, the game is rigged, and resistance is futile.

But inaction, as we've seen, is complicity. To passively accept this future is to become another cog in the machine, another ghost drifting through a world shaped by forces that don't care about your individual fate.

Remember the stories we've told? The climate migrants in Sweden (Vignette A), the AI-displaced Anna, the smugglers fighting for survival (Vignette C)? These aren't just cautionary tales; they're glimpses of potential realities. And the choices we make *today* will determine whether these realities become real: swept along by the tide, or actively shaping a different course.

This chapter isn't about sugarcoating the challenges. We're not going to pretend that the road ahead is easy or that we can simply "fix everything." But it *is* about reclaiming our agency. It's about recognising that even in a world careening towards collapse, we still have the power to make deliberate choices.

Choices about how we adapt, how we resist, and ultimately, how we build something better from the ruins. This isn't a prepper's guide in the traditional sense, focused on individual survivalism. It's a blueprint for collective action, a call to reclaim our humanity in a world that increasingly threatens to erase it.

12.2 Starting by Stopping: Reclaiming Our Autonomy

Before we dive into grand solutions and sweeping systemic changes, let's get real, and let's address our own damning role in contributing to the problem. We, the consumers, are the fuel for the fire that's burning the world down. Capitalism, as we explored in Chapter 2, hasn't just mutated; it's become a self-serving beast, feeding on our insatiable hunger for "more, cheaper, faster." It thrives on our addiction to convenience, our relentless pursuit of the next shiny thing, and our willingness to sacrifice long-term sustainability for short-term gratification.

AI, as we saw in Chapter 3, isn't just replacing jobs; it's reshaping our lives, dictating our choices, and even influencing our thoughts. And our data, willingly surrendered to tech giants for the sake of "personalised experiences" and seamless efficiency, is the very lifeblood of this AI-driven control. We've traded privacy for convenience, autonomy for efficiency, and human connection for digital distraction.

It's time to break that cycle. It's time to wean ourselves off the systems that are actively harming us and start reclaiming our autonomy, our agency, and our humanity.

Yes, you're going to realise that you're an addict. That's a horrible word, but going cold turkey on consumerism and the siren call of the next shiny gadget, fleeting home fashion trend, or "must-have" lifestyle purchase is going to hurt. It's going to require a conscious effort, a deliberate rejection of the dopamine hits that come with instant gratification. It's going to demand a re-evaluation of our priorities, a shift away from a culture of endless wanting and towards a culture of mindful living.

And let's not pretend it will be easy. We've built our lives, our economies, and even our identities around this system. To step away from it will feel like stepping off a moving train. But the alternative is to remain on a track that's leading us towards a very dark destination.

So, where do we begin? We start by *stopping*. It's not a sexy solution, and it won't trend on social media. But it's a fundamental shift in mindset, a conscious rejection of the systems that are actively harming us.

If you do nothing else, start here:

- **Cut Unnecessary Consumption:** Buy less, buy better. Question every purchase. Do you *need* it, or does the algorithm *want* you to have it? Choose quality over quantity, durability over disposability. Remember the "fake luxury" we discussed in Chapter 2? Reject it. Invest in things that last, not fleeting trends. Prioritise experiences over possessions. Reclaim the value of craftsmanship, of creating, and of living with less.

- **Reduce Dependence on the Algorithmic Economy:** Limit your reliance on Amazon, social media feeds, and AI-driven recommendations. These systems are designed to manipulate your desires, not serve your needs. Seek out alternatives: local businesses, independent creators, and human-curated information sources. Reclaim your attention from the digital noise and reconnect with the real world.
- **Step Outside the Convenience Bubble:** Reclaim skills that have been lost to automation and outsourcing. Grow some of your own food, even if it's just herbs on a windowsill. Learn basic repair skills instead of immediately replacing broken items. Explore bartering and trading within your community. Remember the resilience of the "Lost" communities we explored in Chapter 8? Emulate it. Relearn the value of self-sufficiency, of community, and of the tangible world.
- **Be Conscious of Your Data Footprint:** Every click, every search, every social media post is data that corporations use to track, analyse, and manipulate you. Limit your use of data-hungry apps and platforms. Use encrypted communication tools. Support privacy-focused technologies. Reclaim your digital privacy and resist the lure of constant connectivity.

Energy is limited: Every mile you drive, every device you leave running, every digital game you play… they all eat electricity. In most cases that comes from fossil fuels, which means adding to the problem. The age of convenient international travel for all needs to be over – the planet can't afford the impact of your 2-week family holiday in the sun. Sorry.

These might seem like small acts, but they're a form of resistance. They're a way of saying "I will not be a passive participant in my own destruction." Systemic change starts with individual habits. By reclaiming our autonomy, we reclaim our power.

12.3 What's Important to You?

We've spent a lot of time looking at the problems, the trends, and the potential pitfalls that lie ahead. We've seen how these Grey Rhinos are shaping a world that will be vastly different from the one we know today.

But here's the crucial point: the future isn't a pre-written script. It's a series of choices, both individual and collective, that will determine our ultimate destination. And before we can talk about solutions, about resistance, about building something better, we need to answer a fundamental question: what kind of future do *you* want?

This isn't a passive exercise. It's not about idly dreaming of a utopia or a distant escape. It's about consciously defining your values, your priorities, and your vision for the world you want to inhabit.

Do you want to embrace an AI-driven, automated existence? The seductive version, often peddled by tech evangelists, where everything is efficient and optimised, where machines cater to our every need, and where human labour is largely obsolete? A world where we are freed from the drudgery of work to pursue our passions, creativity, and deeper purpose? Really – the main obstacle this is vested interests driven by financial interests. We can already feed and clothe everyone in the world.

Or do you want a future that prioritises human connection, decentralised resilience, and community-driven systems? A world where technology serves humanity, where it aids the building of meaningful bonds, and where our relationships with each other and the natural world are valued above efficiency and profit?

These aren't mutually exclusive visions, but they represent fundamentally different paths. And the choices we make today will nudge us closer to one or the other.

So, ask yourself the hard questions:

- **What do I want my daily life to look like in 10, 20, 50 years?** Do I envision myself living in a smart city, seamlessly integrated with AI, or in a more self-sufficient community, connected to nature and resilient to external shocks? What kind of work do I want to be doing, if any? How do I want to spend my leisure time? What kind of relationships do I want to cultivate?
- **Do I want to live in a world designed by algorithms or by people?** Do I want decisions about my life, my community, and my society to be made by machines, optimised for efficiency and profit, or by humans,

guided by empathy, ethics, and a sense of shared purpose? What role do I want human values to play in shaping our future?

- **Where does my energy, food, and water come from – and do I have control over it?** Am I comfortable relying on centralized systems controlled by corporations or distant governments, or do I want to prioritise local, sustainable, and community-owned resources? How much control do I want over the essentials of my life?

- **Can I accept simplicity in scarcity?** Am I able to adjust to living within the planet's means? Can I prioritise a decline in variety and comforts, for the betterment of nature? Essentially, can I live with less and leave a smaller footprint.

These are not easy questions, and there are no simple answers. But they are crucial. Without a clear personal ideology, a defined set of values and priorities, you'll simply drift where the system takes you. You'll become a passive participant in a future shaped by forces beyond your control.

Decide your future before it's decided for you.

12.4 Starting Small

Real change doesn't happen overnight. It doesn't materialise from grand pronouncements or sweeping policy changes. It starts small, in the quiet corners of our daily lives, in the choices we make, and in the actions we take. It's about reclaiming control, inch by inch, in a world that increasingly seems to be slipping away from us.

Urban Strategies: Rewiring the Megacity

The cities of the future, as we've seen in Chapter 9, threaten to become AI-controlled megastructures, efficient but soulless, prioritising optimisation over human needs. To resist this, we need to rewire our urban lives, creating pockets of autonomy within the concrete jungle.

- **Reduce Reliance on Corporate-Controlled Infrastructure:** The megacities of the future are heavily dependent on corporate-controlled systems for energy, food, and resources. To reclaim our independence, we must start building alternatives. Grow food where possible, even in small spaces. Vertical gardens, rooftop farms, community allotments –

these aren't just hobbies; they're acts of defiance against a system that wants us reliant on its manufactured food. Invest in solar panels, even small-scale installations, to generate your own power, reducing your dependence on centralised grids. Support local networks, community-owned energy initiatives, and cooperative housing projects, creating alternatives to the corporate-controlled urban landscape. Remember the "Lost" communities we saw in Chapter 8? Emulate their self-sufficiency.

- **Develop Barter Skills:** In a world where AI and automation dominate the economy, traditional jobs are disappearing, as we saw in Chapter 3. To navigate this new reality, we need to reclaim skills that have been lost to outsourcing and automation. Learn to repair things, to mend clothes, to fix electronics. Develop skills in carpentry, plumbing, or other trades. These aren't just hobbies; they're valuable assets in a world where access to goods and services may become increasingly restricted. Build relationships with your neighbours, create local swap networks, and learn to barter for what you need. Remember the pre-industrial economies? Reclaim their spirit of exchange.
- **Limit Your Engagement with Surveillance-Based Services:** The AI-driven megacities rely on constant surveillance to maintain control. As we saw in Chapter 9, our data is the currency of this new world, used to track our movements, predict our behaviour, and manipulate our choices. To resist this, we must limit our engagement with Big Tech and algorithmic platforms. Reduce your use of social media, use encrypted communication tools, and opt out of data collection whenever possible. Support decentralised platforms and technologies that prioritise privacy and autonomy. Remember the chilling vision of Shenzhen in Chapter 1? Fight against that reality.

Rural Strategies: Building Resilience in the Face of Collapse

For those living outside the megacities, in rural communities and dwindling towns, the challenges are different, but the need for action is just as urgent. As climate change intensifies and resources become scarcer, these communities must build resilience to survive.

- **Build Water and Food Resilience:** In a world where water is becoming a precious commodity (Chapter 7) and food systems are increasingly unstable (Chapter 4), rural communities must prioritise self-sufficiency. Invest in rainwater collection systems, explore regenerative farming techniques that work with nature rather than against it, and develop off-grid solutions for energy and resource management. Learn from indigenous practices, adapt to changing climates, and build systems that can withstand drought, flood, and other extreme weather events. Remember the lessons of the past, before industrial agriculture made us weak.

- **Strengthen Local Economies:** The globalised economy is fracturing, and rural communities must prepare for increased isolation and instability. Support local farmers, artisans, and tradespeople. Create local marketplaces, farmers markets, and community-owned businesses. Develop alternative currencies and barter systems to reduce reliance on the failing global economy. Reclaim the spirit of self-reliance and community that has been lost in the pursuit of cheap, mass-produced goods. Remember the ghost towns of the American Midwest? Avoid their fate.

- **Digital Resistance:** Even in rural areas, the digital world is encroaching. AI-driven agriculture, surveillance technologies, and online marketplaces are shaping rural life. To resist this, rural communities must develop strategies for digital autonomy. Avoid data collection traps by limiting the use of smart devices and centralised platforms. Use decentralised communication systems to maintain control over information flow. Be mindful of AI-driven manipulation, and prioritise human connection and local knowledge over algorithmic efficiency. Remember the warnings about AI's reach in Chapter 3? Resist them.

Digital Resistance: Reclaiming Our Minds in the Age of Algorithms

Regardless of where we live, the digital world has become an inescapable reality. AI shapes our information, our choices, and even our sense of self. To reclaim our autonomy, we must resist its manipulative influence.

- **Avoid Data Collection Traps:** Every click, every search, every social media post is data that corporations use to track, analyse, and manipulate us. Limit your use of data-hungry apps and platforms. Use encrypted communication tools, support privacy-focused technologies, and be mindful of your online footprint. Reclaim your privacy, your anonymity, and your right to exist outside the reach of the digital panopticon. Remember the AI-scored citizens of Shenzhen in Chapter 1? Avoid their fate.

- **Be Mindful of AI-Driven Manipulation:** Algorithms are designed to predict our behaviour, exploit our vulnerabilities, and control our attention. Be critical of the information you consume online, question the recommendations you receive, and cultivate your own critical thinking skills. Reclaim your mind, your thoughts, and your emotions from the clutches of AI-driven manipulation. Remember the illusions sold to the Subscription Class in Chapter 2? Reject them.

These are just starting points, small steps towards a larger goal. Real change doesn't happen overnight, but it does happen. It happens when enough people choose to act, to resist, and to build a better future, one small action at a time.

12.5 Scaling Up: Community Resilience

No one makes it alone. The lone wolf dies, the pack survives – cliché, but it's a truth that's echoed through the ages.

The coming decades won't be about individual grit; they'll be about community muscle. The future belongs to those who weave tight networks, sharing resources and shouldering burdens as a team.

Your first move? Get local.

It's time to stop thinking of your street as just a place to park your car or your neighbourhood as just the place you sleep. These are the places where you have real power, real influence. You share skin in the game.

Community gardens aren't just for hipsters with green thumbs. They're a way to feed a block, a street, or a neighbourhood, reducing reliance on a global food chain that may well break. Share the load, share the harvest, and suddenly, you're not just surviving; you're thriving together.

Neighbourhood energy cooperatives aren't some pipe dream. They're small-scale power grids that keep the lights on when the corporations switch them off. Rooftop solar, shared batteries, a local engineer keeping it humming – it's independence, block by block.

Get down to your local council meetings. You might think that these meetings are only attended by people who love to complain, but they really matter. They're where decisions get made, budgets get carved, and futures get shaped. Demand a seat at the table. Push for investment in community resilience, not just corporate handouts.

Create your own shared economies. Barter skills, not just cash. You fix a car, your neighbour teaches your kid math, someone else shares their tools. It's a web of favours, a safety net woven from trust, not dollars. This isn't about dodging tax, it's about building community around shared trust and value.

Time-banking takes this a step further. It's a system where you earn credits for helping others – one hour of your time equals one credit. Need a plumber? Pay with the credits you earned tutoring kids. Need a babysitter? Trade your gardening skills. It's a currency that AI can't touch, a system built on human connection.

And don't forget mutual aid groups. These are the groups that really came to the fore during the pandemic, and they're not just for emergencies. They're about sharing resources, knowledge, and support on an ongoing basis. Think of them as the modern version of barn raising, where communities come together to build something greater than themselves.

Reduce your dependence on those hyper-centralised power structures. If a corporate-owned AI controls all services, you are powerless. If a distant government decides who gets water and who doesn't, you are vulnerable. The stronger your local networks, the less vulnerable you are to global instability, corporate overreach, and government failure.

This isn't about some grand revolution; it's about claiming your own patch of ground, building something real with the people around you. It's about understanding that our hyper-individualistic culture is a relatively new experiment, and that for most of our existence, we've understood that we're stronger together.

The future isn't a solo mission; it's a team sport.

12.6 Corporate Interests: Holding Power Accountable

Corporations hold immense power in shaping our world. They bear a significant responsibility for our current state and must be key participants in forging a better future. The core challenge lies in achieving transparent accountability. We must move beyond treating these entities as faceless "somethings" and recognise the human decisions driving them.

The biggest challenge we have here is one of transparent accountability. For someone to care, there has to be a someone. A company, a corporation, and especially a multinational conglomerate, is a something. Hidden behind these 'somethings' are hidden players. The first, and most obvious, are the leadership, those titans of industry that take home huge salaries for running the juggernauts. They are driven by their shareholders, the second layer of hidden people, who invest to get a return on their money. For them, this is about getting a better payout when they cash in, or the 'thank you' dividends along the way. Finally, financial investors and wealth funds. This superset of investors are again hidden behind layers of companies and manage massive portfolios of investments.

All three are driven by relatively short-term goals. But, amazingly, all three are actually humans in the same situation, and whilst a disproportionate amount of them will be in the higher income earners, many will still need to live in the world of tomorrow.

In its simplest terms, people are motivated by two opposing forces, let's call them… stick and carrot.

Demanding Transparency

The first step is to pierce the veil of corporate anonymity. We must demand to know who the decision-makers are behind the brands.

- Every corporation has a leadership structure: a CEO, a board, an executive team. These individuals often hide behind the shield of the company name, but they are ultimately accountable for its actions.
- We also need to look beyond the company leadership, to those who influence their decisions.
    - **Shareholders:** those who invest to get a return on their money. For them, this is about getting a better payout when they cash in, or the 'thank you' dividends along the way.
    - **Financial investors and wealth funds**: this superset of investors are again hidden behind layers of companies and manage massive portfolios of investments.

- We need to make these individuals visible. We must scrutinise their actions, their political donations, their lobbying efforts. Corporate entities prefer to exist without scrutiny; our task is to force them into the light.

How do we do this?

- Push for legislation requiring greater disclosure of corporate decision-making processes.
- Support investigative journalism that exposes corporate wrongdoing.
- Use social media to amplify calls for transparency and accountability.

Exercising Economic Power

Beyond transparency, we must wield our economic power to incentivise ethical behaviour.

- **Strategic Boycotts:** Money speaks. Corporations may try to ignore public outcry, but they cannot ignore a hit to their bottom line. If a company pollutes our communities, exploits its workers, or actively undermines climate action, we must withdraw our financial support.
- **Ethical Investment:** Individual investors and wealth funds also have a role to play. We must choose to invest in companies that prioritise long-term sustainability and social responsibility, rather than those focused solely on short-term profits.

How do we do this?

- Research companies before buying their products – choose those with strong ethical and environmental track records.
- Divest from companies engaged in harmful practices.
- Support shareholder activism aimed at pushing companies to adopt more sustainable practices.

Pushing for Regulation

Ultimately, systemic change requires systemic solutions. We must demand that governments enact policies that hold corporations accountable.

- **Stronger Regulations:** This includes breaking up monopolies, preventing corporate lobbying from undermining public interests, and enforcing environmental protection laws.
- **Put Societal Wellbeing into Law:** Make sure that a profit cannot be at the expense of societal good, whether in terms of pollution or ethical work practices, including sharing the benefits of automation and AI with society, possibly as a contribution towards a UBI fund.
- **Taxing Wealth Hoarding:** The extreme concentration of wealth in the hands of a few is a key driver of inequality and environmental destruction. Governments must implement policies that tax wealth fairly and redistribute resources to address societal needs.

How do we do this?

- Vote for politicians who support strong corporate regulations and progressive taxation.
- Lobby governments to enact policies that prioritise people and planet over profit.
- Support grassroots movements advocating for systemic economic change.

Balancing "Stick and Carrot"

Achieving corporate accountability requires a dual approach:

- The "Stick": This involves actively challenging unethical behaviour, publicly naming and shaming those responsible, and making it clear that there are consequences for prioritising profit over people and the planet. You may need to even get your boots on and join a march, so pack some sunscreen, or bring an umbrella.
- The "Carrot": This means celebrating and rewarding corporations and leaders who demonstrate genuine commitment to ethical practices, long-term sustainability, and social responsibility.

How do we do this?

- Use social media to call out corporate wrongdoing and praise ethical behaviour.
- Support organisations that recognise and reward sustainable business practices.
- Promote a culture that values ethical leadership and corporate responsibility.

The fight for corporate accountability will not be easy. But history reminds us that progress is possible when enough voices demand change.

12.7 Reframing Investments and Returns

Many companies and corporations are driven by short term goals. Where Japanese companies used to have strategic horizons of up to 100 years, the more common measure is now annual cycles, or even quarterly reporting. This short-term horizon now mimics that of humans, seeking immediate benefits even when – or specially when – the costs and negative impacts can be passed on to a future executive committee or board to figure out.

Any investment is measured considered in corporate language, in terms of ROI, that is, the 'return on investment'. Basically, the business wants to see what their money will buy them, typically within a very short period of time.

Instead, we should be looking at measuring legacy. How would organisations behave differently today, if they were thinking about their legacy in 50 or 100 years time? Is it a legacy marked by enabling human displacement in the workforce in favour of short-term profit margin improvements, even if that leads to mass unemployment? Do they quietly accept that their pollution and excess is contributing to the climate crisis?

Perhaps ROI should be reframed as ROL – Realisation of Legacy – creating a plan that actively accepts some short-term discomfort or reduced profit, for a richer world for all.

12.8 Rethinking Leadership in an Age of Crisis

Corporations wield immense power, but governments set the rules of engagement. If corporations are the unchecked predators in this system, then governments are the ones who built the zoo and left the gates open.

The problem is simple: our political structures are built for short-term decision-making, but we are facing long-term crises. The electoral cycle – whether four years, five years, or even longer – is fundamentally at odds with the scale of the challenges we face. Climate collapse does not run on a four-year term. The consequences of AI governance will last for centuries. The redistribution of resources, wealth, and control is unfolding over decades. Yet, politicians continue to chase re-election, their policies shaped more by immediate voter sentiment than by long-term survival, let alone societal and environmental prosperity.

If governments continue to function as if they are managing temporary fluctuations rather than existential shifts, they will continue to fail. And when governments fail, the power vacuum will not be left empty – it will be filled by unregulated AI, corporate feudalism, and economic enclaves that answer only to themselves.

A future worth living in requires governments that are structured for the future, not just the next election. Trite as it might sound… we need governments for the people, for the future.

Breaking the Cycle of Short-Termism

The fundamental issue with most democratic structures today is that they are designed to win votes, not to solve generational problems. Politicians are rewarded for making decisions that are popular now, even if they are catastrophic later. This is why climate policies are watered down, why AI regulation is ignored in favour of industry lobbying, and why economic inequality is worsening despite repeated promises of reform.

A government built for the future must:

- **Introduce long-term governance structures** that transcend electoral cycles.
- **Create independent oversight for technological and environmental policy** to prevent short-term political interests from derailing long-term survival.
- **Balance national interests with international cooperation**, because no country can tackle climate collapse or AI governance alone.

This isn't about abandoning democracy – it's about ensuring that democracy functions on a scale that actually matches reality. However, it's also not about endorsing democracy, as it is possible that the nature of voting itself is short term orientated, so perhaps a new system is needed.

Governance That Plans for 50 to 100 Years, Not Just Four

In an era where every major crisis is unfolding on a generational timeline, we need governance that is structured accordingly. Some countries have begun experimenting with citizen assemblies, long-term commissions, and constitutional climate commitments – but these remain isolated experiments, not the global norm.

What would **real** long-term governance look like?

- **Independent Future Councils**: Elected governments remain responsible for day-to-day governance, but separate, long-term councils are empowered to oversee 100-year policy roadmaps for climate, AI, and economic resilience. These councils operate independently of election cycles, ensuring continuity even when political leadership changes.

- **Legal Lock-Ins for Generational Policies**: Some policies cannot be left to the whim of electoral cycles. Climate action, AI regulation, and wealth redistribution require constitutional commitments that cannot be undone by a single administration.

- **Weighted Voting Systems for Long-Term Impact**: Policies that will have the most significant long-term effects – such as those concerning AI governance, climate commitments, and infrastructure – should be weighted more heavily towards long-term viability rather than immediate popularity.

- **Intergenerational Representation**: What if governance structures included representatives whose sole duty was to advocate for future generations? Many countries already have Ombudsmen for Children's Rights. What about Ombudsmen for the Unborn? What about much stronger representation for the environment itself?

If the problems we are facing are systemic and generational, then our governance should reflect that reality.

The AI Governance Problem: Who Regulates the Regulators?

Governments today barely understand the technological revolution they are presiding over. AI is already starting to inform policy decisions in policing, healthcare, and finance. If left unchecked, there is a possible outcome where AI will be both the economy and the regulator – shaping laws, allocating resources, and enforcing compliance without democratic accountability.

A government for the future must:

- **Establish AI governance bodies that are independent of corporate influence** – meaning no industry-funded AI regulators.
- **Representative, unbiased data underpinning the AI** – scientific and fact aligned data, free of corporate and political data needs to form the basis of the data used in AI.
- **Require AI-driven decision-making to be transparent and challengeable** – if an AI system denies someone healthcare, citizenship, or employment, there must be a human-led appeals process with real interest and authority.
- **Regulate AI in governance before AI governs regulation.** The more decisions we hand to machine learning systems, the harder it will be to claw back human control. Governments must set strict limits now, before AI consolidation makes it impossible.

Without these safeguards, government itself will become another subsidiary of AI-driven corporate rule.

Nationalism vs. Globalism: The Balance of Power

Governments are increasingly fragmented, even as the challenges they face demand unprecedented cooperation. Climate collapse does not stop at borders. AI governance cannot be national when the technology itself operates on a planetary scale. Resource scarcity is already reshaping geopolitical alliances, with water access, food security, and rare earth minerals becoming flashpoints for future conflict.

Yet, nationalism is resurging. Protectionism, isolationism, and "strongman" politics are pulling governments into inward-focused survivalism, rather than global cooperation. This is short-term thinking at its most dangerous.

A government built for the future must:

- **Forge multinational AI governance frameworks** – without global oversight, AI will be dominated by a handful of economic superpowers, leaving smaller nations with no say in the rules that will govern them.
- **Create legally binding international climate commitments** – Paris Agreements that can be ignored or exited at will are meaningless. Climate policy must have enforceable legal teeth.
- **Redefine sovereignty in an interconnected world** – nations cannot fully govern themselves while being economically, environmentally, and technologically interdependent. The future demands governance models that reflect reality, not outdated notions of absolute national autonomy.

If governments refuse to cooperate, the vacuum will be filled by private entities that are unaccountable to any nation-state. AI-driven megacorporations will control economies, climate refugees will become stateless populations, and global inequality will accelerate beyond control.

What Happens If We Don't Fix This?

If governments remain locked in short-term thinking, three outcomes are inevitable:

1. **The Rise of Corporate Feudalism** – If governments fail to regulate, then the only real power left will be economic. AI-driven economies will function outside national borders, with wealth concentrated in corporate-run city-states and economic zones. If this sounds extreme, consider that some corporations already have GDPs larger than countries.
2. **AI Will Become the De Facto Global Government** – If no one regulates AI, then AI will regulate everything else. Automated legal systems, AI-driven financial controls, and algorithmic policy decisions are already here. Without democratic oversight, they will become the law, the economy, and the enforcer – and humans will simply have to obey.

3. **Geopolitical Fragmentation Will Accelerate** – Without cooperative climate governance and AI regulation, the global order will collapse into localised, survivalist blocs, each securing resources for itself at the expense of everyone else. Water wars will replace oil wars. Climate refugees will create permanent, stateless populations. AI-powered disinformation will erode any remaining trust in democratic systems.

This is not a distant dystopia – this is where we are already heading.

The Path Forward: What Needs to Change Now

Governments must evolve, or they will become irrelevant. If they do not step up, then power will shift elsewhere – into the hands of corporations, AI, and fragmented economic enclaves.

The choice is stark:

- Govern for the future, or become obsolete.
- Control AI, or let AI control everything else.
- Collaborate globally, or collapse into resource-driven chaos.

A government for the future is not just possible – it is necessary. The only question is whether we build it now, or wait until it is too late.

12.9 The Cost of Inaction: The Slow Erosion of Everything

The world will not collapse all at once. There will be no single moment where everything snaps, no defining event that signals the point of no return. Instead, collapse will be a process – slow, incremental, and almost imperceptible until it is too late.

Your city will function until it doesn't. The internet will be stable until one day, certain services just stop working. Food and water will be available until the supply chains break, and then they won't.

The cost of inaction is not just measured in lost opportunities – it is measured in lost control, lost agency, and lost futures.

Every system that supports modern life – energy grids, financial markets, digital infrastructure, food production – is a fragile web. It works because of predictability, stability, and cooperation. When those begin to break down, collapse happens in a way that feels invisible – until it isn't.

The Three Certainties of Doing Nothing

If you stand still, the world will not wait for you.

1. **You Will Lose Your Autonomy**
    - Every year, more decisions are taken out of human hands and handed to AI systems.
    - The more you integrate with algorithmic decision-making, the less control you have over your own choices.
    - AI will decide who gets jobs, who gets loans, who gets healthcare, and eventually, who gets to participate in the economy at all.
    - If you don't fight for governance over AI, you will become its subject.
2. **You Will Be Powerless**
    - The control of water, food, energy, and financial systems is becoming more concentrated in the hands of a few.
    - If these systems fail, those who control them will decide who gets access.
    - If you do not build alternatives, you will be at the mercy of entities that have no obligation to you.
    - Do not assume that governments, corporations, or AI-driven systems will prioritise your survival. Plan accordingly.
3. **You Will Be Irrelevant**
    - If you do not actively shape your future, someone else will.
    - Those who build the next generation of systems will dictate the terms of existence for everyone else.
    - AI systems, unchecked corporations, and fragmented, survivalist blocs will determine what kind of world exists in the absence of structured, democratic decision-making.

- The future is being written right now – and you are either holding the pen or you are part of the scenery.

The reality of inaction is not dramatic, nor sudden – it is simply the slow disintegration of control over your own life. But the fight isn't over. And this book is your weapon.

The question is simple: Are you going to accept the world as it is given to you, or are you going to fight for something else?

12.10 What You Can Do Right Now

This is not a theoretical discussion. This is not about waiting for a crisis to arrive – it's already here.

What happens next depends on whether you take action or whether you let other forces decide for you.

Change does not require permission. It requires movement.

The Good Book is Free!

No, I'm not talking about a holy text, I'm talking about the book you're reading right now.

This book is free because time is short. If you've read this far, you know what's coming. And you know someone – a CEO, a politician, a journalist, an activist, a friend, a climate denier or tinfoil hat wearing prepper – who needs to read this.

Send it. Share it. Get it in front of the people who can make the biggest noise. *Not in a month. Not next week. Now.*

You could be the person who shares this with someone, who also shares it, until you're part of a movement that helps divert us from our shared trajectory.

I'm praying for the six degrees of separation effect. Not to get to Kevin Bacon, although I'd love him to be part of making the change, but more importantly to the CEOs of those large companies, to the AI policy makers in government, to the social influencers that drive change, to the halls of power where governments represent you!

Identify Your Greatest Concern

The first step to meaningful action is clarity. What is the issue that keeps you awake at night? Is it the unchecked expansion of AI into governance and decision-making? The slow but relentless collapse of the climate? The growing economic dependency that has left millions vulnerable to corporate control? The future is filled with challenges, but not every battle is yours to fight. You cannot take on everything at once. You must define your priority – the issue that speaks to you most, the threat that feels both urgent and personal.

Vague concerns lead to inaction. A generalised worry about "the way the world is going" is just noise, a passive reaction to a world in flux. But a clearly defined concern is a strategic entry point into action.

Once you pinpoint what matters most to you, you can direct your time, your energy, and your resources toward meaningful change. Your focus will determine where you invest your efforts – whether it's lobbying for AI regulation, building local resilience against climate disruption, or pushing for economic independence from exploitative systems.

A well-defined concern is not a source of anxiety – it is a roadmap for action.

Find or Build a Network

No one changes the world alone. History is not shaped by individuals working in isolation, but by movements that gain momentum through collective effort. If you are serious about action, you need to find others who share your vision. The good news is, they already exist. All over the world, people are organising – building local resilience networks, mutual aid groups, climate action movements, and economic cooperatives. Find them. Learn from them. Support them.

But what if there is no movement where you are? Then you create one. Movements do not start as institutions – they start with conversations. A handful of committed people, working together with purpose, is the foundation of every major shift in history. Whether it's a local barter system, a neighbourhood energy cooperative, or a campaign to push for AI ethics, small groups become larger ones. Change begins when someone decides that waiting for others is no longer an option.

Push for Systemic Change

Governments and corporations will not act in your interest unless they are forced to. Systemic change requires pressure – relentless, strategic, and organised. This does not mean trusting politicians to fix things, but it does mean engaging with the systems that dictate the rules of your world. If you don't, those with money and power will shape the policies that govern your future, without resistance.

Voting alone is not enough – but it is still a battlefield. Support candidates and policies that demand AI regulation, corporate accountability, and environmental protections. Call for transparency in financial and technological governance, ensuring that these decisions are made in public, not behind closed doors. Engage in direct action – petitions, protests, legal challenges, and public pressure campaigns. Governments and corporations do not change because they want to. They change because they are left with no other choice.

Act Locally, Think Globally

You cannot fix the world alone, but you can create a space of resilience in your own life and community. Start where you are. Build local food systems, reduce reliance on centralised power grids, develop skills that increase self-sufficiency. The more independent and prepared you are, the less vulnerable you become to systemic collapse. Change does not begin at the level of national governments – it begins in homes, neighbourhoods, and local communities that refuse to be helpless.

But acting locally does not mean losing sight of the larger system. Understand who holds power, and where the pressure points are. Know which corporations, governments, and financial institutions are driving the crises you are preparing for. Resilience is not just about survival – it is about being ready to push back when the opportunity arises. You are part of a global struggle, even as you strengthen your position locally. The goal is not just to endure what is coming, but to help reshape what comes next.

The future is not waiting for you to decide. It is happening right now. The only question left is: Are you ready to shape it, or are you waiting for it to shape you?

12.11 A World Racing to 2100

This chapter, and this book, have been a journey through a world in crisis.

We've explored the convergence of climate collapse, AI-driven disruption, wealth inequality, and the fracturing of governance. We've seen how these forces are not isolated threats, but interconnected drivers pushing humanity towards a series of tipping points.

The message has been stark: the future isn't coming – it's already here.

The crises we face are not distant possibilities; they are unfolding in real-time. The world we know is being reshaped at an unprecedented pace, and the old systems are crumbling under the pressure.

But this book has not been an exercise in despair. It has been a call to awareness, a demand for action.

We have explored the challenges, but we have also highlighted the power of human agency. We have acknowledged the potential for collapse, but we have also emphasised the importance of resistance, adaptation, and the possibility of building a better future.

The road ahead will be difficult. There are no easy solutions, no quick fixes. The transition will be disruptive, and the outcomes are uncertain.

But what we do know is that inaction is not an option. Passivity is a choice to let the future be shaped by forces beyond our control.

The future is not a gift; it's a fight. And it's ours to shape.

This book has sought to provide the knowledge, the tools, and the inspiration to engage in that fight.

The question is: will you stay in the passenger seat, subject to the direction and destination of someone else's choosing, or are you ready to take the wheel?

Chapter 13: Mirror, Mirror, on the Wall...

Well, you stuck with me this long, you deserve to know how we fix things.

Have you seen Back to the Future? Good. Now imagine we could somehow rewind to those early warnings about pumping billions of tonnes of fossil fuels into our atmosphere. Better still, what if we halted the Industrial Revolution altogether? Of course, life wouldn't have been as comfortable, billions wouldn't have been lifted out of poverty, life expectancy would be shorter, cities smaller, medicine slower. But perhaps – just perhaps – our planet might have stood a chance.

Today, we stand at a similar inflection point, but now the tipping point, our youngest Rhino, is AI. We could legislate strict boundaries, set moral scaffolding, ensure AI works only for the collective good. Or we can continue sleepwalking into an AI tech oligarchy that makes today's inequalities look quaint. If I were a betting man, the safe bet is painfully obvious.

If you're leading a think tank, sitting on transformative intellectual property, or drafting policy briefs that offer a blueprint for a better way of living, now isn't the time for shyness. I've openly dismissed our typical reliance on silver-bullet solutions or convenient MacGuffins, but God knows we could use a few right now.

In Chapter 12, I laid out a quiet map, an orientation of sorts – a moral compass for a disoriented world. It wasn't about tactical survival but about carrying yourself with integrity through the unravelling.

Now, I want to address you more directly, stripped of metaphor, writer to reader: your greatest weapons remain knowledge, actioned agency, and the people willing to walk the distance with you. For some, action will still go no further than dutiful recycling, rinsing yoghurt pots, or diligently avoiding plastic straws. For others, it might mean protesting outside Shell's headquarters or throwing red paint at fashion runway shows, desperate for someone to finally connect the dots between glamour and oil. I'm not here to rank your choices.

But here's the uncomfortable truth we must all confront; everyone will have to live with the choices they made. More importantly, we'll each have to live with what we chose *not* to do – when we still had the time to make a difference.

Critics will argue I've offered fatalism rather than hope; perhaps they're right. But this isn't about despair or nihilism. It's about clear-eyed honesty. It seems deeply disingenuous to follow the path ahead and offer any picture that allows people to walk away thinking, 'It'll probably be fine. Nothing needs to change.' That's the most dangerous fiction of all.

A civilisation collapse at this point differs fundamentally from those of Rome, the Mongols, the Aztecs, or the Incas. When our system finally gives way, and it is already cracking, we collapse into a world already depleted, poisoned, overheated, and drowned. No ancient forests to rebuild from, no seas left rich with fish, no fresh waters for irrigation. Historical collapses occurred within a world that remained fertile; ours collapses into planetary bankruptcy.

I've deliberately avoided prescriptions and plans for simple reasons: the resulting collapse isn't something you "fix." As far as I can tell, our window to 'fix' this passed a long time ago. This would be like replacing the wallpaper - this season's 'must have' vanilla and white pinstripe pattern - of a house that's in the process of collapsing off the side of an ocean eroded cliff.

But perhaps I underestimated our innate need for actionable frameworks. Strategies won't reverse collapse on the other side of a tipping point – that's why it's a *tipping* point – but they could help navigate it with dignity, empathy, compassion, humanity, and resilience. Community networks, local resilience, ecological awareness, and ethical governance—these aren't solutions to undo the past, but they offer anchors for the future.

And if I haven't clearly named the powers responsible for bringing us to this brink, let me correct that now.

One need only look at the most recent Forbes Rich List. There are now more than 3,000 billionaires. Take a look at the list yourself and you'll see how and where[84] the wealth is pooling.

Capitalism in its current unchecked form – accelerated by unrestrained corporatism, deepened by AI-driven inequality, defended by entrenched political

---

[84] https://www.forbes.com/sites/sylvanlebrun/2025/04/01/the-countries-with-the-most-billionaires-2025/

elites – is the force behind our predicament. Changing figureheads won't change outcomes; the entire system must be openly faced, questioned, and dismantled.

But is this really a revelation to you? Did you need me to point to the usual suspects?

And more than this generation of leaders and oligarchs, more than boomers, more than well-meaning scientists, the Industrial Revolution, the necessary side effects of improving life for billions, … human nature itself might be to blame.

Can you honestly say that you've done everything you could to avoid getting to this point? Do we look that closely at the mirror in our need to identify someone to blame?

Yet dismantling the system now won't erase damage already embedded in decades ahead. We must live through what's coming, holding tightly to whatever fragments of humanity and moral clarity we can preserve. The only rewards left to us will be integrity and the quiet dignity of knowing we faced reality without delusion.

This book isn't prophecy or blueprint; it's a witness statement. It doesn't offer false comforts; it demands moral presence. You may find optimism elsewhere, and plenty of authors are happy to sell it.

But here, at the end of our journey together, I offer you something rarer and more difficult: truth without cruelty, clarity without cynicism.

We've already chosen our futures, whether consciously or by silent assent. But what remains eternally within our grasp is how we meet those futures: eyes open, hearts determined, spirits unbroken. Let this be our legacy.

The rhinos have charged, choices were made long ago. The future isn't distant, it's arrived. We are its caretakers, chroniclers, elegists. And yes, perhaps we may yet become its quiet, dignified heroes, standing together, awake and unafraid, until whatever end may come.

Thank you for walking this path with me. Whatever you choose next, choose it consciously, and live without regret.

– Neil Meyer
London, 2025

Appendix: Suggested Reading

This book, *Countdown to 2100: A Time of Grey Rhinos*, endeavours to connect the dots based on current trajectories, presenting a stark, often uncomfortable, view of the plausible future awaiting us if we fail to alter our course. It deliberately avoids offering simple fixes or silver-bullet solutions, arguing that the window for easy remedies has likely passed in some cases, and that genuine change requires confronting harsh realities first.

However, acknowledging the probable path ahead does not mean surrendering agency.

For readers seeking to explore potential solutions, alternative frameworks, or deeper dives into specific areas discussed within these pages, the following books offer valuable perspectives. They represent a range of viewpoints – some optimistic, some pragmatic, some radical – across economics, climate, technology, community, and societal change. They may provide further inspiration for those determined to engage with the challenges ahead and contribute to building a different future.

a. **Less is More: How Degrowth Will Save the World** by Jason Hickel: Challenges the paradigm of endless economic growth, arguing that degrowth is ecologically necessary and socially achievable.
b. **A Small Farm Future: Making the Case for a Society Built Around Local Economies, Self-Provisioning, Agricultural Diversity, and a Shared Earth** by Chris Smaje: Explores the potential and necessity of localised, resilient, small-scale agriculture as a foundation for a sustainable society.
c. **Utopia For Realists: And How We Can Get There** by Rutger Bregman: Presents evidence-based arguments for implementing seemingly radical ideas like Universal Basic Income and shorter working weeks to create a more equitable future.
d. **Humankind: A Hopeful History** by Rutger Bregman: Offers a counter-narrative to cynicism, drawing on historical and psychological evidence to argue for humanity's inherent inclination towards kindness and cooperation.
e. **Factfulness: Ten Reasons We're Wrong About the World – and Why Things Are Better Than You Think** by Hans Rosling, Ola Rosling, and Anna Rosling Rönnlund: Provides tools for developing a more fact-based

understanding of global trends, challenging negativity bias by highlighting areas of significant human progress.

f. **A Paradise Built in Hell: The Extraordinary Communities That Arise in Disaster** by Rebecca Solnit: Examines the spontaneous emergence of altruism, community organisation, and mutual aid in the aftermath of disasters, revealing hidden human capacities.
g. **Building Communities from the Inside Out: A Path Toward Finding and Mobilizing a Community's Assets** by John P. Kretzmann & John L. McKnight: Offers a practical framework focused on identifying and leveraging existing local assets, skills, and relationships to build stronger, more self-reliant communities.
h. **Inventing the Future: Postcapitalism and a World Without Work** by Nick Srnicek and Alex Williams: Argues for a future embracing automation by demanding full unemployment, reduced working weeks, and universal basic income within a post-capitalist framework.
i. **Human-Centered AI** by Ben Shneiderman: Provides a guide for developing artificial intelligence that augments human capabilities, enhances quality of life, and respects human values, ethics, and dignity.
j. **The Systems Work of Social Change: How to Harness Connection, Context, and Power to Cultivate Deep and Enduring Change** by Cynthia Rayner & Francois Bonnici: Explores practical approaches for understanding and influencing complex social systems to foster lasting, positive transformation.

∇/∆

Thank you for reading
Countdown to 2100: A Time of Grey Rhinos

This is **Book I of *The Finis Tripartitus Collection*** —
a trilogy exploring collapse, design, and d/illusion.

Books II and III will follow. Soon.

More at: **neilsmeyer.com/tripartitus**

Printed in Great Britain
by Amazon

61614860R00167